THE LONGEVITY
OF ATHLETES

THE LONGEVITY
OF ATHLETES

Edited by

ANTHONY P. POLEDNAK, Ph.D.

Radiological and Environmental Research Division
Argonne National Laboratory
Argonne, Illinois

CHARLES C THOMAS • PUBLISHER

Springfield • Illinois • U.S.A.

Published and Distributed Throughout the World by

CHARLES C THOMAS • PUBLISHER

Bannerstone House

301-327 East Lawrence Avenue, Springfield, Illinois, U.S.A.

© 1979, by CHARLES C THOMAS • PUBLISHER

ISBN 0-398-03867-8

Library of Congress Catalog Card Number: 78-11338

Printed in the United States of America
V-OO-2

Library of Congress Cataloging in Publication Data

Main entry under title:

The longevity of athletes.

    Includes index.
    1. Athletes--Health and hygiene. 2. Longevity.
3. Athletes--Mortality. 4. Sports--Physiological
aspects. I. Polednak, Anthony P. [DNLM:
1. Life expectancy. 2. Longevity. 3. Sports.
4. Exertion. 5. Sport medicine. 6. Physical
fitness. QT260 L852]
RC1235.L66   617'.1027   78-11338
ISBN 0-398-03867-8

to the memory of

Albert Damon, M.D., Ph.D.
(1918-73)

To all *H* men
Not only is the "H-man" an alphabetic step ahead of the "G-man," but he even achieves a kind of immortality.
"Once an H man means always an H man" (Blanchard, J. A., 1923, *The H Book of Harvard Athletics*, Harvard University Press, Cambridge, Mass., p. 595).

PREFACE

CONSIDERABLE information on the possible long-term consequences on health of participation in athletic competition has been gathered. This book summarizes and critically examines this evidence, and the data reported here should help to dispel some common misconceptions regarding the longevity and health of former athletes. These misconceptions are probably often due to biased sources of information. The early death of a former prominent athlete from heart disease is a newsworthy event, but such anecdotal sources provide an incomplete and biased picture. Within the medical profession, misconceptions about the long-term health effects of athletic participation also appear to be common.

Meaningful studies on the life span of athletes require the recognition of the relevance of many scientific disciplines. Athletes (whether college, Olympic, or professional) are very select individuals. Acquiring data on the physique or body build of athletes and comparable nonathletes requires the skills of physical anthropologists. Psychological studies are relevant to our understanding of the motivation and success of athletes, as well to the assessment of the possible effects of the stressful aspects of athletic competition. Proper follow-up of human populations (athletes and nonathletes) over many years makes epidemiological and biostatistical methods appropriate. Mechanisms for possible effects of exercise and physical training suggested by such studies, such as those on cardiovascular disease, may be provided by physiologists. Workers in all of these disciplines may be interested in how their methods have been (and could be further) applied to the study of the longevity of athletes.

Information on the longevity and health of athletes should be of interest to a wide range of readers. The admiration of, and identification with, successful athletes by laymen is evident in the great interest shown in their professional and private lives. The question of whether or not prolonged physical training and athletic competition is beneficial or harmful to health in later life, therefore, should also be of interest. It will perhaps be surprising for some readers to find that most of the data bearing on this question has come from studies of college athletes. The lack of evidence on athletes who are selected and motivated to step out from the college ranks to the professional level will become apparent, as will the problems involved in studying such highly selected athletes. College athletes, however, have always been a colorful group. One cannot overlook the competitiveness and roughness of college sports, even around the turn of the century (a period relevant to studies discussed in this book). Witness, for example, the "flying wedge," which was outlawed because of the injuries that occurred.

The general medical practitioner, as well as the physician specialist in "sports medicine," should find herein much information relevant to answering questions posed by athletes (and others) on the effects of sports. This book does not deal with athletic injuries, but does provide information on disease (e.g., heart disease) risk in later life, which should be useful to physicians. Physical educators and athletic coaches, at all levels, should also find the material in this book of interest, if only for its historical aspects. Included here are studies on Harvard College athletes and their classmates, which involved Doctor Dudley A. Sargent (1849-1924), a founder of physical education in the United States. Harvard played a role in the 1905 football controversy, which led to the formation of the Intercollegiate Athletic Association (later the National Collegiate Athletic Association).

We have noted that misconceptions may exist regarding the adverse effects of athletics on health. On the other hand, the case for a protective role of athletics or exercise in preventing cardiovascular disease or promoting health has been overstated by some enthusiasts. A more balanced viewpoint, based on available evidence, is constantly striven for in the discussion sections of this book. A number of reviews of the literature on the health and longevity of athletes have been published recently. This book is intended as a sourcebook for those interested in examining the original studies. The discussion of these studies provided in this volume is aimed at relating their findings to those of other studies, and to provide critical analysis of the methods and results.

As mentioned above, critical review of studies on the longevity of athletes requires recognition of the relevance of many disciplines. Included in our discussion, for example, are such controversial topics as the effects of exercise on physiologic and biochemical variables, where the results of studies are conflicting. Hopefully, investigators in these controversial areas will be tolerant of the present attempts to integrate some of the results of selected studies into the discussion of the topic at hand.

INTRODUCTION

STUDIES of the health and longevity of athletes involve several fields of study — for example, medicine, epidemiology, physiology, physical anthropology, and psychology. We are concerned here mainly with epidemiologic studies of athletes. Epidemiologic methods involve the description of disease distributions in human populations according to person, place, and time. Explanation of differences in disease frequency according to these characteristics is one goal of epidemiology. One method of examining possible causes of disease involves cohort studies. A cohort is a group of persons who share a common experience, such as exposure to an environmental agent (e.g., a chemical or toxic agent). The "exposed" cohort is compared to another cohort (nonexposed) which is similar in various respects. The two (or more) groups are followed over time, and the frequency of the disease under study is compared in the groups.

College or other athletes may be considered as cohorts, since they share a common experience (exposure to physical training and athletic competition), and they may be compared with nonathletes (e.g., college classmates). Various outcome measures (causes of death) may be compared in the two groups. We would like to determine whether or not "exposure" to physical training and athletic competition has any long-term consequences in terms of longevity or mortality from specific diseases or conditions. Ideally, we would also like to analyze separately the effects of (1) strenuous physical exercise and training; and (2) "stress" or the psychophysiological aspects of athletic competition.

In attempting to meet the objectives stated above, there are many difficulties involved in epidemiologic studies of athletes. First, humans live long lives relative to experimental animals such as mice, rats, and guinea pigs. Thus, studies of factors affecting human longevity require long follow-up periods, during which some participants may be lost from the study; this raises the question of possible bias in the results. Such studies are costly, and this may be a deterrent to obtaining support.

Short-term studies of various characteristics (morphological, physiological and biochemical) have been done to assess the effects of physical training; athletes and sedentary adults (mostly young men) have been used. Such data may be relevant to the effects of exercise on longevity or "aging" processes. Again, however, studies of longer duration are needed to assess the long-term effects of exercise programs; different subgroups need to be examined, including both long-term participants and nonparticipants. These types of studies are discussed in Section I.

Other problems involved in long-term studies, covering entire life spans of athletes, concern their design and the interpretation of results. These problems are related to self-selection of persons for sports, and selection by others (coaches and physicians). Athletes are selected on the basis of characteristics which are (known or suspected to be) related to longevity. Perhaps one example familiar to most readers is medical selection (i.e., past or present health). Other criteria for selection that are relevant to health include physique (body build), physiological characteristics, personal habits (e.g., smoking), and personality. Some of these characteristics are discussed below.

Ideally, we would like to "control for" or remove the effects of all of these factors, to achieve the goals stated above. With animal experiments, comparability of experimental (i.e., exercised) and control groups is more easily accomplished. The animal experimenter can select a control group which resembles the experimental group, with respect to genetic strain or physical size, and environmental conditions can be controlled (or at least monitored closely). Few animals are lost from the study; ordinarily, the animals cannot refuse to cooperate, or migrate out of their cages to another environment. This is not to say that technical problems do not exist in animal experiments of the effects of physical training.

We would like to approximate the conditions obtained in animal studies by examining the possible effect of characteristics known to differ between athletes and nonathletes; large sample sizes are usually needed. In some studies of college athletes, however, consideration of some differences between athletes and nonathletes, and their effect on mortality, has been possible. Such factors, other than the one of main interest (i.e., physical training and competition), that differ between the groups compared and are related to outcome (mortality) are sometimes called "confounding" variables (Susser, 1973). That is, they confound our attempts to study the effects of the factor of interest, thus complicating the study design and our attempts to explain the findings.

It seems reasonable to assume that the more prominent the athletic group, the more select that group is likely to be on various characteristics. Some characteristics are obvious (e.g., physique, motor skills), while others may be more subtle (e.g., personality, psychological characteristics). This makes the interpretation of studies on the longevity of Olympic and professional athletes more difficult than that of studies of less prominent athletes. Most of the studies included in this book deal with college athletes, particularly those who attended college around the turn of the century (as we have noted, the long life span of humans necessitates long periods of follow-up). This does not imply that these college athletes were not select groups, and that college athletics were not strenuous enough to require special qualities for success. A brief glimpse at the history of college football will attest to this. At the beginning of this century, intercollegiate football contests were dangerous. For example, the Chicago *Tribune* reported on a number of injuries and deaths in football games at the end of the 1905 season (Brubacher and Rudy, 1958). The adoption of the minimum yardage rule in 1882 resulted in mass play, which, along with the "flying wedge," increased roughness and injuries (Danzig, 1971). President Theodore Roosevelt played some role in the 1905 football controversy which led to the formation of the Intercollegiate Athletic Association (later the National Collegiate Athletic Association) (Lewis, 1969). Roosevelt, a Harvard College graduate, had a great interest in Harvard football; Harvard football players, and other athletes, are included in studies presented in this book.

It is worthwhile noting that studies of athletes may suggest hypotheses involving variables other than exercise in disease or longevity. In epidemiology, characteristics of persons that may be related to disease susceptibility are termed "personal" or "host" factors. These include the "constitution" or individual make-up of anatomic, physiologic, biochemical, and psychological characteristics.* Studying the possible effects of exercise and athletic competition on mortality may also provide clues to the importance of host characteristics of athletes that may be relevant to disease; a few examples are provided in the studies included in this book.

Finally, this introduction has emphasized the problems involved in studying the longevity of athletes. Despite the limitations of human studies, they provide important and relevant information; the relevance of results of animal experiments to the human situation is always questionable. Also, it would be difficult to find more interesting or colorful groups to investigate than athletes.

REFERENCES

Brubacher, J. and W. Rudy 1958 Higher Education in Transition. Harper and Row, New York, p. 129.

Danzig, A. 1971 Oh, How They Played the Game. The Early Days of Football and the Heroes Who Made it Great. Macmillan, New York.

Dubos, R. 1965 Man Adapting. Yale University Press, New Haven.

Lewis, G. M. 1969 Theodore Roosevelt's role in the 1905 football controversy. Res. Quart. *40*:717-724.

Susser, M. 1973 Causal Thinking in the Health Sciences. Oxford University Press, New York.

---

*For an excellent introductory discussion of the host in disease, see Dubos (1965).

CONTENTS

SECTION VI
SUDDEN DEATH OF ATHLETES

SECTION VII
CONCLUDING REMARKS

THE LONGEVITY
OF ATHLETES

Physical Activity and "Aging"

As mentioned in the Introduction, short-term studies have been conducted on the effects of physical training on physiological and biochemical characteristics. Exercise may conceivably alter basic "aging" processes, or reverse or stabilize the deterioration in body functions ordinarily seen with advancing age. The first article presented here, by Shock, describes briefly some changes in functional capacities with age and reviews some evidence on the effects of physical activity. The second paper, by Siegel et al., presents evidence for short-term changes in various characteristics during a physical training program in sedentary men; these changes run counter to those ordinarily seen with increasing age in Western populations. These two articles are discussed at the end of this section, along with similar studies on sedentary men and athletes.

Chapter 1

PHYSICAL ACTIVITY AND THE "RATE OF AGEING"*

N. W. SHOCK, Ph.D.

IT is widely assumed that continued physical activity will increase life span. This assumption follows from the observation that physical fitness can be improved by programs of exercise. Since elderly people have many of the characteristics of younger subjects who are physically unfit, it is easy to assume that improvement of physical fitness in young and middle-aged people will increase their life span and consequently reduce their "rate of ageing."

Before examining the experimental evidence for these beliefs, it is necessary to define what is meant by ageing and to agree on appropriate indices of "rate of ageing." For me, ageing represents the progressive changes which take place in a cell, tissue, or organism with the passage of time. The end result of these changes is an increase in mortality rate with increasing age. Thus, ageing of a population can be characterized in terms of a mortality curve. Figure 1-1 illustrates such a mortality curve for the population of the United States.[1] It may be seen that the mortality rate increases progressively with age. As early as 1825, Gompertz[2] showed that this mortality curve becomes linear when the logarithm of the mortality rate is plotted against age. Figure 1-2 represents the Gompertz plot of the same mortality data illustrated in Figure 1-1. This transformation makes it possible to characterize a mortality curve in terms of two parameters, namely, the slope of the curve and its intercept.

---

*Originally published CMA Journal, 96:836-840, March 25, 1967. (Reprinted without Figure 7.)

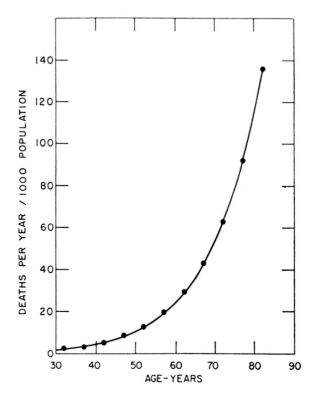

Figure 1-1. Age-specific rate from all causes as a function of age for U. S. males, 1949. (From Curtis, H. J.[1])

Studies of mortality curves for different animal species have shown that the slope of the Gompertz plot is characteristic for the species. Figure 1-3 shows Gompertz plots of mortality data for fruit flies, rats, and humans.[3] In this plot, the age scale has been altered for each species but it is clear that, if the same time scale is used for all curves, the slope of the curve for short-lived species is much greater than that for long-lived species. It is apparent that the *slope* of the Gompertz plot may be regarded as an index of the "rate of ageing" in a population.

The average life span in humans varies widely among different countries and has increased substantially in the past 50

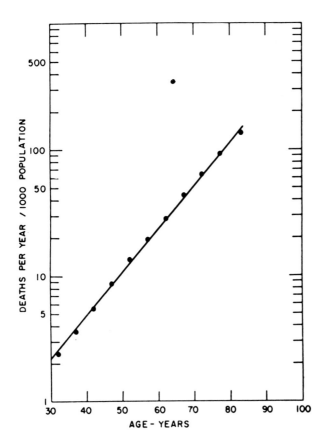

Figure 1-2. Log age-specific death rate as a function of age (same data as in Fig. 1-1). (From Curtis, H. J.[1])

or 100 years. Figure 1-4A compares the Gompertz mortality plots for India (top) and the United States (bottom). Figure 1-4B shows similar plots of mortality data for 1850 and 1950 from the United States.[4] In both instances, it may be seen that improvements in living conditions and medical services have shifted the mortality curves to the right; that is, a given rate of mortality is reached by individuals 10 to 15 years older in the United States than in India. Some investigators have claimed that this shift in the intercept of the curve indicates a difference

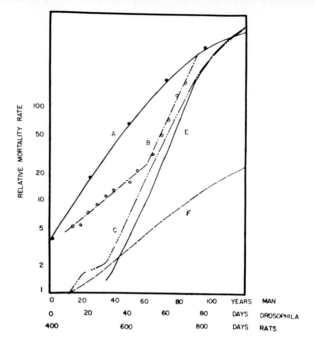

Figure 1-3. Mortality rate versus age for various species of animals. A. Male rats; B. Human male (Egypt, 1947); C. Human male (U. S., White — North Central Division, 1949-51); E. Human Female (U. S., White — North Central Division, 1949-51); F. *Drosophila melanogaster.* (From Mildvan and Strehler.[3])

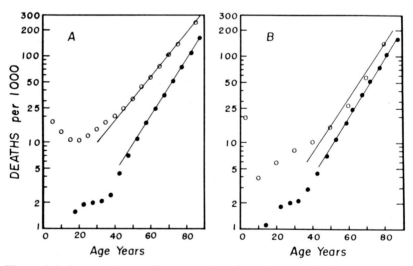

Figure 1-4. Log total mortality rates plotted against age. A. Comparison of mortality rates for India (open circles) and the United States (solid circles). B. Improvement in mortality rates in the United States between 1900 (open circles) and 1951 (solid circles). There is a displacement of the curves to the right, with little change in the slopes of the linear part of the curves. (From Shock, N. W.[4])

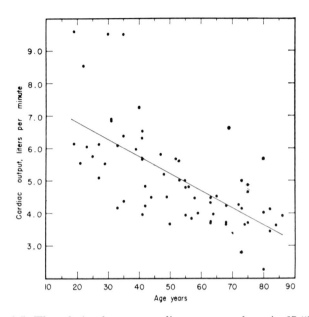

Figure 1-5. The relation between cardiac output and age in 67 "basal" males without circulatory disorder. Each point represents the average of two measurements in 49 subjects, of three measurements in 4 subjects, and a single measurement in 14 subjects. The line indicates the simple linear regression for the data. (From Brandfonbrener et al.[5])

in "physiological age" between the two populations. This may be true, but the "rate of ageing" of the two populations is no different, since the slopes of the two curves are substantially similar. Therefore, the rate of increase in mortality with age has not been altered — the improvements in living conditions and medical care have simply postponed the time when a given level of mortality is reached.

On the basis of these results, it seems probable that if exercise can reduce the incidence of disease and improve "physical fitness" there will be a further shift of mortality curves to the right and total life span will be increased, but there is no evidence that the "rate of ageing" as indicated by a change in the slope of the Gompertz mortality plot will be altered.

It may be argued that mortality curves do not offer a good

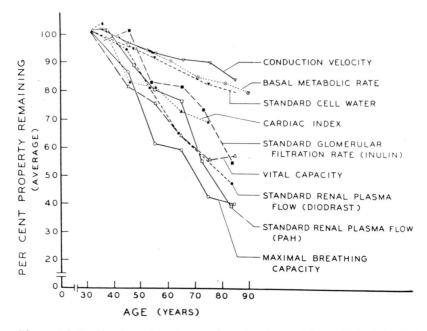

Figure 1-6. Decline in various human functional capacities and physiological measurements. Values are adjusted so that the value at age thirty equals 100 percent. Other values are expressed as the average percentage of the value at age thirty remaining at the specified age. (From Strehler, B. L.[6])

index of ageing and that a more appropriate index would be found in estimates of age differences in specific physiological measurements. One of the primary activities of the Gerontology Branch of the U. S. Public Health Service has been to describe the age regression for a number of physiological variables. Figure 1-6 shows measurements of resting cardiac output in different subjects, carefully screened to eliminate those with diagnosable cardiac disease.[5] Although the variability among subjects is large, there is a statistically significant decrement in resting cardiac output with increasing age.

Figure 1-6 summarizes the age regression for a number of physiological tests.[6] In order to compare tests with different units of measurement, all curves have been plotted as percentage deviations from the mean values of 30-year-old subjects. If we now define "rate of ageing" as the slope of the regression of a test against age, it becomes apparent that there is no single index of ageing. In fact, the rates of change with age vary greatly for different tests. The rate of conduction of a nerve impulse falls only 10-15% between the ages of 30 and 80 years, while resting cardiac output falls by 50% over the same age span. One must therefore decide which physiological variable to choose as the most appropriate index of "ageing," or a single score, based on a combination of a number of measurements, must be devised. This is in itself a formidable research problem to which we are devoting our efforts.

If the slope of the age regression is to be used as an index, an answer to the question "does activity alter the rate of ageing?" requires observations on a sufficiently large number of "active" and "non-active" subjects to establish reliable slopes of the age regression line for each group — and, furthermore, to demonstrate a statistically reliable difference between the two slopes. At present no such data exist.

Although cross-sectional observations, where different subjects are measured at each age, can give an estimate of average age trends, they can never evaluate age changes in an individual. For this purpose, it is necessary to conduct a longitudinal study in which the same measurements are made repeatedly on the same subject as he ages. This approach, expensive and difficult as it is, may be the only method which can answer the question posed. Such a study would require serial measurements on both "active" and "inactive" subjects over their entire life span.

Another approach to the problem involves the use of animals. In terms of life span, the rat or mouse represents the animal of choice, since these animals have life spans of only two to two and one-half years. It is difficult to design experiments in which different levels of physical activity can be induced and controlled in these species. Investigators have attempted to vary activity by swimming, or by running on a treadmill or activity wheel, and some have reported a slight increase in average age of death in exercising *vs.* sedentary rats or mice.[7] However, the data are not extensive enough to permit a reliable estimate of the slope of the mortality curve, and estimates of average age of death are notoriously unreliable, especially in small groups of animals. It can only be said that at present the available data do not prove conclusively that activity or exercise significantly alter the "rate of ageing."

Because of his capacity for training, the dog is an excellent animal for studies on the effects of exercise. However, the dog's life span of 12 to 15 years has limited its use in studies of ageing. The establishment of several long-term dog colonies — for example, at Davis, California; Salt Lake City, Utah; and Ft. Collins, Colorado — raises the possibility of conducting long-term ageing studies on dogs. Whether studies on the effects of exercise on ageing can be carried out on these animals will depend on the interest of the investigators and the supplementary financial support which will be needed.

Ageing is also associated with changes at the tissue and cellular level. Some of the decrements in physiological functions can be attributed to the loss of cells and functional units from organs. For example, a large part of the age reduction in kidney function can be accounted for by a gradual loss of nephrons from the kidney.[8] Similarly, there is a loss of muscle tissue with advancing age which may also be observed histologically.[9] In some respects, the biochemical changes found in aged rat muscle are similar to those found in young muscles which have undergone atrophy due to experimental immobilization.[10] In view of these changes, it might be possible to alter age changes in muscle by subjecting animals to systematic exercise and examining the muscle for histological and biochemical changes.

Summary

It must be admitted that at present there are no data which offer proof that activity significantly alters the "rate of ageing" as evidenced by a change in the slope of the Gompertz mortality curve or an alteration in the slope of the regression of any physiological measurement on age. Experiments can be designed to answer the question, but they will be time-consuming and expensive. Other experiments on the effects of ageing can be conducted with rats and dogs in which less time is needed than in studies on humans to test the effects of exercise on specific functions which are known to change with age. Among these, studies on the biochemical and histological changes in skeletal muscle in the rat could provide important information on the effects of exercise on ageing of muscle.

Although there is ample evidence that age influences exercise performance, data are not available at present to determine the effect of exercise on ageing — or rate of ageing.

REFERENCES

1. CURTIS, H. J.: The biology of aging, Brookhaven National Laboratory, Upton, N.Y. (BNL-854), March 18, 1964, p. 1.
2. GOMPERTZ, B.: *Phil. Trans. A.*, 115: 513, 1825.
3. MILDVAN A. S. AND STREHLER B. L.: A critique of theories of mortality. *In:* The biology of aging. edited by B. L. Strehler, American Institute of Biological Sciences, Publication No. 6, Washington, 1960, p. 216.
4. SHOCK, N. W.: *Bull. N.Y. Acad. Med.*, 32: 268, 1956.
5. BRANDFONBRENER, M., LANDOWNE M. AND SHOCK N. W.: *Circulation*, 12: 557, 1955.
6. STREHLER B. L.: *Quart. Rev. Biol.*, 34: 117, 1959.
7. RETZLAFF E., FONTAINE J. AND FURUTA, W.: *Geriatrics*, 21: 171, 1966.
8. SHOCK N. W.: Age changes in renal function. *In:* Cowdry's problems of ageing, 3rd ed., edited by A. I. Lansing, The Williams & Wilkins Company, Baltimore, 1952, p. 614.
9. ANDREW, W. *et al.: J. Geront.*, 14: 405, 1959.
10. EICHELBERGER L., ROMA, M. AND MOULDER, P. V.: *J. Appl. Physiol*, 12: 42, 1958.

Chapter 2

EFFECTS OF A QUANTITATED PHYSICAL TRAINING PROGRAM ON MIDDLE-AGED SEDENTARY MEN*

WAYNE SIEGEL, M.D., GUNNAR BLOMQVIST, M.D.,
AND JERE H. MITCHELL, M.D.

Abstract

The effects of a 15-week quantitated training program were evaluated in nine men, 32 to 59 years old. All had been blind for 10 years or more but were otherwise in good health. They were sedentary with a stable activity pattern. Training sessions were held three times per week and consisted of four 3-minute exercise periods on a bicycle ergometer, each followed by a rest period of equal duration. Heart rates at the end of the fourth exercise period averaged 27 beats below individual maximal heart rates.

Maximal oxygen uptake increased from 24.0 to 28.5 ml/kg × min or by 19%. Total heart volume and mean serum cholesterol decreased significantly, and psychological tests showed improvement.

Five subjects continued exercising at the same intensity but only once weekly for another 14-week period. Mean maximal oxygen uptake decreased to 6% above the control level. Four subjects who discontinued training after 15 weeks were retested at the same time and had a mean value 5% below control maximal oxygen uptake.

*From *Circulation XLI*:19-29, January 1970. By permission of the American Heart Association, Inc. (Abridged.)

This study was supported by grants from the U. S. Public Health Service (HE 06296), the Texas Heart Association, the Tarrant County Heart Association, and the Southeast Texas Health Foundation.

PHYSICAL training is now widely used in the treatment of angina pectoris and as a preventive measure against coronary heart disease. The literature on the effects of training in various groups of patients and normal subjects is rapidly expanding,[1] but sufficient information to provide a firm basis for exercise prescriptions is not available. Studies on the effect of training programs characterized in detail with respect to type of activity, duration, frequency, and intensity of exercise are clearly needed, particularly from groups with low initial levels of physical fitness. However, strict control of a training program is difficult to accomplish in a normal, free-living population.

Few studies[2,7] on the effect of physical training in middle-aged and older sedentary men have included direct measurement of changes in maximal oxygen uptake (Vo_{2max}). Maximal oxygen uptake is the product of maximal cardiac output and arteriovenous oxygen difference and reflects both the performance of the heart as a pump and the efficiency of distribution of blood flow.[8] Vo_{2max} has been widely accepted as an index of the functional capacity of the circulatory system and of aerobic physical work capacity. Measurements may be repeated at frequent intervals since the technic is noninvasive. Thus, Vo_{2max} constitutes a relevant and convenient standard by which the effect of a physical training program may be judged.

It was suggested by Lamm[9] that blind subjects may constitute an ideal experimental group since they are restricted to a low level of physical activity and to a stable pattern of life. In the present study a group of middle-aged men who all had been blind for many years was recruited. A simple, closely monitored program of interval-training type was administered; that is, exercise sessions consisting of repeated short periods of relatively heavy exercise with intervening short rest periods. An attempt was made to gain specific information on the amount of training required to produce and to maintain a significant increase in maximal oxygen uptake. A preliminary report of this study has been presented.[10]

The Longevity of Athletes

Methods

Subjects

Nine male subjects from the Dallas Lighthouse for the Blind were studied. The group was interviewed in August 1967. The details of the proposed study were carefully explained to each man.

Basic data on age, weight, height, and the duration and etiology of blindness of each subject were determined. The age of the subjects ranged between 32 and 59, with a mean age of 46. They had been restricted in their physical activity for at least 10 years because of blindness. A medical history was obtained, and a physical examination was carried out by an independent physician at the beginning of the study. All subjects appeared to be in good health except for their blindness and a slightly elevated diastolic blood pressure (92 to 100 mm Hg) in subject TC. None of the men had diabetes.

Laboratory Determinations

Methods of measurements of maximal oxygen uptake, blood lactate, hemoglobin, hematocrit, serum cholesterol and triglycerides, and for recording of the Frank lead ECG have recently been described in a report from this laboratory.[11] Total heart volume was calculated according to the formula given by Larsson and Kjellberg[12] by biplane radiographs taken simultaneously with the x-ray tubes at 90° angles and the subject in the prone position. Measurements of cardiac diameters were made independently by three observers and averaged.

A standard psychological test (Minnesota Multiphasic Personality Inventory, MMPI)[13] was administered. Questions were prerecorded and answers recorded on magnetic tape during the control and post-training periods.

Exercise during testing and physical training was performed on a mechanically braked bicycle ergometer.* Bicycle ergometer work loads were measured in kilopond meters per minute

---

*Cykelfabriken Monark, Varberg, Sweden.

(kpm/min). One kilopond is the force acting on the mass of 1 kg at normal acceleration of gravity. One hundred kilopond meters per minute equal 723 foot pounds per minute, or 16.35 watts. Standard pedaling rate was 50 rpm. Actual rpm counts were recorded mechanically.

Each submaximal work period lasted 6 minutes and the maximal run 3 to 6 minutes. The subjects rested 5 to 10 minutes between initial submaximal work loads and 20 to 30 minutes before the maximal run. A warm-up period of 1 to 2 minutes at the second submaximal work load immediately preceded the maximal run. Collection of expired air for measurement of oxygen uptake at submaximal loads was started after 5 minutes of exercise and completed within 1 minute. Duplicate measurements of the oxygen uptake were made at maximal levels. Expired air was collected over 30-second periods. Maximal oxygen uptake was established by the criterion of leveling of the oxygen consumption with increasing work loads. Age-specific maximal heart rates for normal subjects and postexercise lactic acid levels were used as ancillary criteria to establish that a true maximal level had been reached. The laboratory was air conditioned, and the temperature varied between 20 and 23 C.

The ECG was continuously monitored during exercise and recovery. A Frank lead ECG was recorded during the last minute of exercise, immediately after, and 3 minutes after exercise.

Experimental Design

Control studies were carried out over a 3-month period. The response to submaximal and maximal exercise was studied in each subject on three separate occasions with intervals of approximately 6 weeks. Blood chemistry and radiological and psychological studies were made at the initial visit to the laboratory.

All nine subjects took part in the training program during the first 15 weeks. Results after 7 weeks were evaluated by measurement of maximal oxygen uptake and heart rate during submaximal and maximal exercise. After 15 weeks' training the subjects underwent the full complement of tests performed during the control period. Maximal oxygen uptake was determined twice on separate days.

The subjects were then arbitrarily divided into two groups. One group (five men) continued to exercise but only once per week as compared to 3 times weekly initially. The second group (four men) discontinued training. Both subgroups were restudied after 14 weeks of this regimen, that is, 29 weeks after the beginning of the intervention.

The training program during the first 15 weeks was aimed at production of an increase in maximal oxygen uptake. The reduced frequency of training sessions in the five men who exercised during the final 14 weeks of the study represented an attempt to define the minimum amount of exercise required to maintain an improved $\dot{V}O_{2\max}$.

Paired *t*-tests were used to evaluate the results.

Training Program

The format of the training sessions was kept the same throughout the study and may be characterized as interval training. The exercise room was not air conditioned. Room temperature varied between 21 and 28 C. Each session was supervised by one of the authors and consisted of four periods of bicycle ergometer exercise, each lasting for 3 minutes and followed by a 3-minute rest period. The ECG was continuously displayed on an oscilloscope for monitoring and recorded during the last 15 seconds of each work and rest period (Fig. 2-1). A simple transthoracic bipolar ECG lead was used. Heart rate at the end of the fourth 3-minute period of interval exercise was used as an indicator of the intensity of work. Maximal heart rate varied widely within the group. The heart rate during the final 15 seconds of exercise at each session was therefore measured in terms of beats below individual maximal heart rate rather than as absolute values in order to provide a more precise index of relative load. Average heart rate data representing the intensity of exercise for each training session are presented in Figures 2-1 and 2-2.

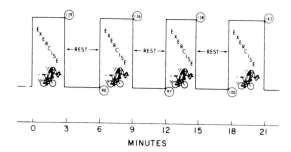

Figure 2-1. Format of all training sessions with mean heart rates (circled numerals) during the last fifteen seconds of each exercise and rest period. Heart rate data based on complete sets of measurements in all subjects during all sessions of the fifteen-week training program.

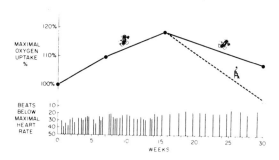

Figure 2-2. Relative changes in mean maximal oxygen uptake (in percent of mean control value) related to duration, frequency, and intensity of training. Each bar in the lower panel represents a training session, and the height indicates the beats below maximal heart rate during the last exercise period of each session (*cf.* Fig. 2-1). The broken line represents the subgroup of four subjects who discontinued training after fifteen weeks.

Work loads were adjusted during the course of the experiment to produce a heart rate at the end of the fourth exercise period within 20 to 30 beats of maximal heart rate of each subject. Somewhat lighter loads were used in subject TC because of diastolic hypertension during exercise and in subject LL because of frequent premature ventricular beats occurring during heavy exercise. Average final heart rates during exercise in these two men were 39 and 35 beats per minute below the maximal level. The group average was 29 beats below maximal heart rate during the first 7 weeks of training. Corresponding figure for the following 8 weeks was 24. This difference, implying a higher intensity of training during the second period, was significant (*P* < 0.01). The five subjects who continued to meet once weekly during the last 14 weeks of the study after the group was divided had an average final heart rate during exercise of 17 beats below their maximal level. This did not represent a significant change as compared to their heart rates during the first 15 weeks.

During the initial 15 weeks the group met three times weekly. Mean attendance rate for the group was 2.6 times per week (range of individual averages 2.4 to 3.0). The five subjects who continued to exercise after this period met once weekly for 14 weeks with a mean attendance rate of 0.9 times per week (range 0.6 to 1.0).

Results

Maximal Work

Changes in mean maximal oxygen uptake values are displayed in Figure 2-2. The relation between individual changes

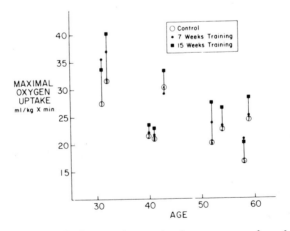

Figure 2-3. Individual changes in maximal oxygen uptake related to age. Subject identification within the circle indicates maximal oxygen uptake at the control study.

in $\dot{V}O_{2max}$ and age is presented in Figure 2-3.

Mean maximal oxygen uptake was 1.63 L/min or 24.0 ml/kg ×min for the nine subjects at the control study. The mean difference between repeated determinations of $\dot{V}O_{2max}$ during the 3-month control period was 0.04±0.005 L/min, with a standard deviation of 0.02 L/min.

The initial 7 weeks of triweekly training sessions resulted in an increase in mean $\dot{V}O_{2max}$ to 1.79 L/min and 2.64 ml/kg× min at the end of the 15-week period of triweekly exercise, representing an increase of 19% above control levels. Thus, the rate of improvement was nearly equal during the first and second halves of the conditioning period. The increase in $\dot{V}O_{2max}$ resulting from an average of 30 minutes of actual exercise per week for 15 weeks was highly significant (P <0.001).

The 14-week maintenance regimen in five men, consisting of only one session per week, resulted in a decrease in $\dot{V}O_{2max}$ to a mean value only 6% above the control level (Fig. 2-2). The four men who did not exercise during the final 14 weeks had a mean $\dot{V}O_{2max}$ 5% below their control level at the end of the study.

Mean maximal heart rate in the nine men was 167 during the control period, 165 after 7 weeks, 169 after 15 weeks of triweekly exercise, and 164 after the final 14 weeks of once weekly or control level activity. These differences were not significant.

Peak lactic acid levels of arterialized fingertip blood after maximal work were similar at each test session. Mean concentrations were 109, 104, 113, and 100 mg/100 ml. The differences were not significant.

Maximal work load data were determined. Average duration of work at the maximal level, 3.5 min, did not change. The average maximal load during the control period was 626 kpm/min and increased to 790 kpm/min after 7 weeks of triweekly exercise. Mean maximal work load was 869 kpm/min at the end of 15 weeks of conditioning, representing an increase of 243 kpm/min or 39% above control levels. This difference was highly significant (P<0.001) and larger than the change in $\dot{V}O_{2max}$.

A dissociation between changes in maximal work load and in VO_{2max} was also evident when mean maximal work loads were calculated separately for the two subgroups with different regimens during the last phase of the study. The group of five men who continued exercising during the final 14 weeks had reached a mean maximal work load of 796 kpm/min or 44.5% above the control level after the initial 15 weeks of training. The maximal load decreased to 733 kpm/min after 14 weeks of exercise only once per week or a final maximal load 33% above the control value. Corresponding figures for the group of four men who did not train during the last 14 weeks were 959 kpm/min at the end of conditioning and 843 kpm/min at the end of the study or 17.4% above their control value.

Submaximal Work

The submaximal work load required to produce a heart rate of 130 beats/min (W130) was calculated from individual work load-heart rate data by interpolation. Results are presented in Figure 2-4. Mean W130 was 357 kpm/min during the control period, 500 kpm/min after 7 weeks of triweekly exercise, and 516 kpm/min after 15 weeks. The increase of W130 to 44.6% above control levels after 15 weeks was highly significant ($P < 0.001$). Less work was required to reach W130 after 14 weeks of either no conditioning or once weekly exercise. The heart rate of the men who continued once weekly exercise had declined to a mean W130 of 30% above control levels. The four subjects who did not exercise showed a decrease in mean W130 to 34% above their control W130. Thus, changes in W130 reflected changes in VO_{2max} even less accurately than changes in maximal work load.

Heart Volume

Total heart volume was measured in seven of the nine subjects from biplane radiographs taken during the control period and after 15 weeks of triweekly exercise. The x-rays were of poor technical quality in RW and were not available after

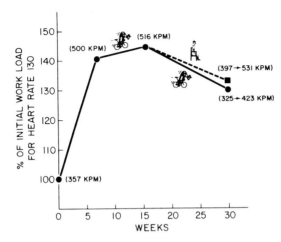

Figure 2-4. Relative changes in the work load required to produce a heart rate of 130 beats/min during the sixth minute of exercise. Mean work loads are given for the total group for the studies performed during the control period and after seven and fifteen weeks of training. Separate mean control and final values (far right) are listed for the subjects who discontinued training after fifteen weeks (broken line) and subjects who continued to exercise once weekly.

conditioning in JP.

Heart volume decreased in all seven subjects during conditioning from a mean of 980 to 895 cc ($P < 0.05$).

Electrocardiograms

The analysis of Frank lead electrocardiograms at rest and during exercise did not show any abnormalities in six of the nine men. Horizontal ST depression of 0.05 mv or more was present during maximal exercise in subjects DA, LL, and TC. TC also developed frequent premature ventricular contractions during maximal work. These ECG changes were not altered by physical training.

Other Measurements

Mean total body weight did not change significantly during the study. The largest individual changes noted during tri-weekly exercise were gains of 2.2 kg each in subjects LL and

DA.

Mean serum cholesterol levels decreased significantly ($P < 0.01$) from 247 mg/100 ml to 210 mg/100 ml during the initial 15 weeks of training. Mean triglyceride levels also declined from 137 mg/100 ml to 82 mg/100 ml; however, this change was not significant.

The subjects experienced a uniform subjective improvement in mood during training. The group mean scores for the Minnesota Multiphasic Personality Inventory show profiles nearer the T-50 value after 15 weeks of triweekly conditioning, demonstrating a change to a more "healthy" profile.[14]

Discussion

The results of this study are in keeping with the contention that blindness of long standing is associated with a stable and low level of habitual physical activity that results in a low maximal oxygen uptake. The mean control Vo_{2max} value of 24.0 ml/kg × min is lower than values reported from other groups of sedentary men in the same age range.[4,7,15] This difference probably reflects a more severe limitation of the level of physical activity among men who are restricted by blindness rather than being sedentary by choice. Only one subject had Vo_{2max} above 31 ml/kg × min. Variations in Vo_{2max} during the 3-month control period were small. Furthermore, the rapid return to control levels in the group who stopped training after 15 weeks supports the view that the training program represented an isolated change in the subjects' physical activity pattern. There is no evidence that the low Vo_{2max} was related to clinical cardiopulmonary disease in any of the men. The appearance of asymptomatic horizontal ST-segment depression during maximal work in one third of the men during heavy exercise parallels the findings of other studies.[16,17] Serum lipids were within normal limits.

The discrepancy between changes in Vo_{2max} and changes in maximal work load and W130 is larger than expected and may reflect an unusually large increase in mechanical efficiency during training of this population. No measurements of oxygen uptake at submaximal work loads were made, but the combination of data on external work performed at the maximal level and the lack of significant changes in work time and lactic acid concentration after maximal work indicates an improvement in mechanical efficiency that was retained past the point of decreasing $\dot{V}O_{2max}$ during the final phase of the study.

Five of seven studies on physical training in sedentary middle-aged and elderly men, including our own (Table 2-I), show remarkably similar results, that is, an increase in $\dot{V}O_{2max}$ from 16 to 19%. The results of the two studies dealing with 70-year-old men are divergent. Benestad[2] was unable to demonstrate any training effect on $\dot{V}O_{2max}$, whereas Barry and co-workers[3] reported a large increase, 38%. The lack of trainability shown in the report by Benestad[2] may have been related to the short training period, initial level of fitness, and low intensity of exercise during training, or it may reflect a true age difference. The results reported by Barry and co-workers[3] may at least be partially explained by the data obtained in the control period. Significantly lower peak heart rates and blood lactic acid levels at the control study suggest that the subjects did not reach a true maximal oxygen uptake before training.

The degree of similarity between our study and those by Hartley,[5] Naughton,[6] Hanson,[4] Mann,[7] and their co-workers may be fortuitous. There is evidence from studies of both young[11] and middle-aged[5] men to suggest an inverse relation between the relative change in $\dot{V}O_{2max}$ and initial $\dot{V}O_{2max}$. This trend was not apparent in our series. The control level was uniformly low, but the groups listed in Table 2-I cover a wide range. Average initial $\dot{V}O_{2max}$ varies between 40 ml/kg × min in the group studies by Hartley and associates[5] and 24 ml/kg × min in our series.

It seems reasonable to postulate that the number of sessions per week, the total duration of training, the effective duration of each session, and the intensity of exercise influence the degree of improvement. The number of training sessions per

Table 2-1

TRAINING DATA FROM SEVEN STUDIES ON TRAINING OF MIDDLE-AGED AND OLD MEN

	Siegel et al.[10]	Naughton et al.[6]	Hartley et al.[5]	Hanson et al.[4]	Mann et al.[7]	Barry et al.[3]	Benestad[2]
Number of subjects	9	18	48	7	62	8	13
Mean age (range)	46	41	(35-50)	49	(25-60)	70	75
Initial $\dot{V}_{O_2max}$ (ml/kg × min)	24.0	31.3	(2.89 L/min)	34.8	34.0	16	27
$\Delta\dot{V}_{O_2max}$ (ml/kg × min)	+4.5	+5.5	(+0.55 L/min)	+6.1	+5.6	+6.1	No change
$\Delta\dot{V}_{O_2max}$ (%)	+19	+17.8 =	+19	+17.6	+16	+38	No change
Maximal heart rate Δ	No change	No change	−7	−4	−	+14	+2
Maximal lactate (mg/100 ml)	100-109	−	−	−	−	Pre Post 49.2 70.7	−
Training duration (weeks)	15	28	8	28	~24	12	6
Frequency (sessions/week)	3	3	3	3	5	3	3
Work minutes per session (excludes "warm-up")	12	30	30	60	40	16-25	5-12
Heart rate during training (beats below max heart rate)	27	−	−	−	*	max	22-36

*In the series published by Mann and co-workers[7] heart rates reached a level of 120 to 140 beats/min during warm-up and increased episodically during work-outs to 160-190 beats/min.

week was the same in four of the series compiled in Table 2-I with a variation in the total duration of training from 8 to 28 weeks. The group studied by Mann and co-workers[7] trained 5 days per week for 6 months. The average rate of improvement in $\dot{V}O_{2max}$ in our own series was approximately equal during the first and second halves of the conditioning program, suggesting that a longer period of training may have produced a larger increase in $\dot{V}O_{2max}$. The effective duration of each session in the five series ranged from 12 to 60 minutes. Sufficient data on the intensity of work to permit a meaningful comparison are not available. Bidirectional variations with respect to duration and intensity may be responsible for equalization of the results.

Data from the literature and from our study offer some support for an alternate hypothesis. The dose-response curve characterizing the relation between the quantity of training and the improvement in $\dot{V}O_{2max}$ may be hyperbolic (S-shaped) with virtually no improvement in $\dot{V}O_{2max}$ below a certain threshold quantity of training and rapidly diminishing returns once a critical level has been exceeded. The quantity of training may in turn be a nonlinear function of intensity, frequency, duration of session, and duration of program, but lack of data makes it impossible even to approximate this function. A threshold effect has been demonstrated with respect to the intensity of training measured as heart rate during exercise. The critical level approximately corresponds to resting heart rate plus 60% of the difference between resting and maximal heart rates[18,20] or about 130 beats/min in the age group 40 to 50. Furthermore, Mann and associates[7] found no significant difference in the degree of improvement between subjects who had an attendance record of 50 to 79% and those who participated in 80 to 100% of their available five sessions per week over 6 months. Once-weekly half-hour sessions with caloric expenditures varying as widely as from 300 to 1,175 proved equally effective in maintaining the improvement in $\dot{V}O_{2max}$. Consistent with the hypothesis also is the fact that training 2.6 times per week for an effective total of 30 minutes resulted in a significant increase in $\dot{V}O_{2max}$ in our series, but 0.9 session per week or 10 effective minutes failed to maintain the improvement.

Previous studies[11] have demonstrated that the increase in $\dot{V}O_{2max}$ after training in sedentary normal young subjects is due to both an increase in maximal stroke volume and a widening of the maximal arteriovenous oxygen difference. Hemodynamic data from the series studied by Hartley and associates[5] suggest that the improvement in $\dot{V}O_{2max}$ in sedentary middle-aged men may be attributed solely to an increase in maximal stroke volume. Cross-sectional studies have shown that there is a linear relation between total heart volume and maximal oxygen uptake[16,21] in both young and middle-aged normal men. Changes in total heart volume closely paralleled changes in stroke volume, cardiac output, and maximal oxygen uptake in a series of five young normal subjects studied in this laboratory after bed rest and after physical training.[11] A significant decrease in total heart volume after training is surprising in the present series of middle-aged men against this background, but similar results have been reported from a study of a comparable group.[22] However, Mann and associates[7] found an increase in heart volume after training, and Hartley's group[5] reported no significant change. X-rays for determination of total heart volume were taken with the subject in the prone position to minimize measurement errors[12] and to conform to previous studies relating heart volume to physical performance.[5,11,16,21]

The decline in mean serum cholesterol values after conditioning was small but significant, whereas the decrease in mean serum triglyceride levels was variable. Other investigators[23,24] have found more reduction in triglyceride levels than in cholesterol. On the other hand, Mann and associates[7] reported a decrease in cholesterol and an increase in triglycerides after training. It should be noted that the decrease in serum cholesterol occurred without any loss in total body weight. The possibility that the fall in serum cholesterol reflected seasonal changes[25] cannot be excluded. Control samples were drawn during September and October, and the training phase was concluded during May.

The psychological improvement after conditioning may be related to several factors in the study, for example, the medical and personal attention that the subjects received. The men were able to improve their self-image as a result of this factor, and they also realized that their work capabilities were improving. Therefore, the effect of increased physical work capacity on mood and anxiety cannot be evaluated independently. Similar changes in MMPI factors have also been reported by Hellerstein and associates[26] after training in patients with clinical coronary disease.

The subjects tolerated the interval training program quite well, with only trivial muscular pain during the first week of the program. This is in keeping with the current concepts that interval training technics allow heavy central circulatory loading without producing progressive skeletal muscle metabolic changes.[27] The appeal of pedaling a bicycle indoors may be limited. Many subjects will undoubtedly find it boring to use only one type of exercise and one particular pattern. On the other hand, the program requires a minimum of time and is extremely simple to administer and monitor. The general pattern of activity may be applied to any type of exercise involving large muscle groups.

REFERENCES

1. FRICK MH: Coronary implications of hemodynamic changes caused by physical training. Amer J Cardiol 22: 417, 1968
2. BENESTAD AM: Trainability of old men. Acta Med Scand 178: 321, 1965
3. BARRY AJ, DALY JW, PRUETT EDR, ET AL: The effects of physical conditioning on older individuals: I. Work capacity, circulatory-respiratory function, and work electrocardiogram. J Gerontol 21:182, 1966
4. HANSON JS, TABAKIN BS, LEVY AM, ET AL: Long-term physical training and cardiovascular dynamics in middle-age men. Circulation 38:783, 1968
5. HARTLEY LH, ÅSTRAND I, KIHLBOM Å, ET AL: Improvement of maximal oxygen uptake and cardiac output by physical training in sedentary middle-age men. Proc Internat Union Physiol Sci 7: 183, 1968
6. NAUGHTON J, NAGLE F: Peak oxygen intake during physical fitness program for middle-aged men: Measurement of changes by laboratory and field testing. JAMA 191: 899, 1965
7. MANN GV, GARRETT HL, FARHI A, ET AL: Exercise to prevent coronary heart disease: An experimental study of the effects of training on risk

factors for coronary disease in men. Amer J Med 46: 12, 1969

8. MITCHELL JH, SPROULE BJ, CHAPMAN CB: The physiological meaning of the maximal oxygen intake test. J Clin Invest 37: 538, 1958

9. LAMM G: Discussion. *In* Physical Activity and the Heart, edited by MJ Karvone, AJ Barry. Springfield, Illinois, Charles C Thomas, Publisher, 1967, p 248

10. SIEGEL W, BLOMQVIST G, MITCHELL JH: Effect of physical training on maximal oxygen uptake in middle-aged sedentary men. Circulation 38 (suppl VI): VI-180, 1968

11. SALTIN B, BLOMQVIST G, MITCHELL JH, ET AL: Response to exercise after bed rest and after training: A longitudinal study of adaptive changes in oxygen transport and body composition. Circulation 38 (suppl. VII): VII-1, 1968

12. LARSSON H, KJELLBERG SR: Roentgenological heart volume determination with special regard to pulse rate and the position of the body. Acta Radiol 29: 159, 1948

13. HATHAWAY SR, MEEHL PE: An Atlas for Clinical Use of the MMPI. Minneapolis, University of Minnesota Press, 1951

14. FLEESON W, GLUECK B JR, HEISTAD G, ET AL: The ataraxic effect of two phenothiazine drugs on an outpatient population. Minn Univ Med Bull 29: 274, 1958

15. FOX SM, III SKINNER JS: Some planning in the United States for further studies to define the relationship between physical activity and coronary heart disease. *In* Physical Activity and the Heart, edited by MJ Karvonen, AJ Barry. Springfield, Illinois, Charles C Thomas, Publisher, 1967, p 231

16. BLOMQVIST G, STENBERG J: The Frank lead electrocardiogram in young and middle-aged male controls during light, moderate, and maximal exercise. Acta Med Scand 178 (suppl. 440): 40, 1965

17. HORNSTEN TR, BRUCE RA: Computer analysis of ST responses to submaximal exercise. Circulation 38 (suppl. VI): VI-102, 1968

18. HOLLMANN W, VENRATH H: Die Beeinflussung von Herzgrösse, maximaler O_2-Aufnahme und Ausdauergrenze durch ein Ausdauer training mittlerer und hoher Intensität. Der Sportarzt 9: 189, 1963

19. KARVONEN MJ, KENTALA E, MUSTALA O: The effects of training on heart rate: A longitudinal study. Ann Med Exp Biol Fenn 35: 307, 1957

20. ROSKAMM H: Optimum patterns of exercise for healthy adults. Canad Med Ass J 96: 895, 1967

21. ÅSTRAND P-O, CUDDY TE, SALTIN B, ET AL: Cardiac output during submaximal and maximal work. J Appl Physiol 19: 268, 1964

22. CURETON TK: Shrinkage of the heart size associated with improved cardiovascular condition. J Ass Phys Ment Rehab 10: 75, 1956

23. SHANE SR: Relation between serum lipids and physical conditioning. Amer J Cardiol 18: 540, 1966

24. HOLLOSZY JO, SKINNER JS, TORO G, ET AL: Effects of a six month

program of endurance exercise on the serum lipids of middle-aged men. Amer J Cardiol 14: 753, 1964

25. DOYLE JT, KINCH SH, BROWN DF: Seasonal variation in serum cholesterol concentration. J Chron Dis 18: 657, 1965

26. HELLERSTEIN HK, HORNSTEN TR, GOLDBARG AN, ET AL: The influence of active conditioning upon coronary atherosclerosis. *In* Atherosclerotic Vascular Disease, edited by AN Brest, JH Moyer. New York, Appleton-Century-Crofts, 1967, p 115

27. ÅSTRAND I, ASTRAND P-O, CHRISTENSEN EH, ET AL: Intermittent muscular work. Acta Physiol Scand 48: 448, 1960

DISCUSSION

SHOCK concludes that the "available data do not prove conclusively that activity or exercise significantly alter the 'rate of aging'." There is ample evidence that athletes and nonathletes differ in various physiological measures, such as maximal oxygen uptake ($\dot{V}O_{2max}$), maximal cardiac output, maximal stroke volume, and maximal heart rate, as well as in body composition; all of these variables show changes with age. Cross-sectional studies, however, provide little evidence that the *rate* of change with age differs between athletes (including those who remain active) and nonathletes.

Hodgson (1971) has reviewed the evidence for age changes in maximal oxygen consumption in various groups. These cross-sectional data suggest that active athletes retain a greater capacity for endurance than nonathletes (sedentary persons), but that the rate of deterioration is similar. Similarly, Lester et al. (1968) found that trained men (including high school, college, and Olympic athletic champions) and nontrained men showed the same rate of change in heart rate with age. As in other studies, the maximal heart rate of the trained men was significantly lower for all age groups.

Shock (see Chp. 1), however, noted the important distinction between cross-sectional and longitudinal studies of aging. The idea of the importance of longitudinal studies is defensible on theoretical and empirical grounds. Damon (1965) gives some examples of discrepancies between findings of cross-sectional and longitudinal studies of physique and physiology; only longitudinal studies provide data on age changes in *individuals*. Dehn and Bruce (1972) reviewed data from longitudinal studies on changes in $\dot{V}O_{2max}$ with age, in inactive and active men (Figure I-1). The rate of change is greater in longitudinal than in cross-sectional studies (Hodgson and Buskirk, 1977). More relevant to our discussion is the greater change with age in inactive than in active groups in some studies (reviewed by Alexander, 1975); more longitudinal studies are needed, however, to clarify this issue (Hodgson and Buskirk, 1977).

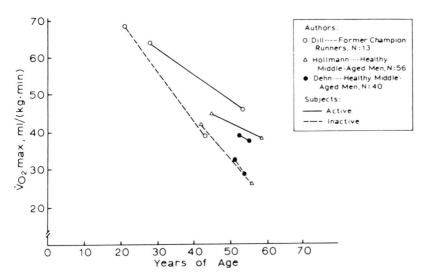

Figure I-1. Longitudinal decline of $\dot{V}o_{2max}$ according to habitual physical activity status. From M. M. Dehn and R. A. Bruce: Longitudinal variations in maximal oxygen intake with age and activity, *Journal of Applied Physiology, 33*:805-807, 1972. Courtesy of American Physiological Society.

Several lines of evidence suggest that exercise can increase maximal oxygen uptake only within certain limits, perhaps determined in part by genetic factors (Klissouras, 1971). Physical training appears to have an effect on $\dot{V}o_{2max}$ during growth. In a longitudinal study of boys followed from age 11 to 15 years (Parizkova, 1968), and a short-term study of 8- to 12-year-old children (Lussier and Buskirk, 1977), physically trained groups showed increased functional aerobic capacity compared with untrained groups. As noted by Siegel et al. (see Chp. 2) several short-term studies on young men also show an increase in $\dot{V}o_{2max}$ with physical training. The levels attained by training in later life in sedentary men, however, do not approach those attained by trained athletes.

Several studies, as reviewed by Siegel et al., show short-term changes in physiological and biochemical characteristics during exercise programs in sedentary men. These studies are in general agreement in showing that such changes are reversible; that is, there is a tendency to revert to original levels after training ceases. This is also true for changes in body composition, including reduction in body fat (or increase in "lean body mass").

Figure I-2 shows some results of a study (Garrett, Pangle, and

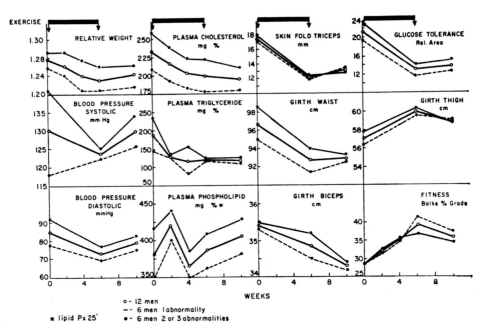

Figure I-2. The trends observed for twelve variables measured to evaluate the effects of strenuous physical training. The mean values are shown for six men with one risk factor originally (solid circles with broken lines), for six other men with two or more risk factors (solid circles with solid lines), and for all twelve men (open circles). The period of supervised exercise is shown as a heavy bar at the top. The initial values represent a mean of two measurements of each variable for each man, measured two weeks apart before training started. The glucose tolerance is shown here as relative area under the three-hour curve. Reprinted with permission from *Journal of Chronic Diseases*, Vol. 19, H. L. Garrett et al.: Physical conditioning and coronary risk factors, copyright 1966, Pergamon Press, Ltd.

Mann, 1966) on the effects of a 6-week program of physical exercise (90 minutes on each of 5 days per week) among 12 men recruited from a graduate school setting. Selection was based on high initial levels of "risk factors" (serum cholesterol, blood pressure, and obesity) associated with coronary heart disease. Levels of various characteristics were compared before the training program, at intervals during the 6-week program, and 4 weeks after completion of the program. Some significant changes were observed during training (Figure I-2), but many measurements tended to revert toward original levels 4 weeks after completion of the program.

The evidence for an effect of physical training on plasma triglyceride level is conflicting. Long-term changes have not been fully supported in some studies but evidence from recent studies (Shorey, Sewell, and O'Brien, 1976; Gyntelberg et al., 1977) support the idea of a role of exercise in lowering plasma triglyceride in some persons with high lipid levels. Plasma triglyceride levels were much lower among 14 active long-distance runners than among nonathletes matched on age, height, and weight. In the nonathletes, but not in the athletes, a statistically significant positive correlation was found between age and plasma triglyceride level (Hurter et al., 1972). Somewhat similar results were reported by Wood et al. (1977) on 84 "runners" in California compared with 1,679 controls randomly selected from nearby towns. It should be noted, however, that these are all cross-sectional data.

Men and women exhibit marked increases in fat content with increasing age (Parizkova, 1964). With exercise training, changes in body composition (Parizkova, 1964, 1965) and anthropometric measures (Seltzer, 1946; Tanner, 1952; Skinner et al., 1964; Garrett et al., 1966) run counter to this trend. These changes, including weight reduction, are transient and are maintained only by continued exercise. There have been few long-term longitudinal studies of exercise and body composition. Among boys followed from age 11 to 15 (Parizkova, 1968), an increase in proportion of lean body mass was found in the most active group. Although most of 16 champion runners restudied after 20 years showed decreased lean body mass, those currently active showed the least decline (Dill et al., 1967).

The transitory nature of physiologic changes related to physical training, and the importance of longitudinal data, are emphasized by Robinson et al. (1973). Ten men who underwent a 6-month strenuous athletic training program at 18-22 years of age were restudied at age 41-44 and again at age 50-54. The changes observed during the 6-month training period, including improvement in aerobic work capacity, had disappeared after about 22 years of sedentary life; the men had gained an average of 11 kg (24.2 lbs) in weight and the percentage of body fat had increased.

There have been a number of detailed studies of old athletes who continue exercise and competition, as reviewed by Kavanagh and Shephard (1977) and Webb, Urner and McDaniels (1977). These data suggest that in these highly select individuals physical training may influence the age-related decline in cardiopulmonary function observed in ordinary sedentary men. The relevance of such small studies on select volunteers to the general population, however, is open to question (Taylor, Buskirk and Remington, 1973) — a point which will be discussed further in the *Concluding Remarks*.

It should be noted that several animal experiments have reported greater life expectancy among exercise versus control animals. If this is a real effect, the mechanisms are unclear. Among albino rats (Retzlaff, Fontaine, and Furuta, 1966) the effect appeared to be related to a change in metabolism in the exercised group, which purportedly "retards the rate of biologic aging." In another study of (male) albino rats, however, the effect of exercise on longevity appeared to be unrelated to metabolic rate (Drori and Folman, 1976). The incidence at autopsy of pneumonia and nephritis, but not of tumors, was significantly lower in the exercised than in the control rats; the immediate cause of death was not evaluated, but pneumonia is known to be the most common cause of death in these animals (Drori and Folman, 1976). The relevance of these findings to the human situation is uncertain.

In summary, physical training may produce changes in physiologic and biochemical factors, and in body composition, that run counter to the changes ordinarily seen with increasing age. To maintain most (if not all) of these changes, however, physical training must be continued. There is some evidence that the long-term rate of decline with age in certain body functions may be affected by physical training, but more (longitudinal) studies are needed. An apparent advantage with respect to work tolerance and disease susceptibility could exist for physically trained, active persons. Even if the rate of decline with age in various characteristics differs little between athletes (or other physically trained men) and inactive men, the advantages of the former group may still hold at each age. For such variables as body fat, heart rate, blood pressure, and plasma triglycerides, such relative advantages could favorably affect longevity by reducing risk of disease (e.g., hypertension, coronary heart disease, diabetes mellitus).

It should be apparent from this brief review that there are many uncertainties in our understanding of the long-term effects of physical exercise on "aging." These uncertainties are related in part to more fundamental problems in aging research, and to the need for long-term studies of the effects of exercise in large populations.

REFERENCES

Alexander, R. 1975 Physical fitness, cardiovascular function and age — Discussant's perspective. *In:* Ostfeld, A.M. and D.C. Gibson (Eds.) Epidemiology of Aging. DHEW Publication No. (NIH)75-711. U.S. Public Health Service, Washington, D.C., pp. 243-247.

Damon, A. 1965 Discrepancies between findings of longitudinal and cross-sectional studies in adult life: Physique and physiology. Human Develop. *8:*16-22.

Dehn, M.M. and R.A. Bruce 1972 Longitudinal variations in maximal oxygen uptake with age and activity. J. Appl. Physiol. *33:*805-807.

Dill, D.B., S. Robinson, and J.C. Ross 1967 A longitudinal study of 16 champion runners. J. Sports Med. Phys. Fitness *7:*4-27.

Drori, D. and Y. Folman 1976 Environmental effects on longevity in the male rat: Exercise, mating, castration and restricted feeding. Exper. Gerontol. *11:*25-32.

Garrett, H.L., R.V. Pangle, and G.V. Mann 1966 Physical conditioning and coronary risk factors. J. Chron. Dis. *19:*899-908.

Gyntelberg, F., R. Brennan, J.O. Holloszy, G. Schonfeld, M.J. Rennie, and S.W. Weidman 1977 Plasma triglyceride lowering by exercise despite increased food intake in patients with type IV hyperlipoproteinuria. Amer. J. Clin. Nutrition *30*:716-720.

Hodgson, J.L. 1971 Age and aerobic capacity of urban midwestern males. Thesis, University of Minneapolis, Minneapolis.

Hodgson, J.L. and E.R. Buskirk 1977 Physical fitness and age, with emphasis on cardiovascular function in the elderly. J. Amer. Geriat. Soc. *25*:385-392.

Hurter, R., J. Sivale, M.A. Peyman, and C.W.H. Barnett 1972 Some immediate and long-term effects of exercise on the plasma lipids. Lancet *2*:671-675.

Kavanagh, T. and R.J. Shephard 1977 The effects of continued training on the aging process. Ann. N.Y. Acad. Sci. *301*:656-670.

Klissouras, V. 1971 Heritability of adaptive variation. J. Appl. Physiol. *31*:338-344.

Lester, M., L.T. Sheffield, P. Trammell, and T.J. Reeves 1968 The effect of age and athletic training on the maximal heart rate during muscular exercise. Amer. Heart J. *76*:370-376.

Lussier, L. and E.R. Buskirk 1977 Effects of an endurance training regimen on assessment of work capacity in prepubertal children. Ann. N.Y. Acad. Sci. *301*:734-747.

Parizkova, J. 1964 Impact of age, diet and exercise on man's body composition. *In*: Jokl, E. and E. Simon (Eds.) International Research in Sport and Physical Education. Charles C Thomas, Springfield, Illinois.

Parizkova, J. 1965 Physical activity and body composition. *In*: Brozek, J. (Ed.) Human Body Composition: Approaches and Applications. Pergamon Press, Oxford.

Parizkova, J. 1968 Longitudinal study of the development of body composition and body build in boys of various physical activity. Human Biol. *40*:212-225.

Retzlaff, E., J. Fontaine, and W. Furuta 1966 Effect of daily exercise on life-span of albino rats. Geriatrics *21*:171-177.

Robinson, S., D.B. Dill, J.C. Ross, R.D. Robinson, J.A. Wagner, and S.P. Tzankoff 1973 Training and physiological aging in man. Federation Proc. *32*:1628-1634.

Seltzer, C.C. 1946 Chest circumference changes as a result of severe physical training. Amer. J. Phys. Anthropol. *4*:389-393.

Shorey, R.L., B. Sewell, and M. O'Brien 1976 Efficacy of diet and exercise in the reduction of serum cholesterol and triglyceride in free-living adult males. Amer. J. Clin. Nutrition *29*:512-521.

Siegel, W., G. Blomqvist, and J.H. Mitchell 1970 Effects of a quantitated physical training program on middle-aged sedentary men. Circulation *41*:19-29.

Skinner, J.S., J.O. Holloszy, and T.K. Cureton 1964 Effects of a program of endurance exercises on physical work capacity and anthropometric measurements of fifteen middle-aged men. Amer. J. Cardiol. *14*:747-752.

Tanner, J.M. 1952 The effect of weight-training on physique. Amer. J. Phys. Anthropol. *10*:427-462.

Taylor, H.L., E.R. Buskirk, and R.D. Remington 1973 Exercise in controlled trials of the prevention of coronary heart disease. Federation Proc. *32*:1623-1627.

Webb, J.L., S.C. Urner, and J. McDaniels 1977 Physiological characteristics of a champion runner: Age 77. J. Gerontol. *32*:286-290.

Wood, P.D., W.L. Haskell, M.P. Stern, S. Lewis, and C. Perry 1977 Plasma lipoprotein distributions in male and female runners. Ann. N. Y. Acad. Sci. *301*:748-763.

Section II

Some Characteristics
of Athletes

Chapter 3

SOME CHARACTERISTICS
OF ATHLETES

ANTHONY P. POLEDNAK

As noted in the Introduction, athletes are select groups with respect to many characteristics; some of the
differences between athletes and nonathletes, and among various groups of athletes, have been documented rather exten-
sively. This chapter will discuss the findings of some studies on
the physique of athletes. The relevance of physique to longevity and correlations between physique and specific diseases
are also reviewed. Finally, selection of athletes according to
other characteristics is discussed briefly.

Body Build and Body Composition

Various methods have been developed for measuring or de-
scribing human physique. Anthropometry is the measurement
of body height and weight, surface dimensions, and dimensions
of body segments. Studies of body composition involve such
methods as densitometry, hydrometry, radiology, and measurement of skinfold thickness. In the description of human body
form, the technique of somatotyping was developed by Sheldon
(1940) and modified by several subsequent investigators.
Briefly, somatotyping is a system of rating components of physique using photographs of persons (without clothing). These
components are endomorphy (roundness, softness), mesomorphy (robustness, boniness, and muscularity) and ectomorphy (linearity, fragility). The "somatotype" consists of the
ratings, on a scale of 1 to 7, for each component; for example,
the 3-5-2 somatotype indicates that mesomorphy is dominant
(see Figs. 3-1, 3-2, 3-3). Studies of the physique of athletes have
involved all of these methods.

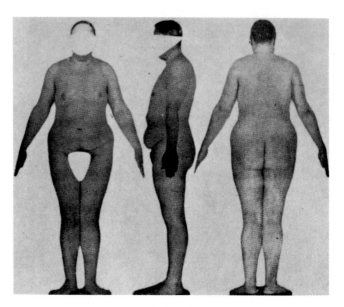

Figure 3-1. Extreme endomorph (somatotype 7-1-2). From W. H. Sheldon: *Atlas of Men: A Guide for Somatotyping the Adult Male at All Ages,* New York, Harper & Row, Publishers, 1954.

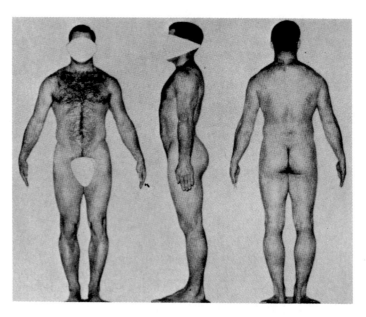

Figure 3-2. Extreme mesomorph (somatotype 1-7-1). From W. H. Sheldon: *Atlas of Men: A Guide for Somatotyping the Adult Male at All Ages,* New York, Harper & Row, Publishers, 1954.

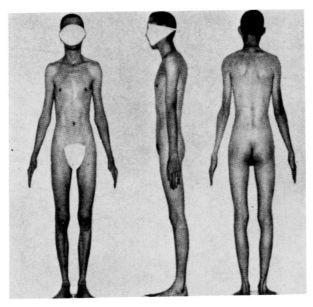

Figure 3-3. Extreme ectomorph (somatotype 1-1-7). From W. H. Sheldon: *Atlas of Men: A Guide for Somatotyping the Adult Male at All Ages,* New York, Harper & Row, Publishers, 1954.

Numerous studies have demonstrated that athletes (at various ages and levels of achievement) differ from nonathletes in body build, and that athletes in different sports also differ in body size and shape. Carter (1970) has reviewed some of these studies, as summarized in Table 3-I where height, weight, and somatotype data on various types of athletes and a small group of nonathletes are summarized. Carter's (1970) data on nonathletes, however, are not extensive, since only a small sample of selected college students are included, i.e., 18 men whose rating on endomorphy exceeded that for mesomorphy. Further data on somatotype and body size among nonathletes compared with athletes are provided in Chapters 6, 7, and 12 (Polednak and Damon, 1970; Polednak, 1972a, 1972b).

It is interesting to note that body size (height and weight) of college athletes in various sports has shown secular (long-term) changes (Malina, 1972; Polednak, 1975). Lettermen in football

Table 3-I

MEAN VALUES FOR SELECTED GROUPS OF MALE CHAMPION ATHLETES

Sample	N	Age (yr)	Ht. (cm)	Wt. (kg)	Endo-morphy	Meso-morphy	Ecto-morphy
San Diego State Swimmers	24	19.9	179.3	74.9	2.4	5.4	2.6
Cureton's Champion Swimmers	21	21.4	183.4	79.6	2.9	5.4	2.7
English Channel Swimmers	11	N.A.	171.5	86.4	4.1	5.1	2.0
San Diego State Football players	35	21.3	184.4	94.4	4.2	6.3	1.4
U. of Iowa Football players	20	19.9	182.1	86.1	3.2	6.2	1.6
"Oregon" Football players	66	20.3	181.6	84.9	3.6	5.5	2.1
Cureton's Track & Field Champions	19	24.2	179.6	72.6	2.5	5.2	3.1
1960 Olympic Track & Field Throwers	14	23.6	189.2	100.3	2.8	6.7	1.4
San Diego State Cross-Country Runners	17	20.2	179.3	65.7	1.8	3.9	4.0
Monte Vista H.S. Cross-Country Runners	8	17.3	175.0	61.6	2.2	4.2	3.9
Olympic Distance Runners	34	25.9	176.5	63.2	1.5	4.6	3.6
Danish Gymnasts	15	24.6	172.7	74.9	2.6	6.2	1.5
U. of Iowa Gymnasts	10	22.3	176.5	71.8	2.0	5.8	2.6
U.S.S.R. Gymnasts	5	N.A.	172.7	72.2	2.6	6.0	2.1
San Diego State Basketball Players	10	20.6	190.0	83.4	2.4	4.9	3.3
U. of Iowa Basketball Players	10	19.6	186.9	79.7	2.7	4.9	3.0
U.S.S.R. Basketball Players	8	N.A.	192.5	87.5	2.9	4.6	4.1

Table 3-1 (Continued)

MEAN VALUES FOR SELECTED GROUPS OF MALE CHAMPION ATHLETES

Sample	N	Age (yr)	Ht. (cm)	Wt. (kg)	Endo-morphy	Meso-morphy	Ecto-morphy
San Diego Baseball Players	151	19.7	179.3	78.2	3.8	5.0	2.7
U. of Iowa Baseball Players	10	20.3	180.3	80.7	3.8	5.2	2.2
British Empire Games Wrestlers	33	27.0	173.2	77.2	2.1	6.2	1.6
U.S.S.R. Wrestlers	34	N.A.	167.1	77.1	3.5	6.4	1.3
A.A.U. Champion Weightlifters	43	N.A.	N.A.	N.A.	2.9	6.5	1.2
British Empire Games Weightlifters	29	26.2	167.9	73.1	1.8	7.6	0.9
U.S.S.R. Weightlifters	54	N.A.	164.6	77.2	4.2	6.6	1.0
British Empire Games Boxers	39	N.A.	171.5	65.8	3.0	5.1	2.8
San Diego State Golfers	9	21.1	181.4	81.0	4.1	5.0	2.3
San Diego State Rowers	21	20.2	183.6	79.8	2.7	5.1	2.6
N.Z. Physical Education Majors	60	20.7	176.3	72.6	2.5	5.4	2.1
Finnish Champion Lumberjacks	40	33.0[a]	173.7[b]	73.1[b]	2.0	5.5	3.0
U.S. College "non-athletes"	18	19.5	181.9	76.8	5.0	3.3	3.4

[a] Karvonen (1955)
[b] N = 60
N.A. = not available.

Reprinted with permission from *Human Biology*, Vol. 42, J.E.L. Carter: The somatotypes of athletes: A review, copyright 1970, Wayne State University Press.

and crew showed greater increase in height and weight than lettermen in various other sports (baseball, ice hockey, track, and two or more sports) around the turn of the century (Polednak, 1975). Changes in the rules of the game of football probably led to the selection of larger-sized men, since success in the game depended in part on body size.

Large body size is apparently an important contributor to success in many sports. Tallness is an apparent advantage in many Olympic events (Khosla, 1968, 1971). For some sports or events, however, large body size may be less important. College athletes in baseball, distance track events (Carter, 1970), and gymnastics (Carter, 1971) include a wide range of body sizes and shapes. Distance runners in collegiate (Parnell, 1951; Behnke and Royce, 1966; Carter, 1970) and Olympic events (Khosla, 1968; Tanner, 1964, 1976) and elite class distance runners (Pollock et al., 1977) appear to be selected for leanness and shorter stature, relative to other athletes.

In addition to studies of body measurements and somatotype, a number of studies of the body composition of different types of athletes have been reported. Such data are of particular interest with regard to longevity, since the amount of body fat may be determined in body-composition analyses, and obesity is related to mortality (as noted below). Among college athletes, Novak, Hyatt, and Alexander (1968) found that football and baseball players had large amounts of body fat relative to track men and gymnasts (who were extremely lean). This is not unexpected in view of the differences in somatotype (i.e., in endomorphy or roundness) noted above (Carter, 1970; Polednak, 1972b — Chp.12). Endomorphy is highly (positively) correlated with percentage of body fat (Damon and Goldman, 1964).

Relative to "normal" standards, however, many football players are lean, in terms of percentage of body fat (Behnke and Royce, 1966). Novak et al. (1968) reported that several college football backs had only about 5% body fat, while the heaviest linemen had 26% fat; less than 21% body fat is considered "lean" for males. Football players also had the highest average excretion of creatinine (an estimate of muscle mass) among several types of college athletes studied (Novak et al., 1968). Again, this latter finding is in agreement with the relatively high mesomorphy ratings of football players (see Carter, 1970; Polednak, 1972b).

As Carter has observed, descriptive data on the physique of athletes and nonathletes represents the influence of physique on the selection of sport (or type of sport) and any effect of physical exercise on the development of physique (or on changes in physique with age). In a longitudinal study of a socioeconomically homogeneous group of boys followed from age 11 to 15 years and divided into four subgroups based on physical activity, there was a significant decrease in total body fat (and an increase in lean body mass) in the most-active group (Parizkova, 1968). There were few significant changes in anthropometric characteristics (height, weight, etc.); the most-active group, however, developed a narrower pelvis relative to body height and shoulder (biacromial) breadth. Malina (1969) has reviewed the meagre evidence on the effect of exercise on growth, and noted the need for further work. After the growth period, changes in body composition and anthropometric measures with exercise (described in Section I) are transient and are maintained only by continued exercise.

Physique in Relation to Longevity and Mortality

Data from insurance companies indicate that "overweight" is associated with increased mortality, especially from cardiovascular diseases (Society of Actuaries, 1959). Overweight persons who reduce, and maintain reductions in weight, may substantially increase their life expectancy (Dublin and Marks, 1951). There are few studies of physique in relation to overall longevity in large populations. Follow-up studies on insured persons (Society of Actuaries, 1959) and on college men (Damon, 1971) indicate that stocky men have shorter lives than leaner men.

Considerable work has been done on associations between

physique and specific diseases; of course, physique is not a direct "cause" of any disease, but may be correlated with factors that are causally related. The results of some studies have been reviewed by Damon (1970). Most relevant to our subsequent discussion of the longevity of male athletes are the findings on hypertension, coronary heart disease, and adult-onset diabetes mellitus.

The relationship between physique and risk of various manifestations of coronary heart disease (CHD) is complex and can only be summarized briefly here. Data from the Framingham (Mass) Heart Study indicate that degree of obesity is related to risk of angina pectoris and sudden death (Kannel et al., 1967). Young men (age 35-49) with angina pectoris, coronary insufficiency, or sudden death were significantly more endomorphic and mesomorphic than men without CHD (Damon et al., 1969). The importance of obesity in risk (and prevention) of CHD may be due to the relation between body weight and "risk factors" or "atherogenic traits" (i.e., high levels of serum cholesterol, systolic blood pressure, and blood glucose and uric acid). Evidence suggests that correction of overweight will reduce CHD risk, so that overweight may be "a correctable major determinant of the atherogenic traits so prevalent in the general population" (Ashley and Kannel, 1974). The apparent effect of weight loss, without salt restriction, on hypertension (a major "risk factor" in coronary heart disease) was demonstrated in a recent study by Reisin et al. (1978).

Obesity and stockiness are associated with increased risk of essential hypertension (Robinson and Brucer, 1940; Society of Actuaries, 1959; Goldman et al., 1972) and adult-onset diabetes mellitus (Lister and Tanner, 1955; Paffenbarger and Wing, 1973). In contrast, the linear (or tall, thin) physique is associated with susceptibility to the tuberculosis (Berry and Nash, 1955; Palmer et al., 1957; Edwards et al., 1971), but this disease is no longer a major cause of death in industrialized populations.

The relevance of these findings on physique to studies on the longevity and mortality of athletes will be considered in Section

III. As noted above, athletes tend to be larger in body size than nonathletes and have higher endomorphy ratings, but the amount of body fat varies considerably among athletes. The dominance of the mesomorphic component among athletes must also be considered in comparing CHD mortality in athletes and nonathletes. A question of importance may be the weight gain in athletes versus nonathletes in later life (e.g., after college, for college men), since overweight is an important risk factor in several conditions (hypertension, CHD, and adult-onset diabetes mellitus) that affect mortality in middle age and beyond. As we have already noted, lifetime exercise habits may also be relevant to the longevity of athletes.

Personality and Personal Habits

Only a few of the numerous studies on the personality of high-school and college athletes are cited here, partly because the relationships between psychological or personality factors and health are not well known (although there has been much speculation). Interested readers are referred to literature reviews by Cooper (1969) and Butt (1976).

Studies of high school and college males suggest that athletes, relative to nonathletic classmates, score higher on scales of extroversion, social aggression, competitiveness, dominance, and leadership (Cooper, 1969; Hunt, 1969; Fletcher and Dowell, 1971). These characteristics are mentioned here because they resemble some components of a behavior pattern ("Type A") associated with increased risk of coronary heart disease in some but not all studies (Haynes et al., 1978). The evidence for the role of this behavior pattern has been reviewed recently by Jenkins (1976), and Friedman and Rosenman (1974) have presented a popular account. Further reference to this behavior pattern is made in Chapter 12, which discusses mortality from coronary heart disease among athletes and nonathletes.

Data on the personal habits (smoking, alcohol consumption, diet) of athletes versus nonathletes appear to be limited but are of great interest with respect to longevity studies. Data obtained from questionnaires among former college athletes and their classmates (see Montoye et al., 1956, 1962) indicate significantly higher percentages of "smokers" and "drinkers" among former athletes than among nonathletes who attended Michigan State University. A group of former champion athletes in Finland, comprising international competitors and Olympic gold medal winners, however, contained more nonsmokers and fewer heavy smokers than "controls" (Pyörälä et al., 1967), but the sample sizes were small and the comparability of the groups compared was open to question. Marathon runners also reportedly tend to smoke and drink less than the general population (Milvy, 1977), but not all groups of "runners" may drink less than controls (Wood et al., 1977). None of the follow-up studies on the longevity of athletes in the References have been able to control for differences in lifetime smoking habits between athletes and nonathletes, although Milvy (1977) has presented a theoretical consideration of the possible effect of such differences.

Data on dietary habits among athletes and nonathletes also appear to be meagre. The "anabolic" steroids were introduced too late to have an effect on the athletes involved in studies reported in this book; this is an important point, in view of the possible harmful effects of these compounds (Freed and Banks, 1972; Johnson et al., 1972). Information on weight gain after college among former athletes and their classmates is relevant to the question of dietary habits.

REFERENCES

Ashley, F.W., Jr. and W.B. Kannel 1974 Relation of weight change to changes in atherogenic traits: The Framingham study. J. Chron. Dis. 27:103-114.

Behnke, A.R. and J. Royce 1966 Body size, shape and composition of several types of athletes. J. Sports Med. Phys. Fitness 6:75-88.

Berry, W.T.C. and F.A. Nash 1955 Studies in the aetiology of pulmonary tuberculosis. Tubercle 36:164-174.

Butt, D.S. 1976 Psychology of Sport. Van Nostrand, New York.

Carter, J.E.L. 1970 The somatotypes of athletes: A review. Hum. Biol. 42:535-569.

Carter, J.E.L., D.A. Sleet, and G.N. Martin 1971 Somatotypes of male gymnasts. J. Sports Med. Phys. Fitness *11*:162-171.

Cooper, L. 1969 Athletics, activity and personality: A review of the literature. Res. Quart. *40*:17-22.

Damon, A. 1970 Constitutional medicine. *In*: von Mering, 'O. and L. Kasdan (Eds.) Anthropology and the Behavioral and Health Sciences. University of Pittsburgh Press, Pittsburgh.

Damon, A. 1971 Physique, longevity and number of offspring: Possible stabilizing selection in man. Amer. J. Phys. Anthropol. *35*:276.

Damon, A., S.T. Damon, H.C. Harpending, and W.B. Kannel 1969 Predicting coronary heart disease from body measurements of Framingham males. J. Chron. Dis. *21*:781-802.

Damon, A. and R.F. Goldman 1964 Predicting fat from body measurements. Densitometric validation of ten anthropometric equations. Hum. Biol. *35*:32-44.

Dublin, L.I. and H.H. Marks 1951 Mortality among insured overweights in recent years. Trans. Amer. Life Insur. Med. Direct. of Amer. *35*:235-263.

Edwards, L.B., V.T. Livesay, F.A. Acquiviva, and C.E. Palmer 1971 Height, weight, tuberculous infection, and tuberculous disease. Arch. Environ. Health *22*:106-112.

Fletcher, R. and L. Dowell 1971 Selected personality characteristics of high school athletes and nonathletes. J. Psychol. 77:39-41.

Freed, D., A.J. Banks, and D. Longson 1972 Aerobic steroids in athletes. Brit. Med. J. *2*:761.

Friedman, M. and R.H. Rosenman 1974 Type A Behavior and Your Heart. Alfred A. Knopf, New York.

Goldman, A.G., P.D. Varady, and S.S. Franklin 1972 Body habitus and serum cholesterol in essential hypertension and renovascular hypertension. J. Amer. Med. Assoc. *221*:378-383.

Haynes, S.G., M. Feinleib, S. Levine, N. Scotch, and W.B. Kannel 1978 The relationship of psychosocial factors to coronary heart disease in the Framingham study. II. Prevalence of coronary heart disease. Amer. J. Epidemiol. *107*:403-411.

Hunt, D. 1969 A cross racial comparison of personality traits between athletes and nonathletes. Res. Quart. *40*:704-707.

Jenkins, C.D. 1976 Recent evidence supporting psychologic and social risk factors for coronary disease (Part 2). New Engl. J. Med. *294*:1033-1038.

Johnson, F.L., J.R. Feagler, K.G. Lerner, P.W. Magerus, M. Siegel, J.R. Hartmann, and E.D. Thomas 1972 Androgenic-anabolic steroids and hepatocellular carcinoma. Lancet *2*:1273.

Kannel, W.B., E.J. Lebauer, T.R. Dawber, and P.M. McNamara 1967 Relation of body weight to development of coronary heart disease. Circulation *35*:734-744.

Khosla, T. 1968 Unfairness of certain events in the Olympic games. Brit. Med.

J. *2*:111-113.

Khosla, T. 1971 The community and sport participation. Brit. J. Prev. Soc. Med. *25*:114-118.

Lister, J. and J.M. Tanner 1955 The physique of diabetics. Lancet *2*:1002-1004.

Malina, R.M. 1969 Exercise as an influence upon growth: Review and critique of current concepts. Clin. Pediat. *8*:16-26.

Malina, R.M. 1972 Comparison of the increase in body size between 1899 and 1970 in a specially selected group with that in the general population. Amer. J. Phys. Anthropol. *37*:135-142.

Milvy, P. 1977 Statistical analysis of deaths from coronary heart disease anticipated in a cohort of marathon runners. Ann. N.Y. Acad. Sci. *301*:620-626.

Montoye, H.J., W.D. Van Huss, H. Olson, A. Hudec, and E. Mahoney 1956 Study of the longevity and morbidity of college athletes. J. Amer. Med. Assoc. *162*:1132-1134.

Montoye, H.J., W.D. Van Huss, and J. Nevai 1962 Longevity and morbidity of college athletes: A seven-year follow-up study. J. Sports Med. Phys. Fitness *2*:133-140.

Novak, L.P., R.E. Hyatt, and J.F. Alexander 1968 Body composition and physiologic function of athletes. J. Amer. Med. Assoc. *205*:764-770.

Paffenbarger, R.S. and A.L. Wing 1973 Chronic disease in former college students. XII. Early precursors of adult-onset diabetes mellitus. Amer. J. Epidemiol. *97*:314-323.

Palmer, A.E., S. Jablon, and P.Q. Edwards 1957 Tuberculosis morbidity of young men in relation to tuberculin sensitivity and body build. Amer. Rev. Tubercul. *76*:517-539.

Parizkova, J. 1968 Longitudinal study of the development of body composition and body build in boys of various physical activity. Hum. Biol. *40*:212-225.

Parnell, R.W. 1951 Some notes on physique and athletic training with special reference to heart size. Brit. Med. J. *1*:1292-1295.

Polednak, A.P. 1972a Longevity and cause of death among Harvard College athletes and their classmates. Geriatrics *27*:53-64.

Polednak, A.P. 1972b Longevity and cardiovascular mortality among former college athletes. Circulation *46*:649-654.

Polednak, A.P. 1975 Secular trend in body size among college athletes. Amer. J. Phys. Anthropol. *42*:501-506.

Polednak, A.P. and A. Damon 1970 College athletics, longevity and cause of death. Hum. Biol. *42*:28-46.

Pollock, M.L., L.R. Gettman, A. Jackson, J. Ayres, A. Ward, and A.C. Linnerud 1977 Body composition of elite class distance runners. Ann. N.Y. Acad. Sci. *301*:361-370.

Pyörälä, K., M.J. Karvonen, P. Taskinen, J. Takkunen, H. Kyrinseppa, and P. Peltokallio 1967 Cardiovascular studies on former endurance athletes. Amer. J. Cardiol. *20*:191-205.

Reisin, E., R. Abel, M. Modan, D.S. Silverberg, H.E. Eliahon, and B. Modan 1978 Effect of weight loss without salt restriction in the reduction of blood pressure in overweight hypertensive patients. New Engl. J. Med. *298*:1-6.

Robinson, S.C. and M. Brucer 1940 Body build and hypertension. Arch. Intern. Med. *66*:393-417.

Sheldon, W.H. 1940 The Varieties of Human Physique. Harper and Row, New York.

Society of Actuaries 1959 Build and Blood Pressure Study, Vol. 1. Society of Actuaries, Chicago.

Tanner, J.M. 1964 The Physique of the Olympic Athlete. Allen and Unwin, London.

Tanner, J.M. 1976 Review of Genetic and Anthropological Studies of Olympic Athletes, edited by A.L. de Garay, L. Levine and J.E.L. Carter. Amer. J. Phys. Anthropol. *45*:125-126.

Wood, P.D., W.L. Haskell, M.P. Stern, S. Lewis and C. Perry 1977 Plasma lipoprotein distributions in male and female runners. Ann. N.Y. Acad. Sci. *301*:748-763.

College Athletes: General Longevity and Mortality

Many early studies involved comparison of former prominent college athletes with the general population or with life insurance data (insured men). In general, the athletes were reported to live longer than the control groups. These studies involved Oxford and Cambridge oarsmen (Morgan, 1873; Hartley and Llewellyn, 1939), Harvard oarsmen (Meylan, 1904), Oxford and Cambridge cricketers (Hill, 1927), and Australian oarsmen (Cooper et al., 1937). The control groups used in these studies were inadequate. Initial selection of athletes for socioeconomic class or other factors related to health (such as physical fitness and physique, and medical history) makes it difficult to assess the effects of athletics in these studies.

Several cohort studies* of athletic and nonathletic college men have been reported. These nonathletic controls are more appropriate than the comparison groups mentioned above, as will become evident in our discussion of these cohort studies.

Dublin (1932) reported on 38,269 men who graduated from 8 colleges in the eastern United States between 1870 and 1905. Most (two-thirds) of the graduates came from Harvard, Yale, and Cornell. In the period of observation (up to 1925) 9,640 deaths occurred among these men. If age 22 is taken as the base for a life table, the expectations of life for the various groups compared were

45.56 years for athletes (lettermen);

47.73 years for "honor men"; and

44.29 years for insured men (U.S. and Canada, 1900-15).

This expectation of life, given that age 22 is reached, is the average number of years of life remaining. Thus, the honor

---

*See the Introduction for definition of cohort studies.

men had a life expectancy about two years greater than the athletes. Taking other ages (27, 32, 37, up to 92) as bases, the life expectancy of the honor men was slightly greater than that of the athletes. Dublin observed, however, that athletes graduating in later years, between 1900 and 1905, had a lower mortality rate than all graduates, and even slightly lower than the honor men. Dublin attributed this change to the introduction of medical examinations, which resulted in better selection of athletes in the later years. Further evidence of this trend will be provided in our discussion of other studies. Dublin's findings indicate the importance of considering the time period during which athletes are being compared with control groups.

Dublin also demonstrated that the college graduates as a whole, as well as the athletes, had a greater life expectancy than insured men. This shows that insured men are an inappropriate control group, as mentioned above with reference to early studies of athletes. In the cohort studies included in this section, college athletes were compared with their classmates.

REFERENCES

Cooper, E.L., J. O'Sullivan, and E. Hughes 1937 Athletics and the heart: An electrocardiographic and radiological study of the healthy and diseased heart to exercise. Med. J. Austral. *1*:569-579.

Dublin, L. 1932 College honor men longer lived. Stat. Bull. *13*:5-7.

Hartley, P.H.S. and G.F. Llewellyn 1939 Longevity of oarsmen: Study of those who rowed in Oxford and Cambridge boat race from 1829-1928. Brit. Med. J. *1*:657-662.

Hill, A.B. 1927 Cricket and its relation to the duration of life. Lancet 2:749-750.

Meylan, G.L. 1904 Harvard University oarsmen. Harvard Grad. Mag. *12*:362-376.

Morgan, J. 1873 University Oars. Macmillan, London.

Chapter 4

AN INVESTIGATION INTO THE LONGEVITY OF CAMBRIDGE SPORTSMEN*

Sir Alan Rook, K.B.E., C.B., F.R.S.P.

Some people prescribe frequent and violent labour and exercises . . . ; the most forbid, and by no means will have to go farther than a beginning sweat, as being perilous if it exceed. — Robert Burton.

THE reaction of the human body to the effects of strenuous exertion in youth and early manhood has long been a subject of interest to everyone concerned with the promotion of health and of physical efficiency. Many observers, both in ancient and in more modern times, have pointed out the alleged dangers of such activities, and these opinions have been summarized by Hartley and Llewellyn (1939). How many regard what they consider to be the folly of undue exertion may be exemplified by the story of the elderly don, himself approaching his hundredth year, who deplored the death of a colleague some three years his junior with the remark that in his youth the dead man had been addicted to climbing mountains, and such exertions must unquestionably have shortened his life. Too often when some well-known sportsman has died at an early age the Jeremiahs, shaking their heads mournfully, have connected two quite unrelated circumstances, much in the way that Morgagni recounted the case of the man "who had been too much given to the exercise of tennis." As this man died of a ruptured aortic aneurysm it seems likely that activities other than tennis were to blame.

*From *British Medical Journal*, 1:773-777, 1954. Courtesy of the Editor of *British Medical Journal*.

The effects of physical exertion are felt by every part of the body, but the cardiovascular system is usually regarded as bearing the chief strain of athletic activities. The problem which the doctor who is called upon to advise about participation in strenuous sports and pastimes is asked to solve has at least two aspects. Firstly, can these exertions cause direct damage to any of the organs of the body, particularly the heart; and, secondly, does exertion, in some way that is not immediately obvious, cause trouble in later life which may result in premature demise?

In answering the first part of the problem the doctor is on firm ground. There now seems to be general agreement, the evidence for which has been restated by Abrahams (1951) in his Lumleian Lecture, that strenuous exertion has no immediate ill effect on the normal heart. This opinion, backed as it is by such giants of cardiology as Mackenzie and Lewis, seems incontrovertible. It is the second part of the problem that has never been answered satisfactorily.

Most observers have found that men taking part in sports which entail long-continued exertion have, on the average, hearts that are demonstrably bigger than those of a control group (Bramwell and Ellis, 1931). Where exertion, although strenuous, is maintained for only short periods it has not been so easy to demonstrate an increase in heart size. Whether any differences which have been observed are the result of training or whether the possession of a heart bigger than normal to start with is a factor in the athletic superiority of these men is not certain. An apparent increase in size of the heart has been reported as occurring during periods of active training (Wilce, 1943), a finding which others have failed to confirm (Parnell, 1951). In any case, does an apparently normal heart that is bigger than the average indicate a lasting increase in cardiac efficiency, or does it, as has been suggested, constitute a relative inferiority? If this latter argument is correct it would appear that the hearts of athletes might not last so well and that cardiac disease should figure more prominently among them, and at an earlier age, than it does in nonathletes.

During recent years a great deal of work has been done,

partly in this country but largely in America, to answer the problem by inquiring into the life-histories of sportsmen of earlier days. The conclusions of the various observers have been somewhat conflicting, but the general findings may be summarized as follows. When comparing the expectation of life of these men with that of males in the general population there was no doubt that university sportsmen had an advantage, according to one computation by as much as five years. Comparison between American college sportsmen and other college graduates showed that, while there was little to choose before the age of 50 years, after 50 the advantage was slightly with the other graduates. The difference was even more apparent when comparison was made between sportsmen and a group of "honours men," men of high intellectual status, who had a distinctly greater expectation of life.

This work may be criticized for various reasons; the principal ones are that the number of lives investigated have been too few, the follow-up has been for too short a period, and in some cases comparison has been with standard life-tables made from a population not comparable with the men under investigation. Even in those instances where comparison has been made with groups of people closely allied to the sportsmen, there are so many variable factors to be taken into account that there could be no certainty that any differences in longevity occurring in the groups were the results of strenuous exertion. The influences of inheritance cannot be neglected, while variations in physical development affecting the height-weight ratio are known to play a part. The period of life when strenuous activities are undertaken is usually a limited one, and subsequent factors such as the economic situation, occupation, and, in particular, habits as regards the intake of food, alcohol, and tobacco affect longevity quite apart from the more direct influences of certain diseases. The psychological factors which attract men to take part in strenuous and sometimes hazardous pastimes are often not wholly satisfied by such activities, and sportsmen are more inclined to live dangerously than their less energetic neighbours.

Hence, while a study of the longevity and of the cause of

death of sportsmen is probably the only method at present available of ascertaining whether in the long run strenuous exertion is, or is not, harmful to the cardiovascular system, it is a method that is beset with pitfalls and one which justifies only tentative conclusions.

Scope of the Investigation

An opportunity for reinvestigating the matter has been afforded by the completion of *Alumni Cantabrigienses* (Venn, 1953), a biographical list of all known students, graduates, and holders of office at Cambridge University from the earliest times until 1900, compiled during a period of over 30 years by the President of Queens' College, Dr. J. A. Venn, whose kindness and help in this investigation must be gratefully acknowledged. This work contains information about Cambridge men, including the date of birth, the school, the college, and often details of University distinctions both academic and sporting. In many instances there are notes of the career after leaving the University and, when appropriate, the date of death.

When planning the investigation it was decided to limit inquiries to men who during a certain period had represented the University in the contests with Oxford University (Abrahams and Bruce-Kerr, 1931) at rowing, cricket, rugby football, and certain branches of athletics, the whole group being called the sportsmen group, and to compare them with a control group of men who had been at the University during the same period of time. The years chosen were those between 1860 and 1900 inclusive, the former date because regular contests started about this time, and the latter so that young or middle-aged men should not be included.

The group with which comparison is made, called the control group, has been composed from two sources, the first being selected at random (random group) and the second from men of special academic distinction (intellectual group). It is possible that the men selected at random were enthusiastic sportsmen whose physical activities equalled or even exceeded those of the men who took part in inter-university contests, while the intellectual capacity of some in the sportsmen or random group may have been on a par with that of the men who formed the intellectual group. Similarly, there is evidence that the sporting activities of some of the men in the intellectual group were not inconsiderable. It can only be argued that, despite obvious drawbacks, these men form a better basis for comparison than do those from whom actuarial tables of assured lives or the Registrar-General's tables have been made.

As was to be expected, the after-histories of a number of the men in all the groups could not be ascertained, so that roughly one in every fourteen names had to be discarded. This failure chiefly affected the men whose university careers had not been particularly distinguished, so that after-histories for the group selected at random could not be obtained in one out of every nine cases. This may have been due in some cases to an early death, and life tables made for this group in which the greatest number of unknowns occurred may be somewhat optimistic.

This investigation inevitably suffers, as have previous ones, from the smallness of the numbers involved, so that the differences to be observed in studying the life-tables made from the various groups are never more than might have resulted from chance in so small a sample. Nevertheless, certain trends are apparent both of a positive and of a negative nature.

Composition of the Various Groups (Table 4-I)

Sportsmen

ATHLETES. The athletes chosen for study were those running the short-distance races (the 100 yards and 440 yards), the longer-distance races (the mile and three miles), and those competing in throwing the hammer and putting the weight. The records of inter-university athletic contests start in the year 1864. During the earlier years there were a number of changes in the events, so that in the first sports the distance events were the mile and a steeplechase and there was no hammer or weight contest. In 1865 the steeplechase was altered to a two-mile race

Table 4-I

TOTAL NUMBERS UNDER INVESTIGATION*

Group	No.	Information		Dead	Alive
		Complete	Incomplete		
Sportsmen:					
Athletes	252	221	31	206	15
Cricketers	187	177	10	162	15
Rowing men	178	171	7	155	16
Rugby footballers	217	203	14	180	23
Total	834	772	62	703	69
Controls:					
Intellectuals	382	374	8	332	42
Random group	379	336	43	293	43
Total	761	710	51	625	85
Grand total	1,595	1,482	113	1,328	154

* Double and triple "blues" and "half-blues" have been shown once only. The athletes group includes all men who took part in the interuniversity contests in the sprints, long-distance races, hammer, and weight. The cricket group does not include men who took part in the athletic contests as well as gaining a cricket blue. The rowing group does not include men who, besides gaining a rowing blue, took part in the athletic contests or who played cricket for the university, and similarly the rugby footballers comprise only men not included in the other three groups. Six of the intellectual group obtained blues or half-blues, and have been included in the appropriate sportsmen group, so that there is some duplication, the number of separate individuals for whom information is complete being 1,476 and not 1,482.

and putting the weight was included. The two-mile race was continued in the 1866 and 1867 contests but was omitted in 1868, when a three-mile race was introduced. Throwing the hammer began in 1866 and has been contested since, although in this and in putting the weight the actual weight used and the method of competing varied somewhat in the first few years. The records consulted give the names of all men taking part, and not only the first and second strings. All names mentioned as competing in the selected events in the interuniversity contest have been included in the group.

CRICKET. Cricket was the first of the inter-university contests, beginning in 1827, two years before the first recorded boat race. It was played intermittently after that until 1838 and thereon each year except during the world wars. Cricket was the second game for which a blue was awarded, rowing being the first.

ROWING. The first boat race was rowed in 1829, but it was not until 1856 onwards that it became an annual event. The coxes have not been included in the group, which is confined to oarsmen.

RUGBY FOOTBALL. Rugby football was the last of the four sporting events to be recognized by the award of a blue. The first inter-university contest was in 1872, but it was not till the winter of 1873 that the names of the players were recorded in the *Book of Blues* (Rysden, 1900). Two games were played in 1873 — one in February and one in December. At first the numbers varied, 21 being the usual number on each side, made up of 14 forwards and 7 backs. On one occasion fog prevented a number of players reaching the ground, and the game was played with 14 a side. The present number of 15 a side was first used in 1875, but the team then consisted of ten forwards and five backs and in later games of nine forwards and six backs. It was not until 1893 that the present formation of eight forwards and seven backs came into use. As records of rugby football teams began in 1872, it follows that the men in this group are not spread over the whole of the period studied but belong only to the middle and later year.

DOUBLE AND TRIPLE BLUES. A number of men took part in two of the different sporting events and two men took part in three — in athletics, cricket, and rugby football. In the athletic group five men also played in the cricket side, six rowed in the university boat, and eleven played in the rugby side; one cricketer rowed in the boat race, and eleven played in the inter-university rugby match, as did two of the rowing men. Thus 38 men in the sportsmen group took part in contests against Oxford University in more than one of the four sports under review. In the subsequent tables, when comparing the men who have taken part in the different sports contests with one another, these men have been included in the appropriate groups, so that there has been duplication; when comparing sportsmen with the control groups these 38 men have been entered only once.

Controls

INTELLECTUAL GROUP. This group is made up of men whose names were taken from the honours lists of the Historical Register of the University. It comprises those men included in the first four places of the mathematical tripos for each of the years 1860 to 1900, and similarly those in the first class of the classical tripos for the years 1860 until 1882. In 1882 new regulations came into force which altered the composition of the lists slightly, and from this date until 1900 the first four names in division 1 of the first class were taken. In some years more than four men were bracketed together for the first four places, so that the numbers in the group exceed the estimated total of 328. Included in the group are six men who in addition to their classical or mathematical honours obtained blues or half-blues for one or other of the sports which are under investigation. One man, a fourth classic, obtained blues for both rowing and athletics; two men, a third wrangler and a fourth classic, took part in the inter-university athletics contest; two men, a first classic and a fourth classic, obtained rugby blues; and one, a fourth classic, got a cricket blue. These men have been included in both the intellectual group and the sportsmen group.

RANDOM GROUP. This group, chosen at random, was made up of men who have been at the university in the years under survey and who had not distinguished themselves sufficiently either academically or as sportsmen to be included in the other groups. The man selected was the first one on every tenth page of *Alumni Cantabrigienses* who fulfilled the requirements. In this way 379 names were taken, and it was possible to obtain the after-histories of 336 of them.

Method of Investigation

Probably the simplest method of studying the longevity of a group of people is by the construction of life-tables showing the survival rates experienced during a chosen period of time. If the group is large enough this can be done in yearly periods or with smaller groups in five- or ten-year periods. Where the groups studied are sufficiently large, the rates of mortality are likely to be regular and chances of gross error are remote, but with small groups a methodical progression is unlikely, and any peculiar happening resulting in a few deaths within a short period may distort the tables considerably. Despite these obvious drawbacks it seems probable that for the present purpose these tables are the best way of making comparisons, but it is essential that the failings of the method should be kept in mind.

I am indebted to Dr. W. L. Smith, Ph.D., statistician to the medical school of Cambridge University, for advice and for the construction of the following tables.

One of the striking things about life-tables which have been compiled within the last century has been the improvement in the expectation of life experienced by the general population. This improvement is shown in life-tables published by the Registrar-General and by the Institute of Actuaries, but it does not affect the lives of the men under investigation to any appreciable degree. In the first place the improvement occurred largely in the latter part of the period, not in the earlier years which are being dealt with here. Secondly, advances in hygiene have chiefly benefited the poorer elements of the population and not the group now being investigated. University men of these times were a specially selected group drawn almost entirely from the more prosperous sections of the community, most of them subsequently having successful professional or business careers. When the whole group is divided up into those born (1) before January 1, 1850; (2) from between January 1, 1850, and December 31, 1859; (3) from between January 1, 1860, and December 31, 1869; and (4) those born on January 1, 1870, and thereafter, the survival rates in the four subgroups show surprisingly little variation (Table 4-II).

This is of some importance in reading the subsequent life-tables, for as a result of the fact that rugby football games did not start till 1872, and also to a less extent because the athletic contests did not start till 1864, the spread of the men whose lives are under investigation has not been distributed evenly over the period. Had there been any marked improvement in the expectation of life in the university population it would

The Longevity of Athletes

Table 4-II

COMPARISON OF SURVIVAL RATES
OF MEN BORN IN DIFFERENT DECADES.
EXCLUDING DEATHS DUE TO WAR AND ACCIDENT

Age	No. of Survivors at Each Age			
	Year of Birth			
	Before 1850	1850-9	1860-9	1870 Onwards
20	1,000	1,000	1,000	1,000
25	990	989	997	989
30	957	976	986	967
35	931	952	978	953
40	914	918	967	914
45	881	881	948	872
50	855	851	923	847
55	822	798	873	817
60	776	729	813	736
65	697	634	730	650
Percentage living aged over 70	56.6	51.5	56.7	52.2
No. in group	305	376	362	361

The smaller number in the subgroup born before 1850 is due to the almost complete absence of rugby footballers, as rugby football games against Oxford did not start until 1872.

have given the rugby footballers and the athletes an advantage which would have been difficult to gauge. It seems justifiable, however, to assume that in university men of the period 1860 to 1900 any change in expectation of life as the result of improving medical and social conditions with the passage of time has been negligible, and that the life-tables which follow have not been distorted from this cause.

Comparison of the Various Groups

Comparison of Sportsmen and Controls

It will be seen from Table 4-III that the average age at death

Table 4-III
SURVIVAL RATES OF SPORTSMEN AND CONTROLS.
EXCLUDING DEATHS DUE TO
WAR AND ACCIDENTS

Age	No. of Survivors at Each Age		
	Sportsmen	Intellectuals	Random Group
20	1,000	1,000	1,000
25	996	987	985
30	982	962	964
35	963	948	949
40	934	937	913
45	898	910	889
50	870	888	867
55	825	841	837
60	763	791	754
65	673	738	634
70	523	597	532
75	377	434	364
80	186	231	193
85	82	92	82
90	23	26	23
No. in group	723	362	325
Average age at death	67.97	69.41	67.43
Variance of estimate of average age at death	0.29	0.61	0.74

varied comparatively little, being slightly better for the intellectuals, who lived on the average nearly two years longer than the random group and nearly one and a half years longer than the sportsmen.

From these survival rates it would appear that up to the age of 40 the sportsmen had slightly better prospects, the differences seen in the other two groups probably being the result of deaths of weaklings who from their physical attributes would be unlikely to be drawn to sports. At 40 years the intellectual group has caught up to the sportsmen; after this the sportsmen and the random group keep closely together, while the intellectuals have a slight but distinct advantage at each age.

Comparison of Different Sporting Groups

Comparison of the survival rates of the different sporting groups (Table 4-IV) is not satisfactory in view of the small numbers of men involved. In the groups of men under review those playing rugby football have a slight advantage, closely followed by the cricketers, whose chances of longevity have been commented upon by Bradford Hill (1927). They are followed by the athletes, and lastly come the rowing men. Differences are, however, small and within the limits of statistical error. It is tempting to adduce reasons why the cricketers had

Table 4-IV

COMPARISON OF DIFFERENT SPORTING GROUPS.
EXCLUDING DEATHS DUE TO WAR AND ACCIDENTS

Age	No. of Survivors at Each Age				
	Athletes	Cricketers	Rowers	Rugby Footballers	Random Group
20	1,000	1,000	1,000	1,000	1,000
25	991	995	1,000	1,000	985
30	972	978	983	996	964
35	949	951	959	996	949
40	920	935	930	955	913
45	886	912	888	918	889
50	866	873	841	895	867
55	827	822	787	854	837
60	763	765	733	776	754
65	668	679	650	659	634
70	508	529	487	554	532
75	377	379	362	368	364
80	172	193	181	184	193
85	76	77	82	81	82
90	7	39	31	15	23
No. in each group	203	176	167	218	325
Average age at death	67.41	68.13	67.08	68.84	67.43
Variance of estimate of average age at death	1.10	1.26	1.38	0.82	0.74

the greatest number of nonagenarians, perhaps attributing this to the more contemplative aspects of the game, though such speculations might well lead to another cricket controversy, a state of affairs which too often engenders heat, a good deal of sound, but usually very little light.

Light and Heavy Physiques (Table 4-V)

Physique is a factor which has been shown by life assurance companies to have a bearing on longevity. The assurance companies do not usually cavil at a stature and musculature above the average, but they dislike an increase in abdominal girth, a

Table 4-V

SURVIVAL RATES OF LIGHT AND HEAVY SPORTSMEN.
EXCLUDING DEATHS DUE TO WAR AND ACCIDENT

Age	No. of Survivors at Each Age		
	Light	Heavy	Random Group
20	1,000	1,000	1,000
25	994	1,000	985
30	979	989	964
35	964	969	949
40	933	926	913
45	899	879	889
50	868	859	867
55	830	815	837
60	786	720	754
65	695	624	634
70	542	480	532
75	396	338	364
80	194	166	193
85	95	62	82
90	14	18	23
No. in group	315	251	325
Average age at death	68.46	66.73	67.43
Variance of estimate of average age at death	0.68	0.85	0.74

body build where weight has increased out of proportion to height. Thus it has been computed that at the age of 45 to 50 years an overweight of 20 lb. (9 kg.), when compared with the normal for the height, increases the death rate over average by 18%; for 40 lb. (18 kg.) overweight the increase is by 45%, and for 60 lb. (27 kg.) overweight by 67% (Sinclair, 1953). Conybeare (1937) observes that a deviation up to 15% is usually allowable, especially in the younger age groups; if abdominal girth exceeds the expanded chest it is an unfavourable sign, but overweight due to a heavy frame can be passed. It has been stated that sportsmen tend to put on weight when they have to give up strenuous exercise, and if this is so it would be an adverse factor tending to lessen longevity. So far as is known, there has been no inquiry into this point, and it may well be one of those statements that are copied from book to book without justification.

It has been possible roughly to divide the athletes, rowing men, and rugby men into heavy weight and light weight groups. With the athletes this has been done by taking the running men on the one hand, and the hammer and weight men on the other; the rowing men have been divided into those rowing at a weight below 168 lb. (76 kg.) and those above this figure, and the rugby men into backs and forwards. While this division is distinctly arbitrary, it has probably resulted in a great majority of the light weights and the heavy weights being divided into correct groups.

It will be seen that once again the differences in the average age at death are not outside the range of statistical error. The trend of the table is for the heavy men to have a slight advantage over their lighter confreres up to middle age, a tendency which is reversed with advancing years.

Some further evidence bearing on this point can be found in the group of athletes. In this group, after excluding those who were killed in war or died from accident, there were 61 short-distance men (100 yards and 440 yards), 89 long-distance men (1, 2, and 3 miles and the steeplechase), and 53 men who took part in the hammer and weight contests. Of the short-distance and the long-distance men 57% and 56% respectively lived to be over 70 years of age; of the hammer and weight men only 34%

lived over this age. The numbers involved are again so small that chance may be playing a large part in these findings.

Causes of Death (Table 4-VI)

Another way to tackle the problem is to ascertain the causes of death of those who have died, for if strenuous exertion in youth had damaged the heart, cardiovascular diseases should figure more prominently in the death certificates and at an earlier age in the sportsmen than in the controls.

The use of death certificates as the basis for a statistical analysis of this nature is not entirely satisfactory and numerous difficulties are encountered. Diagnoses are often vague; fashions in diagnosis even on death certificates change with the years, possibly capriciously or possibly as the result of more accurate methods and greater knowledge of pathological causes. Sometimes when two or more possible causes of death

Table 4-VI

CAUSES OF DEATH IN
A SAMPLE FROM EACH GROUP

Group	Athletes	Cricketers	Rowing	Rugby	Intellec- tuals	Random
Size of sample	149	120	171	155	232	230
Alive	10	10	16	18	30	32
Cause of death known	110	99	130	100	172	142
Cause of death unknown	29	11	25	37	30	56

Cause of Death Arranged as Percentages of the Total
where the Cause is Known

Infection	11.8	14.1	14.6	16.0	11.7	16.2
Pneumonia and bronchitis	6.4	13.1	8.4	8.0	8.2	10.5
Cardiovascular conditions	36.4	37.2	31.5	42.0	39.9	41.5
Neoplasms	13.6	10.1	18.4	12.0	12.3	12.8
Genito-urinary diseases	5.5	7.0	4.6	4.0	8.2	7.1
Accident and war deaths	13.6	9.1	10.8	8.0	4.7	7.0
Senility	3.9	5.1	3.8	3.0	6.4	2.8
Suicide	0.9	1.0	–	3.0	4.1	–
Miscellaneous	7.9	3.3	7.9	4.0	4.5	2.1

figure on a certificate it is difficult to choose the most important. For a variety of reasons it was possible to seek the causes of death in only a sample of each group, and only of those who had died in England. The sample chosen comprised all the rowing blues and, of the other groups, all men whose surnames began with the letters A to O inclusive. Though such limitation is unlikely to influence the comparisons here made, it must be acknowledged, on the general grounds given above, that the evidence so obtained is open to serious criticism. Certain points of interest do, however, emerge.

Death certificates were found for roughly half of all those under investigation, and an attempt was made to classify the causes given on the certificates into nine groups: (1) Infections, made up chiefly of cases of phthisis, enteric-group infections, and septic conditions of all sorts. (2) Pneumonia and bronchitis. (3) Cardiovascular conditions, including apoplexy, valvular disease of the heart, coronary disease and angina, heart failure and myocarditis, and arteriosclerosis. (4) Neoplasms. (5) Genitourinary diseases. (6) Accidental and war deaths. (7) Senility. (8) Suicides. (9) Miscellaneous group, including such conditions as the blood diseases, cirrhosis, intestinal obstruction, and various organic nervous diseases.

DEATH FROM CARDIOVASCULAR CONDITIONS. In the sample from the control group, deaths due to cardiovascular conditions formed just over 40% of all causes of death; in the sample from the sportsmen group this figure was slightly exceeded only in the rugby footballers, with the rowing men showing the lowest percentage. It might be suggested that cardiovascular causes of death occurred at earlier ages in sportsmen, but there is no evidence of this. In the control group sample 27.3% of deaths due to cardiovascular conditions occurred before the age of 65, compared with 22.5% in the sportsmen group sample; the percentages between the ages of 65 and 75 years are controls 39.7% and sportsmen 37.5%, and after 75 years of age 33% for the controls and 40% for the sportsmen. There is thus little evidence from these figures either that sportsmen are more likely to die from cardiovascular causes than are the controls or that they were affected at an earlier age.

ACCIDENTAL AND WAR DEATHS. There were 72 deaths in the whole of the sportsmen and control groups known to be due to accident (38) and war injuries (34). In the sample from these groups the number was 32 for accidents and 29 for deaths due to war injuries. It may be that the incidence of war and accident deaths is somewhat exaggerated because such deaths are more likely to be reported, though the generations of young men under review were not those most likely to have been involved in Britain's wars. A few men died in the second Boer war, when the British Forces deployed were small, while the numbers engaged in hostilities in the first world war cannot have been large, for only a small proportion were under 40 years of age in 1914, and more than half were over 50 years. When the rates for the various groups are worked out, the increased liability of sportsmen to die from one of these two causes becomes apparent. While 70.4 per 1,000 of the random group sample and 46.7 of the intellectual group sample died from accident or war injuries, 97.9 per 1,000 of the sportsmen group sample died from these causes. In the sportsmen and random group samples, war deaths and accidental deaths were roughly equal in numbers; in the intellectual group sample the accidental deaths, chiefly due to mountaineering accidents, exceeded the war deaths by 3 to 1.

SUICIDE. This was given as the cause of death of seven men in the sample from the intellectual group, and may conceivably have been the cause in others in which the death certificate was worded ambiguously. In all others forming the rest of the samples (581 men) there were five cases of suicide, which gives rates of 40.9 per 1,000 for the intellectuals and 8.6 for the remainder, a ratio of nearly five to one. The likelihood that these figures are due to chance is less than one in a hundred.

Summary

The longevity of 834 Cambridge University sportsmen has been investigated and information about 772 has been obtained.

As controls, 761 men who were at the University at the same time were chosen and information was obtained about 710 of them. They were made up of a group of intellectuals numbering 374 men and a group of 336 men chosen at random.

There was no evidence that the sportsmen died at an earlier age than the group chosen at random; the intellectuals lived longer by a period averaging about 1.5 years, but this small difference might well be due to chance.

There was some evidence that the prospects of longevity for the heavily built men was not so good as it was for those more lightly built.

No evidence could be adduced from the information available that cardiovascular causes of death were more prominent in the sportsmen or occurred at an earlier age.

REFERENCES

Abrahams, A. (1951). *Lancet*, 1, 1133. 1187.

Abrahams, H. M., and Bruce-Kerr, J. (1931). *Oxford versus Cambridge.* London.

Bramwell, J. C., and Ellis, R. (1931). *Quart. J. Med.*, 24, 329.

Conybeare, J. J. (1937). *Med Wld. Lond.*, 47, 501.

Hartley, P. Horton-Smith, and Llewellyn, G. F. (1939). *British Medical Journal*, 1. 657.

Hill, A. Bradford (1927). *Lancet*, 2, 949.

Parnell, R. W. (1951). *British Medical Journal*, 1, 1292.

Rysden, O. (1900). *The Book of Blues.* London.

Sinclair, H. M. (1953). *British Medical Journal*, 2, 208.

Venn, J. A. (1953). *Alumni Cantabrigienses.* University Press, Cambridge.

Wilce, J. W. (1943). *Amer. Heart J.*, 25, 613.

Chapter 5

STUDY OF THE LONGEVITY AND MORBIDITY OF COLLEGE ATHLETES*

Henry J. Montoye, Ph.D., Wayne D. Van Huss, Ph.D.,
Herbert Olson, M.S., Andrew Hudec, M.S., and
Earl Mahoney, M.S.

Abstract

When 629 athletes were compared with 583 nonathletes with approximately the same college environment, there appeared to be no significant difference in life expectancy, cause of death, or the type of death. The criterion of being called an athlete in this survey was to have been a varsity letter winner. This particular study is in agreement with other recent studies of a similar nature.

THE effects of intensive athletic competition on the heart and other organs and on bodily resistance to disease has long been a subject of controversy. Previous to the work of Morgan[1] in 1873, the viewpoint prevailing in England was that competitive oarsmen did not live beyond 50 years of age and that this reduced longevity was directly caused by athletic competition. The studies of Morgan[1] and Meylan[2] in 1904 refuted this concept. Attempting to gain further insight into the longevity of athletes, Anderson[3] and Greenway and Hiscock[4] compared the longevity and causes of death of Yale University athletes with use of insurance tables. Dublin,[5] Knoll,[6] Hartley and Llewellyn,[7] and Wakefield[8] similarly compared their data on athletes with insurance company or general population statistics. Bickert,[9] Van Mervennee,[10] and Schmid[11] added to the body of information available on the longevity

*From JAMA, 162:1132-1134, 1956. Copyright 1956, American Medical Association. (Abridged.)

77

and morbidity of athletes but presented no control data. Hartley and Llewellyn[7] point out that athletes are a select group and that, therefore, comparisons with data of life insurance company tables are open to serious criticisms. Dublin[5] stated that a comparison of athletes with their classmates might yield more valid information.

Dublin's[12] second study in 1932 and Rook's[13] work in 1954 represent perhaps the best analyses in the literature on the longevity and causes of death among athletes and nonathletes. Dublin's results show the expectation of life in years at age 22 for honor men (47.73) to be greater than for either the average graduate (45.71) or the athlete (45.56). All college groups, however, showed greater life expectation at age 22 than was listed in tables covering the period 1900-1915 for American men (44.29) or was given for American white males listed in the 27 registration states of the United States for 1919-1920 (43.35). Rook's results as to longevity varied from Dublin's, in that the average age of sportsmen at death (67.97) exceeded that of the randomly selected group (67.43) in his study. The intellectual group again, however, had the greatest longevity (69.41). In all studies in which causes of death were investigated, deaths by external violence among athletes markedly exceeded those among controls. Typically, Wakefield[8] in 1944 found 34% of all deaths among former basketball players were due to external violence, as compared with 17.3% for the general population of the state of Indiana. Rook found the death rate due to external violence to be 97.9 per thousand for sportsmen, as compared with rates of 46.7 for intellectuals, and 70.4 for his random group.

The results of studies regarding comparative rates of death due to cardiovascular causes do not indicate clear trends. In Rook's[13] study for instance, 27.3% of the deaths before age 65 among controls were due to cardiovascular conditions, as compared to 22.5% among sportsmen. Wakefield's[8] results, on the other hand, showed 25% of all deaths caused by disease to be due to cardiovascular-renal diseases, as compared to only 16% for the general population of Indiana. Dublin's[5] results in 1928 showed that, of all deaths among athletes over 45 years of age, 32% were due to heart disease, as compared with a rate of about 20% of the total deaths among insured groups from this cause.

Present Study

The present study was undertaken as a pilot study of the larger national research project inaugurated in 1951 and sponsored by the physical education honorary fraternity, Phi Epsilon Kappa. Questionnaires prepared by a national study committee were sent out to 1,130 former athletes and 1,130 others not former athletes, individually matched as to years of attendance at Michigan State University and ranging in dates of birth from 1855 to 1919. (For purposes of this study, athlete is defined as a letter winner in a varsity sport.) Of the 2,260 questionnaires sent out, 1,212 were returned with sufficient information to be included. Six hundred twenty-nine, or 55.66%, of the questionnaires sent to athletes were returned, as were 583, or 51.59%, of those sent to the control group. The distribution of returns by year of birth would seem to indicate that comparisons are justified with respect to longevity or causes of death. Data from the questionnaires were tabulated, punched onto IBM cards, and analyzed, insofar as possible by IBM techniques. The data have been statistically analyzed where appropriate (Tables 5-I and 5-II). One hundred twenty-three, or 9.85%, of the total returned questionnaires were for deceased subjects, of whom 67 were athletes and 56 controls. Since this was a questionnaire study and, hence, subject to response error, particularly with regard to cause of death, it was decided to determine the validity of the responses. Therefore, data from the death certificates were obtained in 104 cases. List B of the "Manual of the International Statistical Classification of Diseases, Injuries, and Causes of Death"[14] was used for the classification of the causes of death. Errors in the causes of death were classified as major, minor, and those of insufficient information. A major error was listed when the questionnaire response was not pathologically related to the cause of death on the death certificate. A minor error indicated that the response and the actual cause were related pathologically although classified differently in the international classification.

The validation results, in which the data from death certificates and the questionnaires were compared, were as follows: 1.

The Longevity of Athletes

Table 5-I

COMPARISON OF ATHLETES
AND NONATHLETES,
BY SELECTED CHARACTERISTICS

Characteristic	Athletes, %	Nonathletes, %
Service in armed forces*	66.4	55.8
Branch of service*		
Army	70.1	82.7
Navy	23.2	13.9
Marine Corps	2.8	. . .
Other	3.9	3.4
Activity in service		
Mild	13.7	18.9
Moderate	50.4	53.9
Vigorous	35.9	27.2
Married	96.9	97.0
Drinker*	77.6	66.5
Smoker*	68.7	60.2
Weight in college*	164 lb.	153 lb.
Weight gain since college	9.7 lb.	10.4 lb.

* These differences are statistically significant, i. e., it is unreasonable that chance would account for them.

Table 5-II

COMPARISON OF AGE AT DEATH OF
ATHLETES AND NONATHLETES

	Mean Life Expectancy, Yr.*	Mean Age at Death Yr.†	Difference, Yr.
All deaths included			
Athletes	65.96	73.86	7.90
Nonathletes	65.97	74.24	8.27
Excluding accidental deaths			
Athletes	65.96	74.43	8.47
Nonathletes	65.99	74.59	8.60

* Computed for the time when the athlete or nonathlete was in college, using the appropriate mortality tables.

† Actual ages of death were used where death has occurred. Otherwise this represents the individual's present age plus remaining years of life predicted from current mortality tables.

In dates of birth, agreement was very good. Only 10 discrepancies were noted, with a mean error of 0.35 years, which was not statistically significant. 2. In ages at death, agreement was good. Twenty-two discrepancies were noted, with a mean error of 0.32 years, which also was not statistically significant. 3. Nineteen discrepancies were noted in causes of death. Two were major errors, 13 minor errors, and 4 were cases in which insufficient information was available to make a decision. Most of the errors noted concerned cardiovascular causes, particularly heart disease. While the layman is apparently oriented to the term heart disease, the death certificate might list the cause of death as coronary thrombosis or angina pectoris, which technically, for classification purposes, is erroneous. Because of this, fine classifications of causes of death from conditions of the cardiovascular area were not possible. Coarse classifications, however, were affected very little when questionnaires and death data were compared.

The age at death of the athletes and nonathletes is compared in Table 5-II. The difference in actual and expected age at death is not surprising when we consider how highly select the men in attendance at college were during these years. Also, since the percentages of returns of the questionnaires in the two groups were 55.66 and 51.59, it is quite probable the sample became even more select due to the difficulty in obtaining data on those who died in the earlier years. What is of interest here, however, is that there is little difference existing between the two groups. This is in agreement with the studies by Dublin[12] and Rook.[13] Differences between the athletes and nonathletes in the distribution of causes of death, type of death (sudden or lingering), and causes of death of parents were statistically insignificant.

Summary

The questionnaire method was employed in securing data on former college athletes (letter winners) and nonathlete controls. The results indicated that the longevity of athletes was approximately the same as that of controls and the distribution of causes of death was very similar. A significantly greater percentage of former athletes served in the armed forces and, of those serving, a significantly larger proportion served in the Navy and Marine Corps. A significantly greater percentage of former athletes smoked and drank, and their weight in college was appreciably greater. There were no significant differences in the number married, weight gain since college days, or strenuousness of activity while in the armed services.

REFERENCES

1. Morgan, J. E.: University Oars, 1873, in Karpovich, P. V.: Longevity and Athletics, Res. Quart. 12: 451-455 (May) 1941.
2. Meylan, G. L.: Harvard University Oarsmen, Harvard Grad. Mag. 9: 362-376 (March) 1904.
3. Anderson, W. G.: Further Studies in Longevity of Yale Athletes, Med. Times 44:75-77, 1916.
4. Greenway, J. C., and Hiscock, I. C.: Preliminary Analysis of Mortality Among Athletes and Other Graduates of Yale University, Yale Alumni Weekly 35: 1086-1088 (June) 1926.
5. Dublin, L. I.: Longevity of College Athletes, Harper 157: 229-238 (July) 1928.
6. Knoll, W.: Welches Lebensalter erreichen die Ruderer von "Oxford-Cambridge"? (Eine Richtigstellung), Med. Klin. 34: 464-466 (April 8) 1938.
7. Hartley, P. H. S., and Llewellyn, G. F.: Longevity of Oarsmen: Study of Those Who Rowed in Oxford and Cambridge Boat Race from 1829-1928, Brit. M. J. 1: 657-662 (April) 1939.
8. Wakefield, M. C.: Study of Mortality Among Men Who Have Played in Indiana High School State Final Basketball Tournaments, Res. Quart. 15: 3-11 (March) 1944.
9. Bickert, F. W.: Einfluss des wettkampfmässig betriebenen Sports auf die Lebensdauer and Todesursache: Eine statistische Studie, Deutsche med. Wehnschr. 55: 23-25 (Jan. 4) 1929.
10. Van Mervenneé, C. J.: Life Span of Athletes, Nederl. tÿdschr. geneesk. 85: 535-543, 1941.
11. Schmid, L.: How Long Sportsmen Live, in Sport and Health, Royal Norwegian Ministry of Education, Oslo, Norway, 1952, pp. 100-107.
12. Dublin, L. I.: College Honor Men Long-Lived, Statist. Bull. Metrop. Life Insur. Co. 13: 5-7, 1932.
13. Rook, A.: Investigation into Longevity of Cambridge Sportsmen, Brit. M. J. 1: 773-777 (April 3) 1954.

14. World Health Organization: Manual of International Statistical Classification of Diseases, Injuries, and Causes of Death: Sixth Revision of International Lists of Diseases and Causes of Deaths, Adopted 1948: Bulletin of the World Health Organization, supp. 1, vol. 1, 1948, vol. 2: Alphabetical Index, 1949.

Chapter 6

COLLEGE ATHLETICS, LONGEVITY, AND CAUSE OF DEATH*

ANTHONY P. POLEDNAK, Ph.D. AND ALBERT DAMON, M.D., Ph.D.

THE relationship between physical exertion and health has been approached in several ways: by experiments on animals, by short- and long-term physiological studies on healthy men, by exercise programs for patients with heart disease, and by epidemiological studies on populations both living and dead. Epidemiologists have investigated exercise mainly in connection with cardiovascular disease because of the high frequency of such disease in industrialized countries and because evidence suggests that lack of physical exercise confers a risk. Furthermore exercise, like diet and smoking habits, can be modified. The consensus seems to be that while the effect of exercise on health has not been proved, the possibility is strong enough to warrant increased research and even experimental trials (Montoye 1962, 1967; Fox and Skinner 1964; Katz 1967). Several such trials are now under way.

There have been few reports of the long-range effects of early exercise on longevity and cause of death. We report here such as study based on 2,090 men who attended Harvard College between 1880 and 1916.

Subjects and Methods

The present subjects initially were 2,631 men who had been measured anthropometrically and photographed, while at Harvard University between 1880 and 1912, by D. A. Sargent and two assistants. The photographs were later rated by F. L. Stagg and the late E. A. Hooton, using a modification of Sheldon's

*From *Human Biology*, 42(1):34-46, 1970. Courtesy of Wayne State University Press. (Abridged.)

(1940) somatotype technique. Mr. Stagg has kindly made his ratings available to us.

The 2,631 photographed men were part of a larger group of some 17,000 Harvard men measured by Sargent and his assistants, roughly half of all men attending Harvard between 1880 and 1920. All applicants of gymnasium locker rental were measured, but not all were photographed. A 1% random sample of 170 measured men, each compared to the next unmeasured classmate starting 10 names after the subject's on the official class list, showed only one difference among 8 personal characteristics (birthplace, parents' birthplace, religion, father's occupation, subject's preparatory schooling, college athletics, and later education and occupation) — namely, that the measured men were more active in college sports. This might have been expected from their basis of selection. Otherwise they were representative of all Harvard men of their era.

The 2,631 men were fairly homogeneous ethnically, 85% being Old Americans of British descent, and 10% of immediate Northern European ancestry. An Old American is a person whose four grandparents were born in the United States.

Information on college sports was obtained from Harvard College records, including Annual Reports of Classes from 1884 to 1916 and a compilation of athletic records (Blanchard 1923). To ensure greater homogeneity and an opportunity for all subjects to have participated in college sports, only those men were included who were born between 1860 and 1889 and who had spent two or more years at Harvard College. Exclusion of dropouts, transfer students, graduate students, instructors, and men born before 1860 or after 1889 reduced the number to 2,152. Further exclusion of men who were lost (20) and of those known to be dead but lacking death certificates (34) or whose certificates had not been received (8) yielded a study group of 2,090 men.

The subjects were classified into three groups, on the basis of their participation in athletics in Harvard College, as follows:

1) Major athletes — men who received one or more letter awards, or "H"'s, in major varsity sports (baseball, football, crew, track, ice hockey, and tennis).

2) Minor athletes — participants in the major sports who did not win letters, plus all regular participants in minor intercollegiate sports of the period for which letters were not awarded — basketball, cricket, fencing, golf, lacrosse, polo, swimming, and wrestling.
3) Nonathletes — men who had no record of having participated in formal intercollegiate sports, or who participated only as freshmen.

Table 6-I shows their distribution by birth decade and athletic category.

Table 6-I

HARVARD ATHLETES,* BY BIRTH DECADE

			Birth decade			
	1860-69		1870-79		1880-89	
	N	Per Cent	N	Per Cent	N	Per Cent
Major athletes	58	10.6	94	9.4	25	4.6
Minor athletes	52	9.5	145	14.4	78	14.4
Non-athletes	435	79.8	766	76.2	437	81.0
Total	545	99.9	1005	100.0	540	100.0

* Alive on 30 June 1967 or dead of known cause.

Age at death and cause of death were obtained from death certificates and were coded according to the International Classification of Diseases (World Health Organization, 1957). Only the first listed cause was used here. By 30 June 1967 all but 4 of the 545 men born in the decade 1860-69 had died (99.3%), as had 951 of the 1,005 men born in 1870-79 (94.6%), and 408 of the 540 men born in 1880-89 (75.5%) — a total of 1,900 deaths out of 2,090, or 90.9%.

Results

In analyzing longevity among 2,090 men alive or dead of known cause, we followed Rook (1954) in discarding deaths from causes other than natural. Such deaths, 111 in number, were examined separately. In Table 6-II appear, for each decade of birth, the percentages of men reaching ages 70 and 75. Of the

Table 6-II

HARVARD ATHLETES,
ALIVE OR DEAD OF NATURAL CAUSES;
PERCENTAGE OF MEN REACHING AGES 70 AND 75,
BY BIRTH DECADE

Birth decade	Reaching Age 70			Reaching Age 75		
	1860-69	1870-79	1880-89	1860-69	1870-79	1880-89
	N % *	N % *	N % *	N % *	N % *	N % *
Major athletes	26 46.4	52 59.7	14 60.9	21 37.5	42 48.3	12 52.2
Minor athletes	29 58.0	86 63.2	55 76.4	21 42.0	72 52.9	48 66.7
Non-athletes	239 57.2	444 60.7	255 62.9	186 44.5	333 45.5	201 49.6

For significance of differences, see text.
* Per cent of men in each athletic category in each birth decade who reached the specified age. Thus, of 56 major athletes alive or dead of natural causes in the birth decade 1860-69, 26, or 46.4%, reached age 70.

subjects alive on 30 June 1967, all had had a chance to reach age 75 but not 80.

Table 6-II shows some interesting points. The increased longevity over time within each athletic category reflects general environmental and possibly medical advances. In 4 of the 6 comparisons — that is, the percentages of men in the 3 birth decades who reached age 70 or 75 — the major athletes were the lowest, and in the other two they were intermediate of minor athletes, who led in 5 of the 6 comparisons and were second in the sixth.

The significance of these differences was assessed in several ways. Chi-square values within each decade were not significant, but the combined chi-square values — sum of chi-squares for each of the three birth decades — for men reaching age 70 was 7.05 which, for 3 degrees of freedom, gave a p-value between 0.05 and 0.10. The combined chi-square for men reaching age 75 was 9.85; for 3 degrees of freedom, p < 0.02.

The combined chi-square technique makes no assumptions as to similarity of the subpopulations. Grouping all three birth decade samples for further statistical tests of longevity is justified by the roughly similar frequency of each athletic category in the three birth decades (Table 6-I). Chi-square tests for the total number of men in each athletic category, combining all birth decades, gave the same significance levels, for men reaching ages 70 and 75, as the combined chi-squares for the separate birth decades — namely, $0.10 > p > 0.05$ for age 70, and $p < 0.02$ for age 75.

Combining all birth decades to obtain percentages of men reaching age 70, the differences between pairs of athletic categories were as follows: minor athletes > nonathletes, $0.10 > p > 0.05$; minor > major athletes, $p < 0.05$; major < nonathletes, not significant. Corresponding differences for men reaching age 75 were: minor > nonathletes, $p < 0.05$; minor > major athletes, $0.06 > p > 0.05$; major < nonathletes, not significant.

In short, not only in consistency of trend across the birth decades but also in statistical significance, minor athletes emerge as the longest lived group of the three. Major athletes and nonathletes did not differ significantly, but the trend favored the nonathletes.

If we count the living rather than the dead, the percentage of men still alive in the birth decades 1870-79 and 1880-89 — all but 4 men born in 1860-69 having died — also favored the minor athletes. In the birth decade 1870-79, percentages still alive were: major athletes, 3/94 or 3.2%; minor athletes, 17/145 or 11.7%; nonathletes, 34/766 or 4.5%. The differences between minor and major athletes, and between minor and nonathletes were both significant ($p < 0.05$); that between major and nonathletes was not. In the birth decade 1880-89, percentages still alive were: major athletes, 7/25 or 28%; minor athletes, 29/78 or 37.2%; nonathletes, 96/437 or 21.8%. The only difference approaching significance was that between minor and nonathletes ($0.10 > p > 0.05$).

Age at death, for men who died of natural causes, is set out by birth decade in Table 6-III. The only consistent trend is that major athletes were the shortest lived in each birth decade, but none of the paired comparisons reached statistical significance. The preceding paragraph noted the preponderance of minor athletes still alive in the more recent birth decades, 1870-79 and 1880-89. We may therefore expect that eventually, when all

Table 6-III
HARVARD ATHLETES: MEAN AGE AT DEATH,
FOR MEN DEAD OF NATURAL CAUSES

Age at death (yrs.)	1860-69			1870-79			1880-89		
	N	Mean	S. D.	N	Mean	S. D.	N	Mean	S. D.
Major athletes	55	67.3	16.8	84	69.8	15.9	16	66.2	14.2
Minor athletes	49	67.9	18.0	119	70.8	14.7	43	67.2	16.8
Non-athletes	416	69.3	17.4	699	70.1	15.0	308	67.7	12.5

Note: Percentage of deaths among original cohort in each birth decade: 1860-69, 99.3%; 1870-79, 94.6%; 1880-89, 75.7%.
Differences among athletic categories within each birth decade are not significant.

subjects have died, the minor athletes will have improved their longevity relative to the other athletic categories.

In view of the possible bearing of physique on longevity (Society of Actuaries 1959) and the well-known muscularity of athletes compared to the general population, somatotype ratings, on a 7-point scale for each "component," were compared among the present subjects (Table 6-IV). Ratings were stable across birth decades. Within each birth decade, endomorphy (fat) was greater in athletes than in nonathletes; mesomorphy (rugged bony muscularity) increased from nonathletes to minor and then to major athletes; and ectomorphy (leanness — here, height/ $\sqrt[3]{}$ weight) generally in the opposite direction. Most of these differences, 18 out of 27, reached statistical significance (Table 6-V). The athletes were fatter, more muscular, and stockier than the nonathletes, and major athletes tended to be more so than minor athletes.

CAUSE OF DEATH. Selected causes of death appear, for each birth decade and athletic category, in Table 6-VI. The omitted causes of death affect too few subjects in any single category to warrant inclusion. Looking first at infections, we see no consistent or significant relationship among the athletic categories. The same is true for neoplasms. In diseases of the nervous system and sense organs, however, both major and minor athletes were slightly but consistently lower than nonathletes. The differences in cardiovascular and specifically in coronary heart

Table 6-IV

HARVARD ATHLETES: SOMATOTYPE

	Major athletes Mean	S. D.	Minor athletes Mean	S. D.	Non-athletes Mean	S. D.
Birth decade 1860-69						
(N)*	(60)		(52)		(448)	
Endomorphy	3.70	0.59	3.79	0.75	3.44	0.79
Mesomorphy	4.10	.86	3.69	.85	3.19	.93
Ectomorphy	4.22	.87	4.15	.83	4.70	.93
Birth decade 1870-79						
(N)	(95)		(146)		(785)	
Endomorphy	3.65	.73	3.56	.62	3.45	.74
Mesomorphy	3.65	.87	3.47	.96	3.10	.95
Ectomorphy	4.42	.87	4.52	.90	4.73	.91
Birth decade 1880-89						
(N)	(25)		(78)		(446)	
Endomorphy	3.60	.65	3.45	.66	3.44	.70
Mesomorphy	4.12	.88	3.53	.77	3.10	.87
Ectomorphy	4.12	1.09	4.45	.80	4.71	.86

* All men are included, whether dead, alive, or lost.
For significance of differences, see Table 6-V.

Table 6-V

HARVARD ATHLETES: SOMATOTYPE;
SIGNIFICANCE OF DIFFERENCES

Birth decade	1860-69 Non- Athletes	Minor Athletes	1870-79 Non- Athletes	Minor Athletes	1880-89 Non- Athletes	Minor Athletes
Endomorphy						
Minor athletes	**		*		n. s.	
Major athletes	**	n. s.	*	n. s.	n. s.	n. s.
Mesomorphy						
Minor athletes	**		**		**	
Major athletes	**	*	**	n. s.	**	**
Ectomorphy						
Minor athletes	**		*		*	
Major athletes	**	n. s.	**	n. s.	*	n. s.

* $p < 0.05$
** $p < 0.01$

Table 6-VI

HARVARD ATHLETES:

SLECTED CAUSES OF DEATH, BY BIRTH DECADE

(PERCENTAGES OF TOTAL DEATHS IN SPECIFIED ATHLETIC CATEGORY)

Birth Decade	1860-69			1870-79			1880-89		
	Major athlete	Minor athlete	Non-athlete	Major athlete	Minor athlete	Non-athlete	Major athlete	Minor athlete	Non-athlete
(N)*	(57)	(51)	(433)	(91)	(128)	(732)	(18)	(49)	(341)
Infections, parasites	10.5	3.9	8.5	5.5	3.1	3.6	5.6	6.1	2.9
Neoplasms	12.3	5.9	8.5	13.2	12.5	9.7	5.6	18.4	11.1
Nervous system	5.3	13.7	14.8	13.2	12.5	15.3	5.6	8.2	12.6
Circulatory system	36.8	37.3	34.2	36.3	46.9	42.5	50.0	36.7	42.2
(Coronary heart disease)	(17.5)	(17.6)	(14.3)	(20.9)	(22.7)	(24.9)	(27.3)	(20.4)	(26.7)
Respiratory system	10.5	13.7	17.8	16.5	10.9	12.8	16.7	2.0	12.6
Accidents (exc. war)	1.8	3.9	1.4	4.4	3.9	2.0	5.6	8.2	5.0
Suicides	0	0	1.6	2.2	2.3	2.5	5.6	6.1	3.5

* N = total deaths in specified decade and athletic category.

disease were patternless and statistically insignificant. In further tabulations, omitted here, men in the three athletic categories did not differ in age at death from cardiovascular or from coronary heart disease; nor did the use of all listed causes of death, not merely the first, change the negative results for cardiovascular diseases.

Death from respiratory disease was least frequent among the minor athletes in the birth decades 1870-79 and 1880-89. Combining all three birth decades, the minor athletes had a percentage of respiratory deaths, in relation to total deaths, of 9.7%, major athletes 14.4%, and nonathletes 14.2%. The differences between minor athletes and nonathletes was statistically significant (p < 0.05).

Accidental deaths were more frequent for athletes than for nonathletes in each birth decade, but by small and statistically insignificant amounts. Suicide rates did not differ among the three athletic categories.

Discussion

LENGTH OF LIFE. In the present study minor athletes were generally and for the most part significantly longer lived than major athletes and nonathletic classmates. Major athletes tended to have shorter lives than nonathletes, the differences being consistent but not statistically significant. Longevity was measured in several ways: percentages of men living to ages 70 and 75, percentages alive on 30 June 1967, and age at death of those dying of natural causes. The three categories of athlete were compared within each of three birth decades, a procedure which minimized time trends in selection of athletes, in relative proportions of the three categories of athletes, in age at death, cause of death, and diagnosis.

All of the present subjects were interested in exercise while at college, to the extent of wishing to rent a gymnasium locker. Exercise was not compulsory at Harvard at that time. The three athletic groups were therefore not as extreme as those of previous authors, a point which adds meaning to the differences found. Our subjects' ethnic and ultimate socioeconomic homogeneity control two other possible sources of variation, while high socioeconomic status increases the chances of a high, uniform standard of medical care and diagnosis. Though death certification is all too fallible, inaccuracies are unlikely to be concentrated in one or another of the three athletic groups.

Our findings confirm those of previous cohort studies of longevity, in that major athletes had shorter lives than their less athletic or less athletically prominent classmates. The differences in all studies seldom reach statistical significance, to be sure, but the consistency of trend is impressive. Slight but real differences may take very large numbers of subjects to establish.

A novel finding was the greater longevity of minor athletes, a group not previously investigated. It is difficult to think of a physiological explanation. Exercise in later life does seem to protect against coronary heart disease, although there is no evidence as to its effect on longevity in general. Are minor college athletes more likely than major athletes to continue to exercise after college? Unfortunately we, like most previous authors, lack data on our subjects' later exercise habits. To speculate, it is certainly easier to swim, play golf, or fence throughout life than to play baseball, football, or hockey. But it is also easy to play tennis or to row, so this cannot be the whole explanation.

Do certain kinds of sports in college conduce to shorter lives, whereas others lengthen the life span? Or is it the kind of participant and not the sport that matter? The single study (Montoye et al. 1956) of weight gain after college showed no difference between varsity athletes and nonathletes.

Analysis of somatotype can help delineate the personal factor in the three athletic categories. Major athletes were markedly fatter, more muscular, and stockier than nonathletes, while minor athletes were intermediate but closer to the major athletes (Tables 6-IV and 6-V). The stocky, muscular person, the endomorphic mesomorph, has been shown to have a shorter life span than the lean person, not only in insurance records (Society of Actuaries 1959) but also in a preliminary analysis of the present subjects plus men in Harvard College less than two years (Damon, Stagg, and Hooton, unpublished). Among some

2400 former Harvard men alive or dead of natural causes, without regard to athletic participation, endomorphy and mesomorphy were negatively associated with longevity, and ectomorphy was positively associated.

Since major athletes had the endo-mesomorphic physique associated with shortened life span, we may speculate that this factor, independently of any effect of athletics, could account for their shorter lives.

How then can one explain the superior showing of the minor athletes, also at some risk in terms of physique, but who lived longer than nonathletes? There is evidence that slight amounts of stockiness have little effect on mortality, most of the risk being confined to the markedly stocky (Seltzer, 1966). But something must have overcome even this slight excess risk — could it have been habits of moderate exercise, learned in college? The present finding requires confirmation among other subjects before one speculates further on what may be an isolated observation.

CAUSE OF DEATH. The three athletic categories did not differ in percentages dying of infections, neoplasms, cardiovascular or specifically coronary heart disease, or suicide. Ages at death for men dying of cardiovascular or coronary heart disease did not differ. The athletes had consistent but slight and statistically insignificant trends toward lower death rates than nonathletes for nervous diseases, and higher death rates for accidents. The minor athletes had significantly fewer deaths from respiratory diseases than the other two groups, possibly a chance finding.

As regards infections, our negative results confirm those of others (Rook 1954, Pomeroy and White 1958). Our suggestion that athletes may have more accidents bears out Rook's finding which was, however, likewise statistically insignificant. Contrary to the reports of Rook and of Pomeroy and White, we found no increased frequency of suicide among athletes.

The present negative results for cardiovascular and coronary heart disease confirm those of Rook and of Pomeroy and White, but not of Paffenbarger et al. (1966), who noted fewer varsity athletes and less participation in sports among early coronary decedents than among classmates still alive. The discrepancies may be reconciled by the observation that the coronary risk factors of concern here, exercise (Fox and Skinner 1964) and body build (Damon et al. 1968), hold for early disease. The subjects of Paffenbarger et al. had died early, whereas the other three studies covered entire life spans. This may also explain why, if the present athletes had physiques particularly susceptible to cardiovascular and coronary heart disease, they showed no excess of such deaths. We can certainly say that college athletes have been no *more* prone to cardiovascular disease, early or late in life, than nonathletes.

To pose still another question: if the three categories of athlete did not differ in rates for the major causes of death, what can account for the generally greater longevity of minor athletes and the reduced longevity of major athletes? Ages at death in some diseases could differ, although the three athletic groups did not differ in mean ages at death from cardiovascular or coronary heart disease. Again, death rates could differ in respect to diseases of early and late adult life. Death rates for neoplasms, a major cause of death which typically appears late in life, did not in fact differ among the athletic groups. Mean ages at death for neoplastic, nervous, and respiratory diseases showed no consistent pattern. The three athletic groups had similar ages at death for nervous diseases; major athletes died earlier from neoplasms, and minor athletes from respiratory diseases. Since a greater proportion of minor athletes than the other two groups were alive on 30 June 1967, their mean age at death will eventually be relatively greater than those of the other two groups, for the various causes of death as well as for deaths generally.

These questions will come closer to solution when the entire cohort has died, but larger numbers may be needed to demonstrate the reality of small differences in longevity or cause of death. Even then, the role of athletics can be fully evaluated only if exercise habits after college are known.

Summary

Among 2,090 men who attended Harvard for at least two

years between 1880 and 1916, athletic status in college was analyzed in relation to longevity and cause of death. All men were interested in athletics to the extent of renting a gymnasium locker for voluntary exercise, but exercise habits after college were unknown.

Major athletes (N = 177) were letter-winners in "major" varsity sports. Minor athletes (N = 275) participated in major sports without winning letters, or in sports for which letters were not awarded at the time. Nonathletes (N = 1,638) played on no teams or squads. Freshman participation was disregarded.

By 30 June 1967, 90.9% had died of known cause. Major athletes tended to have the shortest lives, as reported from previous cohort studies, and minor athletes the longest, a novel finding. In percentages of men still alive and in percentages of men reaching ages 70 and 75, minor athletes were consistently and for the most part significantly higher. In mean age at death for men dead of natural causes, differences were small, between 1 and 2 years, and not significant.

Major athletes were fatter, more muscular, and stockier than nonathletes, with minor athletes intermediate but more like the major athletes. Physique might account for the reduced longevity of the major athletes but not for the increased longevity of the minor athletes.

The three categories of athlete did not differ in death rates from infections, neoplasms, cardiovascular diseases — their leading cause of death —, coronary heart disease, or suicide; or in mean age at death from cardiovascular or coronary heart disease.

REFERENCES

BLANCHARD, J. A. (Ed.) 1923 The H Book of Harvard Athletics (1852-1922). Harvard Univ. Press, Cambridge, Massachusetts.

COOPER, E. L., J. O'SULLIVAN AND E. HUGHES 1937 Athletics and the heart: an electrocardiographic and radiological study of the response of the healthy and diseased heart to exercise. Med. J. Austral., 1: 569-579.

DAMON, A. 1965 Delineation of the body build variables associated with cardiovascular diseases. Ann. N.Y. Acad. Sciences, 126: 711-727.

DAMON, A., S. T. DAMON, H. C. HARPENDING AND W. B. KANNEL 1969 Predicting coronary heart disease from body measurements of Framingham males. J. Chronic Diseases, 21: 781-804.

DAWBER, T. R., W. B. KANNEL AND G. D. FRIEDMAN 1966 Vital capacity, physical activity and coronary heart disease. *In* Raab, W. (Ed.), Prevention of Ischemic Heart Disease. Charles C Thomas, Springfield, Illinois.

DUBLIN, L. I. 1928 Longevity of college athletes. Harper's Mag., 157: 229-238.

_____ 1932 College honor men longer lived. Stat. Bull. Metropolitan Life Ins. Co., 13: 5-7.

FOX, S. M., III AND J. S. SKINNER 1964 Physical activity and cardiovascular health. Am. J. Cardiol., 14: 731-746.

FRANK, C. W., E. WEINBLATT, S. SHAPIRO AND R. V. SAGER 1966 Physical inactivity as a lethal factor in myocardial infarction among men. Circulation, 34: 1022-1033.

GREENWAY, J. C. AND I. C. HISCOCK 1926 Preliminary analysis of mortality among athletes and other graduates of Yale University. Yale Alumni Weekly, 35: 1086-1088.

HARTLEY, P. H.-S AND G. F. LLEWELLYN 1939 Longevity of oarsmen: study of those who rowed in Oxford and Cambridge boat race from 1829-1928. Brit. Med. J., 1: 657-662.

HILL, A. B. 1927 Cricket and its relation to the duration of life. Lancet, 2: 949-950.

KARVONEN, M. J., J. KIHLBERG, J. MÄÄTTÄ AND J. VIRKAJRÄVI 1956 (Cited by Cumming, G. R. 1963. The heart and physical exercise. Canad. Med. Assoc. J., 88: 80-85).

KATZ, L. N. 1967 Physical fitness and coronary heart disease: some basic views. Circulation, 35: 405-414.

MEYLAN, G. L. 1904 Harvard University oarsmen. Harvard Grad. Mag., 12: 362-376.

MONTOYE, H. J. 1962 Summary of research on the relationship of exercise to heart disease. J. Sports Med. & Phys. Fitness, 2: 35-43.

_____ 1967 Participation in athletics. Canad. Med. Assoc. J., 96: 813-820.

MONTOYE, H. J., W. D. VAN HUSS AND J. W. NEVAL 1962 Longevity and morbidity of college athletes: a seven-year follow-up study. J. Sports Med. & Phys. Fitness, 2: 133-140.

MONTOYE, H. J., W. D. VAN HUSS, H. OLSEN, A. HUDEC AND E. MAHONEY 1956 Study of the longevity and morbidity of college athletes. J. Am. Med. Assoc., 162: 1132-1134.

MORGAN, J. 1873 University Oars. Macmillan, London.

PAFFENBARGER, R. S. AND D. P. ASNES 1966 Chronic disease in former college students. III. Precursors of suicide in early and middle life. Am. J. Public Health, 56: 1026-1036.

PAFFENBARGER, R. S., JR., J. NOTKIN, D. E. KRUEGER, P. A. WOLF, M. C.

THORNE, E. J. LEBAUER AND J. L. WILLAMS 1966 Chronic disease in former college students. II. Methods of study and observations on mortality from coronary heart disease. Am. J. Public Health, 56: 962-971.

POMEROY, W. AND P. D. WHITE 1958 Coronary heart disease in former football players. J. Am. Med. Assoc., 167: 711-714.

PYÖRÄLÄ, K., M. J. KARVONEN, P. TASKINEN, J. TAKKUNEN AND H. KYRÖNSEPPÄ 1965 Cardiovascular studies on former endurance runners. Reports from the Institute of Occupational Health, Helsinki, Finland, No. 19.

ROOK, A. 1954 An investigation into the longevity of Cambridge sportsmen. Brit. Med. J., 1: 773-777.

SELTZER, C. C. 1966 Some re-evaluations of the build and blood pressure study, 1959, as related to ponderal index, somatotype and mortality. New Eng. J. Med., 274: 256-259.

SHELDON, W. H., S. S. STEVENS AND W. B. TUCKER 1940 The Varieties of Human Physique. Harper and Bros., New York.

SOCIETY OF ACTUARIES 1959 Build and Blood Pressure Study. Society of Actuaries, Chicago, Illinois.

WEINBLATT, E., S. SHAPIRO, C. W. FRANK AND R. V. SAGER 1966 Return to work status following first myocardial infarction. Am. J. Public Health, 56: 169-185.

——— 1968 Prognosis of men after first myocardial infarction: mortality and first recurrence in relation to selected parameters. Am. J. Public Health, 58: 1329-1347.

World Health Organization 1957 International Classification of Diseases. World Health Organization, Geneva, Switzerland.

Chapter 7

LONGEVITY AND CAUSE OF DEATH AMONG HARVARD COLLEGE ATHLETES AND THEIR CLASSMATES*

Anthony P. Polednak, Ph.D.

THE relationship between physical exercise and health has been approached in several ways, including: (1) experiments on animals, (2) short-term and long-term physiologic studies of healthy men, (3) exercise programs for patients with heart disease, and (4) epidemiologic studies of human populations, including follow-up studies of college athletes.

The evidence indicates that physical training or athletics produces changes — in functional capacity,[1-5] cardiovascular-respiratory physiology,[6] body composition and anthropometric measures,[4,7-12] and biochemical variables such as serum cholesterol level[11] — that generally oppose the trends reported with increasing age. The evidence suggests that such effects, at least on body weight or composition[4,7,11] and serum cholesterol,[11,13-15] are short-term and maintained only by continuous exercise. At present there is no evidence for residual, long-lasting effects of physical training on cardiovascular function, but there are few longitudinal studies. For example: "It is not known whether the cardiovascular changes caused by endurance athletics are wholly reversible. A question of interest is whether taking part in endurance athletics modifies the development and course of cardiovascular disease in later life."[16]

By what mechanisms could physical training such as ath-

---

*Reprinted from *Geriatrics*, 27:53-64, October 1972. Copyright 1972 by Harcourt Brace Jovanovich, Inc.

Part of this work was done under a predoctoral fellowship, National Institute of Mental Health No. 5-F01-MH-4383302, while the author was a graduate student in the Department of Anthropology, Harvard University, Cambridge, Massachusetts.

letics produce long-term, irreversible effects on the cardiovascular system? One possible mechanism involves the number and size of coronary collateral arteries. The presence of collateral vessels may protect against mortality from myocardial infarction.[17-19] Animal experiments,[20-22] autopsy findings on a famous athlete,[23] and meager clinical data[24] suggest that exercise may promote improvement in human coronary collateral circulation. The severity and duration of exercise needed to produce such changes in human beings is unknown.

Epidemiologists have investigated exercise mainly in connection with cardiovascular disease because of the high frequency of such disease in industrialized countries. In several population studies,[25-27] occupational physical activity, independent of other risk factors such as smoking and diet, was a significant variable in determining prevalence of coronary heart disease. Another method of studying the long-term effects of physical exercise on cardiovascular and general health involves follow-up data on college athletes. Such studies permit investigation of the possible long-term effects of exercise programs on longevity in general, as well as on mortality from specific causes.

The literature on longevity and cause of death among college athletes has been reviewed elsewhere.[28] In brief, studies have reported no statistically significant difference in average life expectancy between former college athletes and their less athletic classmates. Four cohort studies[28-31] have reported a slight difference (between one and two years) in mean age at death from natural causes in favor of nonathletes, however. Earlier studies reporting greater longevity of former sportsmen lacked adequate controls. No strong association has been established between participation in college athletics and subsequent death from cardiovascular or other specific groups of diseases. In all studies, however, the number of deaths is small for any given cause, so that larger samples are needed. Such studies may help explain the slightly reduced longevity of prominent athletes reported in all cohort studies.

Ideally, follow-up studies on longevity of former college athletes should consider the type of sport, degree of participation and achievement, the time period covered, the subjects' physique, and later habits of exercise. The present study considers, to some extent, all of these factors except later exercise habits. Neither Dublin,[29] Rook,[30] nor Polednak and Damon[28] had information on the physical activity of men after college, but Montoye[32] did. The occupations and physical activity were "about the same" for former athletes and nonathletes, but a significantly greater percentage of former athletes participated in recreational sports such as golf and bowling. These sports are not strenuous and in any case did not lengthen the former athletes' lives in relation to those of their classmates.[31,32] In one study of former Harvard varsity athletes,[33] however, lifetime exercise habits apparently had an important influence on cardiovascular mortality. Unfortunately, such data on later exercise habits are difficult to obtain.

We are concerned, therefore, with the possible long-term effects of early physical training (i.e. college athletics) on longevity, regardless of whether or not that training was continued in later life. Data on longevity and cause of death are presented on a larger sample of Harvard athletes and their classmates. Data on longevity of prominent athletes (lettermen), subdivided by type of sport and number of awards, are to be presented in a separate publication.

Subjects and Methods

The present series initially included 8,538 men who had been measured anthropometrically by D. A. Sargent and two assistants at Harvard University between 1880 and about 1912. These 8,538 men were part of a larger group of some 17,000 Harvard men (about half of all men attending Harvard between 1880 and 1920) who had been measured. Details of selection of subjects are presented elsewhere.[28] All applicants for gymnasium locker rental were measured but not all were photographed (for somatotype rating). Included in a previous report[28] were 2,631 men who had been both measured and photographed between 1880 and 1912.

Methods were similar to those used in the previous report.[28] Only men born between 1860 and 1889 were included; they were divided into three birth decades (1860-69, 1870-79 and 1880-89). Information on college sports was obtained from Harvard College records, including the First Annual Report of classes 1880 to 1916, and a list of athletic award winners.[34] Only men who had spent two or more years at Harvard College were included. Exclusion of dropouts and graduate students reduced the number of subjects to 6,591. Men who were lost (61) or who were known dead but lacking death certificates (227) were also excluded. This yielded a study group of 6,303.

The subjects were classified into three groups according to athletic participation: (1) Major athletes (668) — men who received one or more awards (letters) in "major" varsity sports — baseball, football, track, ice hockey, tennis, and golf. Only 10 major athletes won letters in tennis or golf. (2) Minor athletes (1,501) — men who participated in "major" sports without winning a letter, in sports for which letters were not awarded (lacrosse, cricket, basketball, swimming, gymnastics, and fencing), or in class sports. (3) Nonathletes (4,134) — men who had no record of having participated in formal college sports or participated only as freshmen.

Table 7-I

DISTRIBUTION OF HARVARD ATHLETES
AND THEIR CLASSMATES DEAD OF KNOWN CAUSE
OR ALIVE ON JUNE 30, 1967

| | Birth decade | | | | | |
| | 1860-69 | | 1870-79 | | 1880-89 | |
	No.	%	No.	%	No.	%
Major athletes	146	11.5	208	10.5	314	10.3
Minor athletes	244	18.9	330	16.7	927	30.5
Nonathletes	899	69.6	1,434	72.7	1,801	59.2
Total	1,289	100.0	1,972	99.9	3,042	100.0

Table 7-I shows the distribution of subjects by birth decade and athletic category. Age at death and cause of death were obtained from death certificates, and cause of death was coded according to the 1957 International Classification of Diseases.[35] Only the first-listed cause was used here. By June 30, 1967, all of the 1,289 men born in 1860-69 (100 percent) had died, as had 1,861 of the 1,972 men born in 1870-79 (94.4 percent), and 2,173 of the 3,042 men born in 1880-89 (71.4 percent). Thus, 5,323 of 6,303 men (84.5 percent) had died.

Separate analysis of the two series of Harvard men — the present series and that previously published[28] — seems justified because of possible differences between the two groups attributable to factors of selection. The photographed men[28] were a smaller and probably more select group since they volunteered to be photographed without clothing. The trends in longevity and cause of death in both series, by athletic group, can now be compared.

Results

LONGEVITY. In analyzing longevity among the 6,303 men alive or dead of known cause, deaths from causes other than natural were excluded, following Rook's[30] procedure.

Table 7-II
HARVARD ATHELTES AND THEIR CLASSMATES,
ALIVE OR DEAD OF NATURAL CAUSES,
REACHING AGES 70 AND 75

	Reaching age 70						Reaching age 75					
	1860-69		1870-79		1880-89		1860-69		1870-79		1880-89	
	No.	%	No.	%	No.	%	No.	%	No.	%	No.	%
Major athletes	62	44.6	101	52.6	170	57.2	46	33.1	84	43.5	145	48.8
Minor athletes	127	55.7	169	54.7	540	62.1	94	41.2	140	45.3	436	50.1
Nonathletes	437	51.9	767	57.2	1047	61.8	318	37.8	588	43.8	848	50.1
Comparison No.	1		2		3		4		5		6	

The focus in this paper is on survival to ages 70 and 75. In Table 7-II are listed, for each birth decade, the percentages of men reaching ages 70 and 75. Of the subjects alive on June 30, 1967, all had had a chance to reach 75 but not 80. An interesting point about Table 7-II is the increasing longevity over time within each athletic category. As previously noted,[28] this probably reflects environmental and medical advances.

In all six comparisons (Table 7-II) the major athletes were last. The minor athletes led in four of the six comparisons, tied for the lead in one (comparison No. 6), and were second in one (comparison No. 2). Except for the first birth decade (1860-69), however, differences were small; only one difference was statistically significant (0.05 level) — that between major and minor athletes born in 1860-69 reaching age 70.

Chi-square values within each birth decade, for men reaching and not reaching age 70 and 75 by athletic category, were not significant.

Men from all three birth decades were combined. For the percentage reaching age 70, two differences were significant (0.05 level) — i.e., minor athletes versus major athletes and nonathletes versus major athletes. For the percentage reaching age 75, none of the differences were statistically significant; the minor athletes lived longest, but by small margins.

Grouping men from all three birth decades for analysis seems justified by the roughly similar frequency of men in each athletic category in the three birth decade samples. The only exception is the higher percentage of minor athletes, and consequent lower percentage of nonathletes, in the last birth decade (1880-89), attributable to the fact that several sports began at the time these men were in college. The relatively greater longevity of all men born in this decade, compared to the other two (Table 7-II), introduces a bias in favor of minor athletes when the three birth decades are combined. The combined chi-square technic,[36] using the sum of chi-square values for each of the three birth decades, helps overcome this bias. The combined chi-square value for men reaching and not reaching age 70 was 8.67, which, at 3 degrees of freedom, is significant (0.05 level). The combined chi-square value for men reaching and not reaching age 75 (3.07) was not significant. The reduced longevity of the major athletes contributed most to the chi-square values.

Longevity cannot be assessed completely, however, until all men have died. The percentages of men still alive for the birth decades 1870-79 and 1880-89 (all men born in 1860-69 had died) favored the minor athletes, but differences were not statistically significant. In the birth decade 1870-79, percentages still alive were: major athletes, 9 of 208 or 4.3 percent; minor athletes, 22 or 330 or 6.7 percent and nonathletes, 80 of 1,434 or 5.6 percent. In the birth decade 1880-89, percentages still alive were: major athletes, 83 of 314 or 26.4 percent; minor athletes, 278 of 927 or 30 percent; and nonathletes, 508 of 1,801 or 28.2 percent.

The mean ages at death for men who died of natural causes are listed in Table 7-III. The only consistent finding is that the major athletes were the shortest-lived group in each birth decade. The only difference approaching statistical significance is that between major and minor athletes born in 1860-69 (0.10 > p > 0.05). Since slightly larger percentages of minor athletes

Table 7-III
MEAN AGE AT DEATH FOR HARVARD ATHLETES
AND THEIR CLASSMATES
DEAD OF NATURAL CAUSES*

	Birth decade								
	1860-69			1870-79			1880-89		
	No.	Mean	S.D.	No.	Mean	S.D.	No.	Mean	S.D.
Major athletes	139	65.7	17.1	184	67.8	17.1	214	64.2	13.8
Minor athletes	228	68.6	16.5	287	67.9	15.1	592	64.5	14.2
Nonathletes	842	67.8	16.9	1,259	68.5	15.4	1,186	65.2	14.6

*Percentage of deaths in each birth decade: 1860-69, 100 percent; 1870-79, 94.4 percent; and 1880-89, 71.4 percent. For significance of differences, see text.

Table 7-IV

HEIGHT AND WEIGHT OF HARVARD ATHLETES
AND THEIR CLASSMATES DEAD OF NATURAL CAUSES

	Birth decade 1860-69						Birth decade 1870-79						Birth decade 1880-89					
	Major athletes		Minor athletes		Nonathletes		Major athletes		Minor athletes		Nonathletes		Major athletes		Minor athletes		Nonathletes	
No.	139		228		842		184		287		1,259		214		592		1,186	
	Mean	S.D.	Mean	S.D.	Mean	S.D.	Mean	S.D.	Mean	S.D.	Mean	S.D.	Mean	S.D.	Mean	S.D.	Mean	S.D.
Height (in.)	68.6	2.6	68.0	2.6	67.7	2.4	69.5	2.6	68.9	2.3	68.2	2.5	70.1	2.3	69.1	2.4	68.5	1.5
Weight (lb)	147.2	18.9	138.3	16.0	131.9	15.0	150.6	20.0	144.6	15.6	136.8	16.4	155.5	19.6	147.1	16.7	139.6	17.8

Table 7-V

SELECTED CAUSES OF DEATH, BY BIRTH DECADE,
OF HARVARD ATHLETES AND THEIR CLASSMATES

Total deaths	Birth decade 1860-69			Birth decade 1870-79			Birth decade 1880-89		
	Major athletes 146	Minor athletes 243	Nonathletes 899	Major athletes 199	Minor athletes 308	Nonathletes 1,354	Major athletes 231	Minor athletes 649	Nonathletes 1,293
	%	%	%	%	%	%	%	%	%
Infections, parasites	7.5	6.6	6.9	7.5	2.9	4.7	2.2	3.5	3.9
Neoplasms	12.3	9.1	7.7	13.1	13.6	12.0	16.9	14.6	14.2
Nervous system	16.4	15.4	13.3	11.6	11.7	14.8	13.4	12.2	13.5
Circulatory system	34.9	41.6	38.3	41.2	44.2	41.7	41.1	42.2	43.9
(coronary heart disease)	14.4	17.3	17.2	23.6	22.1	23.0	26.4	27.0	27.8
Respiratory system	15.8	14.8	16.6	8.5	14.6	10.9	11.3	11.1	9.0
Accidents (excluding war)	4.8	2.9	3.7	3.0	4.9	3.8	2.2	4.3	3.6
Suicides	0.0	2.5	2.4	5.5	1.6	2.4	3.0	2.8	3.6

are still alive in the two most recent birth decades, it is expected that eventually the minor athletes will improve their longevity (although perhaps only slightly) in relation to the other two groups.

In view of the relationship between physique and longevity,[37],[38] height and weight were compared among men dead of natural causes (Table 7-IV). Within each birth decade, major athletes were taller and heavier than nonathletes, and minor athletes were intermediate. All but one of the differences reached statistical significance, at either the 0.05 or 0.01 level. Differences in weight were larger than differences in height, in agreement with the previously reported finding[28] that Harvard athletes were less ectomorphic (linear or lean) than nonathletes.

CAUSE OF DEATH. Selected causes of death, for each athletic category by birth decade, appear in Table 7-V. Causes involving too few subjects to warrant inclusion have been omitted.

The three athletic categories did not differ in percentage of deaths caused by infections or diseases of the nervous system. The differences in cardiovascular and specifically coronary heart disease were also patternless and statistically insignificant. Nonathletes consistently had the lowest percentage of deaths caused by neoplasms, however. Combining all three birth decades, the incidences of neoplastic deaths in relation to total deaths were 11.7 percent for nonathletes, 13.3 percent for minor athletes, and 14.4 percent for major athletes. The difference between major athletes and nonathletes approached statistical significance $(0.10 > p > 0.05)$.

For all other causes of death shown in Table 7-V, differences in percentage of deaths among the athletic categories are small and inconsistent across the birth decades.

In comparing mean ages at death for selected causes by birth decade and athletic category, a few consistent trends were found. Major athletes consistently died earlier from neoplasms than the other two groups. Combining all three birth decades, the mean age at death for neoplastic diseases was 67.1 years for major athletes (83), 68.4 years for minor athletes (159), and 69.2 years for nonathletes (415). None of the differences were statistically significant. Since more than 25 percent of men born in 1880-89 are still alive, the differences in age at death from neoplasms (and other causes) among the athletic groups may become more apparent when the entire. cohort has died.

Differences among the athletic groups in mean age at death from cardiovascular diseases were small and inconsistent in direction. This disease category includes coronary heart disease (CHD) — code 420.1, 1957 International Classification of Diseases[35] — which also was analyzed separately. Major athletes consistently died earliest from CHD in each birth decade. Combining all three birth decades, the mean age at death from CHD was 70.1 for major athletes (129), 70.4 for minor athletes (285), and 72.1 for nonathletes (827). The differences between nonathletes and major athletes and between nonathletes and minor athletes both reached statistical significance (0.05 level).

What could account for these differences in mean age at death from specific causes? For CHD, somatotype differences may be invoked since Harvard athletes from this era were significantly more mesomorphic (muscular and robust) and endomorphic (fat) than their classmates[28] and should, therefore, be at higher risk for early death from CHD.[39] Unfortunately, somatotype was not available for the present series. Weight alone is a poor discriminator of CHD risk since it does not indicate what components (fat, muscle, or bone) are involved. In any case, mean weight and height measured in college did not differ in future CHD decedents compared with the men dead from natural causes.

Differences between the major athletes and the other two groups in percentage of deaths and mean age at death from neoplastic diseases, although not statistically significant, are consistent in direction. If these differences are real, it is difficult to think of an explanation. For this series, mean height and weight did not differ among future decedents from neoplastic diseases compared with the total group of men dead of natural causes, but somatotype differences may conceivably exist. Smoking habits may have differed but such data were unavailable.

Discussion

The three athletic categories were compared by birth decade, a procedure which minimized time trends in relative proportions of the athletic categories, in age at death, cause of death, and diagnosis. The most consistent finding was the reduced longevity of major athletes. Differences within each birth decade were small, however, and rarely statistically significant. The combined chi-square technic, nevertheless, revealed significant differences among the athletic groups in survival to age 70. The reduced longevity of major athletes contributed most to this result.

Major athletes graduating in later years (after about 1890) had a lower mortality rate relative to athletes of earlier classes and only slightly higher than their classmates. This also was reported by Dublin,[29] who attributed the finding to better medical selection of athletes in later years. It should be noted, however, that all men in the first birth decade (1860-69) in the present series had died. The complete picture of longevity will emerge only when all men in the other birth decades have died.

The findings confirm those of previous studies, including one of Harvard men from the same era,[28] in showing the reduced longevity of major athletes (lettermen) compared to their classmates. The differences in all studies are small (between one and three years in mean age at death from natural causes) but the consistency in trend is impressive. The relatively reduced longevity of major athletes may be explained, in part if not entirely, by their physique. In the present series major athletes were significantly heavier and taller than the other two groups. In the previous report on 2,090 photographed Harvard men,[28] major athletes were significantly fatter, stockier, and more muscular than nonathletes, while minor athletes were intermediate. Stocky men have been shown to have shorter lives than leaner men, among insured persons[37] and in a preliminary analysis of somatotype among some 2400 photographed Harvard men.[40]

A limitation of most studies is their comparison of only two categories — prominent athletes who received awards in college and their less athletic classmates. The latter group actually includes men who participated in "major" sports without winning a letter or in other sports for which no awards were given at the time. Polednak and Damon[28] introduced a new category, the "minor" athletes. Although this classification is somewhat arbitrary, it does reflect degree of participation and achievement. Major athletes participated in enough games and with sufficient prominence to receive an award. Minor athletes are a more heterogeneous group, but it may be assumed that they participated less often in athletic competition and thus are intermediate between major athletes and nonathletes. In fact, minor athletes were intermediate in somatotype[28] and body size, being fatter, more muscular, and stockier than nonathletes.

In percentages of men reaching ages 70 and 75 and in percentages still alive, minor athletes generally led by small and insignificant margins. They also led in mean age at death from natural causes in the one birth decade for which all men had died, but differences only approached statistical significance. The same trend was reported in the previous, smaller study,[28] but, in various comparisons of longevity, few differences were statistically significant. The question of whether or not these slight differences are real may be answered better when all men in the present series have died.

The fact that the longevity of minor athletes is at least as great as that of nonathletes, despite the stockier build of the former, awaits explanation. Two possible explanations are that minor athletes are a select group, perhaps in terms of general health while in college, giving them an advantage, and that minor athletes continue their habits of moderate exercise in later life and benefit from this. There are no data to test these hypotheses. Data from other studies should be examined.

It should be emphasized that all subjects were interested in exercise in college to some extent, since all had applied for gymnasium locker rental. Exercise was not compulsory at Harvard at that time. The athletic groups therefore are not as extreme as those in other studies, which makes the difference more meaningful.

The one consistent trend was the higher percentage of neoplastic deaths among major athletes in each birth decade. Combining all three birth decades, the difference between major athletes and nonathletes approached statistical significance. Major athletes also died earlier, on the average, from neoplasms, but the differences were not significant. These same trends held for the series of photographed Harvard men.[28] Combining both series of Harvard men and all birth decades, the differences between major athletes and nonathletes were significant (0.05 level) both for percentage of neoplastic deaths and mean age at death.

Major athletes died earliest from CHD in each birth decade. Combining all three birth decades, the differences between major athletes and nonathletes and between minor athletes and nonathletes both reached statistical significance (0.05 level). This finding does not agree with that from the other Harvard series[28] in which no differences were found; the latter study, however, involved smaller numbers of CHD deaths. The present findings could be explained by physique. Other data[39] indicate that endomesomorphic men, like the Harvard athletes of this era,[28] are at greater risk for early CHD mortality.

The negative results for cardiovascular disease confirm those of Rook,[30] Pomeroy and White,[33] and Polednak and Damon.[28] The present finding on mean age at death from CHD, however, seems to disagree with that of Paffenbarger and associates,[41] who found fewer varsity athletes and less participation in sports among early coronary decedents than among classmates still alive. The present data, however, cover entire life-spans. At what age does the difference in CHD mortality first appear between major athletes and their classmates? For early CHD, Table 7-VI shows consistent differences by athletic category, although admittedly small and statistically insignificant for these small samples. Apparently, then, college athletics did not protect against early death from CHD and did not reduce mean age at death from CHD, perhaps because any possible protective effect of physical training did not offset the increased risk among athletes attributable to body build. The discrepancy between the present findings and those of Paffenbarger and associates[41] is unexplained.

Table 7-VI
DEATHS FROM CORONARY HEART DISEASE
BEFORE A GIVEN AGE IN ALL BIRTH DECADES COMBINED

	Before age 45		Before age 55		Before age 65		Total CHD deaths
	No.	%	No.	%	No.	%	No.
Major athletes	2	1.6	14	10.9	43	33.3	129
Minor athletes	0	0.0	27	9.5	92	32.3	285
Nonathletes	5	0.6	50	6.1	230	27.8	827

The athletic groups did not differ in percentage of deaths or mean age at death from cardiovascular diseases as a group. This suggests that differences for cardiovascular diseases other than CHD must favor the athletes and offset the difference in age at death from CHD, perhaps because of screening of athletes for absence of rheumatic fever and early signs of hypertensive disease.

In general, the present data support Fox and Haskell's[42] conclusion that, "It appears that for exercise to be of benefit it must be continuous throughout one's life, i.e. that one cannot 'store up' the benefits of earlier athletic performance, such as that done in college." Are the minor athletes an exception to this rule? Probably not, because if they are, indeed, slightly longer-lived than nonathletes, as our data suggest, it may be due to their habits of moderate exercise carried into later life. Unfortunately, there are no data to test this hypothesis.

Perhaps the most significant conclusion is a negative one. If the slightly reduced longevity of major athletes is related to their physique, as the data suggest, and if minor athletes are at least as long-lived, if not more so, than nonathletes, then there is no evidence that participation in college athletics reduces the life-span for men.

Summary

Among 6,303 men who attended Harvard College for at least

two years between 1880 and 1916, athletic status in college was analyzed in relation to longevity and cause of death. Major athletes (lettermen) had the shortest lives, but differences were small. In mean age at death (natural causes) differences were not statistically significant, but major athletes were consistently the shortest-lived group — by about one to three years in relation to minor athletes and nonathletes — in each of three birth decades. Major athletes died significantly earlier than nonathletes from coronary heart disease; they also died more often and earlier from neoplasms, although differences were not statistically significant for this series. Physique might account for the slightly reduced longevity of major athletes. Using several methods of analysis, longevity of minor athletes was as great as, or slightly (but insignificantly) greater than, that of nonathletes, despite the larger body size of the former.

REFERENCES

1. Skinner JS, Holloszy JO, Cureton TK: Effects of a program of endurance exercises on physical work capacity and anthropometric measurements of fifteen middle-aged men. Amer J Cardiol 14:747, 1964
2. Hollmann W: Körperliches Training als Prävention von Herz-Kreislaufkrankheiten. Stuttgart, Hippokrates-Verlag, 1965
3. Ekblom B, Astrand PO, Saltin B: Effect of training on circulatory response to exercise. J Appl Physiol 24:518, 1968
4. Parizkova J: Longitudinal study of the development of body composition and body build in boys of various physical activity. Hum Biol 40:212, 1968
5. Siegel W, Blomquist G, Mitchell JH: Effects of a quantitated physical training program on middle-aged sedentary men. Circulation 41:19, 1970
6. Andersen KL: The cardiovascular system in exercise. In Falls HB (Editor): Exercise Physiology. New York, Academic Press, 1968
7. Mayer J, Stare FJ: Exercise and weight control (frequent misconceptions). J Amer Diet Ass 29:340, 1953
8. Hutson EM, Cohen NL, Kunkel ND, et al: Measures of body fat and related factors in normal adults. J Amer Diet Ass 47:179, 1965
9. Seltzer CC: Chest circumference changes as a result of severe physical training. Amer J Phys Anthrop 4:389, 1946
10. Tanner JM: The effect of weight-training on physique. Amer J Phys Anthrop 10:427, 1952

11. Garrett HL, Pangle RV, Mann GV: Physical conditioning and coronary risk factors. J Chronic Dis 19:899, 1966

12. Buskirk EA, Taylor HL: Maximal oxygen uptake and its relation to body composition, with special reference to chronic physical activity and obesity. J Appl Physiol 11:72, 1957

13. Cooper RW, Ritota MC, Steinberg M, et al: Hearts and lipids of veteran handball players: A preliminary report. Angiology 17:192, 1966

14. Grimby G, Saltin B: Physiological analysis of physically well-trained middle-aged and old athletes. Acta Med Scand 179:513, 1966

15. Dill DB, Robinson S, Ross JC: A longitudinal study of 16 champion runners. J Sports Med 7:4, 1967

16. Pyörälä K, Karvonen MJ, Taskinen P, et al: Cardiovascular studies on former endurance runners. Helsinki, Finland. Reports from the Institute of Occupational Health, No. 19, 1965

17. Spain DM, Bradess VA, Iral P, et al: Intercoronary anastomotic channels and sudden unexpected death from advanced coronary atherosclerosis. Circulation 27:12, 1963

18. Scott JC: Physical activity and the coronary circulation. Canad Med Ass J 96:853, 1967

19. Helfant RH, Vokonas PS, Gorlin R: Functional importance of the human coronary collateral circulation. New Eng J Med 284:1277, 1971

20. Eckstein RW: Effect of exercise and coronary artery narrowing on coronary collateral circulation. Circ Res 5:230, 1957

21. Tepperman J, Pearlman D: Effect of exercise and anemia on coronary arteries of small animals as revealed by the corrosion-cast technique. Circ Res 9:576, 1961

22. Stevenson J, Felek V, Rechnitzer P, et al: Effect of exercise on coronary tree size in rats. Circ Res 15:265, 1964

23. Currens J, White PD: Half a century of running. New Eng J Med 265:988, 1961

24. Hellerstein HK, Horsten, TR, Goldberg AN, et al: Influence of active conditioning upon coronary atherosclerosis. In Brest AN, Moyer JH (Editors): Atherosclerotic Vascular Disease: A Hahnemann Symposium. New York, Appleton-Century-Crofts, 1967

25. McDonough J, Hames C, Stulb S, et al: Coronary heart disease among negroes and whites in Evans County, Georgia. J Chronic Dis 18:443, 1965

26. Dawber TR, Kannel WB, Friedman GD: Vital capacity, physical activity and coronary heart disease. In Raab W (Editor): Prevention of Ischemic Heart Disease. Springfield Ill. Charles C Thomas, 1966

27. Paffenbarger RS, Laughlin ME: Physical activity of work as related to death from coronary heart disease and stroke. Circulation 39, 40(suppl 3):158, 1969

28. Polednak AP, Damon A: College athletics, longevity, and cause of death. Hum Biol 42:28, 1970

29. Dublin LI: College honor men longer lived. Statist Bull Metrop Life Insur Co 13:5, 1932
30. Rook A: An investigation into the longevity of Cambridge sportsmen. Brit Med J 1:773, 1954
31. Montoye HJ, Van Huss WD, Neval JW: Longevity and morbidity of college athletes: A seven-year follow-up study. J Sports Med 2:133, 1962
32. Montoye HJ: Participation in athletics. *Ibid,*[18] p 813
33. Pomeroy W, White PD: Coronary heart disease in former football players. JAMA 167:711, 1958
34. Blanchard JA (ed): The H Book of Harvard Athletics (1852-1922). Cambridge, Mass, Harvard University Press, 1923
35. World Health Organization: International Classification of Diseases. Geneva, Switzerland, WHO, 1957
36. Maxwell AE: Analysing Qualitative Data. London, Methuen & Co, 1961
37. Society of Actuaries: Build and Blood Pressure Study. Chicago, Society of Actuaries, 1959
38. Seltzer CC: Some re-evaluations of the build and blood pressure study, 1959, as related to ponderal index, somatotype and mortality. New Eng J Med 274:254, 1966
39. Damon A, Damon ST, Harpending HC, et al: Predicting coronary heart disease from body measurements of Framingham males. J Chronic Dis 21:781, 1968
40. Damon A: Physique, longevity and number of offspring: Possible stabilizing selection in man (abstract). Amer J Phys Anthrop 35:276, 1971
41. Paffenbarger RS Jr, Notkin J, Krueger DE, et al: Chronic disease in former college students. II. Methods of study and observations on mortality from coronary heart disease. Amer J Public Health 56:962, 1966
42. Fox SM, Haskell WL: Physical activity and the prevention of coronary heart disease. Bull NY Acad Med 44:950, 1968

Chapter 8

LIFE EXPECTANCY OF
IVY LEAGUE ROWING CREWS*

BENJAMIN MOORSTEIN, M.D., THOMAS B. QUIGLEY, M.D.,
FRED V. HEIN, Ph.D., AND EDWIN E. WESTURA, M.D.

I *was recently asked whether the extremely rigid and physically demanding training program used by the Ivy League schools for their rowing crews is harmful to the heart in later years. An example was quoted that the members of the Harvard crew of 1948 have all since died of various cardiac diseases. Please discuss this and provide pertinent references.*

— B.M.

I can assure you that all members of the Harvard crews of the 1948 season are alive and well. Specifically, this record encompasses some 36 individuals constituting four crews of nine each. This includes the heavyweight varsity and junior varsity and the lightweight varsity and junior varsity. We are interested in the source of your information "that members of the Harvard crew of 1948 have all since died of various cardiac diseases," and would like to know how such a rumor might have started.

— T.B.Q.

Follow-up studies of rowing crews have been conducted particularly with respect to longevity. Cooper and associates,[1] in 1937, found that the mortality of oarsmen of Ormand College in Australia was lower than that for the average insurance risk. Among these athletes, there were 24 deaths as compared with the expected 31.8 in a control group born between the years 1885 and 1905.

---

*From Questions and Answers, *JAMA,* 205(9):106, 1968. Copyright 1968, American Medical Association.

Knoll,[1] in 1938, studied oarsmen of Oxford and Cambridge in terms of their current age or age at death. The principal purpose of the study was to determine the validity of the claim that oarsmen rarely lived to age 50. The mean age of those studied was 56.1 years, and many were still alive at the time of the study.

Hartley and Llewellyn,[1] in 1939, also studied the mortality of 767 Oxford and Cambridge oarsmen. Mortality was found to be lower among the athletes than among the insured population to which they were compared. However, college students are known to be a select group as far as longevity is concerned. Even if the example quoted in the question were true, which we are very much inclined to doubt, one would not be justified in drawing such conclusions based on the longevity of the members of one particular crew. A more extensive study covering a large sample of athletes undergoing comparable training would seem essential.

— F.V.H.

I have had no personal experience with crew members, either presently active or formerly active in this sport in undergraduate or graduate days. The athletes in our program of research are either track veterans or active professional golfers.

I think the comment is appropriate, that any conclusions regarding favorable or adverse effects of this sport on longevity would require much more data covering a large sample of athletes undergoing a comparable training program.

The sport itself requires extensive effort utilizing all major muscle groups. Energy costs are very high when expressed as mean aerobic cost or mean heart rate. As you are aware, there is little data upon which to make judgments regarding the long-term effects of activity of this type in youth. It may be that the same type of reasoning applies to this group as to other athletes, that is, that following very active lives as young men, if habitual activity is discontinued and replaced by a sedentary type life, overweight and other factors may supervene to increase risk, obliterating any possible benefit accrued from past athletic participation.

The real answer to the inquiry is not yet at hand. Intuitively, we suspect that an active early portion of life has no bearing on longevity, but the real question is, does continued habitual physical activity after age 25 alter longevity, and if so, what is the minimum amount and type required to obtain this beneficial effect?

— E.E.W.

REFERENCE

1. Montoye, H.J. et al: *Longevity and Morbidity of College Athletes.* East Lansing, Mich: Phi Epsilon Kappa Fraternity, Michigan State University, 1957, pp 16-17.

Chapter 9

LIFE EXPECTANCY OF
COLLEGE OARSMEN*

Curtis Prout, M.D.

Abstract

For 100 years, college rowing has been accused of producing injury and early death. Earlier studies indicated that
rowing was safe, and that athletics do not injure the heart or
shorten life. One hundred seventy-two varsity oarsmen, when
compared with random controls, lived longer. The factors
contributing to this longevity do not include height, social
class, or educational level.

THE rigorous training of rowing and the sus-
tained exertion of the races have been alleged, without foundation, for more than a century, to bring about serious physical
damage and occasional early death. This myth was sufficiently
widespread by 1873 to warrant a careful investigation. J. E.
Morgan[1] did a follow-up investigation of the health of 294
oarsmen from Oxford and Cambridge. It remains a valuable
study. Morgan concluded that rowing was usually healthful,
and only harmful to those few who were in poor health before
commencing to row, or to those who had "let themselves go in
later life." Morgan's conclusions are in agreement with several
later writers.[2,3]

In the year 1897, three well-known British oarsmen, all in
their 20s, died. Articles on the dangers of rowing promptly
appeared in the British lay and medical press until Lehmann,[4]
an old oar who knew all three, disclosed that they had died of a
ruptured appendix, tuberculosis, and an overwhelming infection, respectively. In each case the cause of death was evidently

*JAMA, 220(13):1709-1711, 1972. Copyright 1972, American Medical Association.
(Abridged.)

unrelated to rowing.

As recently as 1968, a letter to the *Journal of the American Medical Association* alleged that all the members of the Harvard 1948 crew were already dead,[5] a statement hotly denied by every one of them! The AMA Committee on the Medical Aspects of Sports has attempted to trace similar stories which appear from time to time, all without foundation. Evidently, fiction is more fun than fact.

The nature of crew races perhaps leads to these ideas. The precise timing of a successful eight-oared crew requires each man to exert himself uniformly, continuously, and maximally. The duration of this work is from seven minutes for the classic Henley distance to 22 minutes for a four-mile race. Long distance swimming and running races may last longer, but there the individual performer can vary his pace to suit his own capacity, whereas an oarsman cannot. The examination of a trained oarsman at rest shows some features not usually seen in other healthy persons; resting pulses with normal sinus rhythms in the 50's and even in the 40's, are not rare. Normal bradycardia of this degree is frequently associated with an apical mid-systolic murmur. The electrocardiogram may be interpreted as abnormal unless one has seen a number of such results in trained athletes. The ECGs of oarsmen have shown some coronary nodal rhythm and sinus bradycardias, according to unpublished data on the 1968 Harvard Olympic crew, gathered by William S. Kaden, MD. There was no evidence of atrioventricular block. The QRS complex had a normal configuration but a greater than normal amplitude, and the ST segments in the limb and lateral precordial leads were occasionally elevated. These changes are not thought to be pathologically significant. For these reasons, and to answer the recurring rumors of damage, it is worthwhile to review the literature and to study the lives of oarsmen, and to compare them with a randomly selected control group. This should also involve an attempt to identify the selection factors which produce varsity oarsmen. We need to know the causes of death of those few oarsmen and controls who died at relatively early ages.

The effect of vigorous exercise on the healthy heart of the

trained athlete is harmless. This was stated by Sir James McKenzie in 1912 when he disproved the existence of "athlete's heart." Lee et al[6] studied the heart size of oarsmen at Harvard in 1915 and found no significant enlargement. Deutsch and Kauf,[7] in 1927, studied the heart size of a large series of Viennese athletes, including oarsmen, with similar findings. Pomeroy and White,[8] in following the later lives of former Harvard football players, also found no harmful effects. The standard American textbooks of cardiology nowhere suggest that exertion can harm the previously healthy heart of the trained athlete.

The most convincing proof, however, must be in a study of mortality. The first such attempt was that of J. E. Morgan whose 1873 group contained many men who were still living. He tried, through correspondence, to ascertain the cause of death in the rest. He compared them with Farr's standard tables of British mortality, and while he found that oarsmen lived longer, he admitted that he was dealing with a selected group. The causes of death were listed for only 39 men. This cannot be compared with standard tables, but only three of the deaths were attributed to heart disease.

Hartley and Llewellyn,[2] in 1939, reported 767 Oxford and Cambridge "Old Blues" extending over a period of 100 years of races. Their life spans were compared with insured lives who were certainly better risks than the general population, but perhaps not comparable to a university group. They found the largest margin of superiority of oarsmen to be in the "deaths under 50" group (as has the present study). The mortality experience of these British university oarsmen was "appreciably superior" to the insured population, although the difference grew less with each year of age.

The largest series of data on longevity among athletes was compiled by Dublin and his associates[9] at the Metropolitan Life Insurance Co, and published in 1949. The college students were graduates of eight eastern colleges, classes 1870 to 1905 (closely comparable to our study), observed until 1925. The greater longevity of college students was probably related to social and economic factors. It is of interest that in this group, athletes had a mortality no different from the whole college population. The superior longevity of honors graduates has been noted in other studies.

Another study was reported in 1957 by Montoye and his colleagues[10] at Michigan State University. They sent questionnaires to 1,129 athletes, none of whom were oarsmen. Evidently the same questionnaire was sent to an equal number of "age-matched nonathletes." Six hundred twenty-nine of the former athletes replied (or surviving family members replied for them). Replies were received from about 583 of the nonathletes. The authors thought that, on the basis of the replies they received, there was no difference in the mortality between athletes and nonathletes. The literature, therefore, strongly suggests that rowing does not damage the heart and that the life of oarsmen is not shortened. To date, however, rowers have not been fully compared with their peers.

The group in this study consisted of 172 graduates of Harvard and Yale, each of whom rowed at least once in the four-mile varsity race. The years of the races selected were from 1882 to 1902 to insure a complete mortality experience. For each oarsman, a classmate was picked at random to serve as a control. The number of oarsmen in each class was compared with an equal number of nonoarsmen selected from that class by the random number method. Their ages were the same. There was no way to determine from the alumni reports reliable data on social differences or previous health. The height and weight of each oarsman was recorded, his age while rowing, age at death, and, when available, the cause of death. Every man who rowed in the Harvard-Yale varsity race in these years is included.

The average life span was calculated for the crew members and the control groups (Table 9-I). At both Yale and Harvard the average for the crew was higher than for the controls. The difference between the two groups at Yale was 6.35 years, and at Harvard 6.24 years. The difference between these averages was tested for significance by the standard *t*-test, and at both schools the probability that the difference would have occurred by chance was less than the 5% level. Where this occurred in both samples, one can feel quite secure in stating that the differences

Table 9-I
COMPARISON OF
AVERAGE LIFE SPAN OF
CREW MEMBERS AND CONTROLS AT
HARVARD AND YALE

Group	No. of Subjects	Average Life Span	t-test	P
Harvard crew	90	67.79	2.41	$<.05$
Harvard controls	90	61.54		
Yale crew	82	67.91	2.37	$<.05$
Yale controls	82	61.56		
Combined crew	172	67.85	3.39	$<.01$
Combined controls	172	61.55		

were real ones.

Needless to say, coxswains were not included in this study. There were differences, possibly not very significant, in two other categories; the 35 crew captains had a life span of 66.1 years, slightly less than the general average, and the 27 stroke oars lived to an average age of 69.5 years.

Unfortunately, the otherwise excellent alumni records do not often have a reliable diagnosis of the cause of death. Some information can be gained, however, from a study of the number of early deaths in each group, and the cause where it is available. The superior mortality of the oarsmen is most striking under the age of 50, as was also noticed by Hartley in 1939.[2]

The causes of death for those under the age of 60 are incompletely listed and the numbers are small (Table 9-II). Why

Table 9-II
KNOWN CAUSES OF
DEATH UNDER AGE 60

	Controls	Oarsmen
Stroke and heart disease	7	6
Acute infectious disease	8	2
Appendicitis	7	0
Tuberculosis	5	1

appendicitis caused deaths only in the control group seems unexplainable.

It is tempting to think that rowing itself made these men more long-lived, but other selection factors may be operating. The use of a control group probably excludes two factors known to have a favorable effect on mortality, namely college education and social class. Obviously the oarsmen were in good condition to begin with, otherwise they would not have been chosen.

Height is an obvious attribute of oarsmen, but Dublin found that under age 40, tall men had a higher mortality than short or average men, and after age 40, they had a higher mortality than men of average height.[11] This was confirmed in a study of Harvard and Pennsylvania students.[12,13] A distinct possibility is that former varsity oarsmen tend to continue to exercise and to avoid obesity, but this needs further study. Lastly, there is the speculation that people who are successful in various fields tend to outlive their less successful contemporaries.

REFERENCES

1. Morgan JE: *University Oars.* London, MacMillan & Co Ltd, 1873.
2. Hartley PHS, Llewellyn FIA: Longevity of oarsmen. *Brit Med J 1*:657, 1939.
3. Drinkwater GC, Sanders TRB: *The University Boat Race Official Centenary History.* London, Cassel & Co Ltd, 1929.
4. Lehmann RC: *Rowing.* New York, Edward Arnold & Co, 1897.
5. Moorstein B: Life Expectancy of Ivy League Rowing Crews. *JAMA 205*:652, 1968.
6. Lee RI, Dodd WJ, Young EL Jr: *Boston Med Surg J 173*:499, 1915.
7. Deutsch F, Kauf E: *Heart and Athletics.* St. Louis, Mo, C.V. Mosby Co, 1927.
8. Pomeroy WC, White PD: Coronary heart disease in former football players. *JAMA 167*:711-714, 1958.
9. Dublin LI, Lotka AJ, Spiegelman M: *Length of Life.* New York, Ronald Press, 1949.
10. Montoye HJ, et al: *Longevity and Morbidity of College Athletes.* East Lansing, Mich, Michigan State University, 1957.
11. Dublin LI: *Body Build and Longevity.* Presented at the deLamar lecture at Johns Hopkins University. Baltimore, Williams and Wilkins Co, 1927.

12. Paffenbarger RS, Wing A: Characteristics in youth predisposing to fatal stroke in later years. *Lancet 1*:753-754, 1967.
13. Paffenbarger RS, Wolf PA, Notkin J, et al: Chronic disease in former college students: I. Early precursors of fatal coronary heart disease. *Amer J Epidem 83*:314-328, 1966.

DISCUSSION

IN Rook's study (Chp. 4), the difference in mean age at death (natural causes) between sportsmen and intellectuals was not statistically significant (.15 > p > .10) nor was the 0.54 year difference between sportsmen and random controls. It is interesting to note that the two year difference between intellectuals and random controls reached the 5% significance level. This latter difference may have been due to socioeconomic differences, or possibly health during college, but we shall not speculate further here.

By 1953, 89.6% of Rook's subjects had died; the percentages dead were similar in the three groups compared. Up to the age of 40 years, the sportsmen had better survival rates than the other two groups. Table 4-III is an example of a *life table*.* It represents the rate of loss of persons from the original cohort due to death. The number living at the beginning of each interval may be used to obtain a percentage, or represented as the number surviving per 1,000 as in Rook's table. The cohort life table provides a summary of the mortality experienced by the cohort.

After age 40, the sportsmen and random groups had similar survival rates, while the intellectuals had a slight advantage at each age. Rook attributed this pattern to the early death of "weaklings" among the nonsportsmen. This idea relates to the medical selection of athletes.

Rook considered the possible effect of physique on longevity. The sportsmen were divided into two groups. The "light" group consisted of rowers below 168 lbs. (76 kg.), runners, and rugby backs, and the "heavy" group comprised rowers above 168 lbs., hammer and weight throwers, and rugby forwards.

---

*Discussion of life tables may be found in most books on biostatistics or on aging. The first life table was developed by John Graunt in London in 1662.

The light men lived slightly longer, i.e., a mean age at death of 66.73 years for 251 heavy men and 68.46 years for 315 light men. The difference was not statistically significant, but this evidence suggests a real (if slight) effect of physique on longevity, which could account for part of the difference in longevity between athletes and controls. It is interesting to note that Rook could find no evidence in the literature to support the popular notion that sportsmen tend to gain much weight after giving up athletic competition. Montoye et al. (1956, 1962, 1967) reported that although 629 athletes were heavier than 583 nonathletes in college, their subsequent weight gain was not significantly different (9.7 lbs. vs. 10.4 lbs.). This suggests that the weight gain among former athletes may be more readily noticed by observers, giving rise to the notion that this gain is excessive.

Montoye et al.'s (1956, 1962) study at Michigan State University was based on 1212 questionnaires, out of 2260 sent. In the 1956 report (see Chp. 5) 67 former athletes and 56 controls had died (see Table 5-II). In a seven-year follow-up of 98% of this group of 1212, 114 former athletes and 86 controls had died, at mean ages of 62 and 64 years, respectively (Montoye et al., 1962). This difference is not statistically significant, but favored the nonathletes, as did the simple mortality rates. This study involved small numbers. Also, bias in the findings was possible, since little more than half of the questionnaires were returned. Those who do not return questionnaires in a study are termed "nonrespondents." Nonrespondents almost always differ from respondents in various ways, some of which may be related to the outcome under study (i.e., mortality). In a recent report on the follow-up of this group, a total of 180 athletes and 140 controls had died, at mean ages of 65.37 and 66.91 years, respectively; the difference in mean age at death was reportedly not statistically significant (Olson et al., 1977).

Unlike Dublin or Rook, Montoye (1967) had some information on physical activity of men after college, which could be a crucial matter. Montoye found that occupations and physical activity at work were about the same for athletes and nonathletes. A significantly greater percentage of former athletes participated in later years in recreational sports like golf and bowling. These sports are hardly strenuous.

A limitation of these studies is their comparison, for the most part, of only two categories: prominent athletes who received awards in college and their less athletic classmates. The second group actually includes men who participated in sports but did not achieve prominence or participate in as many games, as well as those who did not participate. Rook defined athletes as participants in intercollegiate sports, but he did not classify them according to prominence or time spent in sports.

When comparing only two groups, there is no statistically significant difference in the average life expectancy of former college athletes and their less athletic college classmates. Several cohort studies, however, have reported a slight difference (between 1 and 2 years) in mean age at death in favor of nonathletes or honor men. Earlier studies reporting greater longevity of former college athletes were based on inadequate controls (the general population or insured men), so that the effect of athletics could not be assessed.

The results of the studies on Harvard athletes (Chps. 6 and 7) serve to reinforce some points made earlier. First, Shock (Chp. 1) noted that the average length of life has increased substantially in many countries over the past 50 to 100 years. Although increases in life expectancy at birth have been greater than those at later ages (Jacobson, 1964; Dubos, 1965; Greville, 1975) increases are evident in the percentages of Harvard men reaching ages 70 and 75 years across the birth decades; of course, all of these men had to reach the age of 17 or 18 years (i.e., at college entrance).

Second, differences in physique between college athletes and nonathletes (see Chapter 3) are quite striking. Somatotype data are presented on a sample of nonathletes (at Harvard) larger than that reported by Carter (1970), along with some unique data on "minor athletes." These data support Carter's conclusion that college athletes are highly selected in terms of physique. Also of interest is the observation that the minor athletes are intermediate between major athletes and nonathletes in physique, as they apparently also are in terms of achievement in athletics. Third, as noted above, these studies on Harvard athletes include some consideration of achievement or prominence in sports in relation to longevity. The apparent slight advantage of minor athletes in terms of survival to certain ages requires further exploration in other populations.

Finally, the results of these studies confirm the above-mentioned finding of slightly reduced longevity of college athletes (lettermen) versus nonathletes found in other studies, and suggest that specific disease categories may be involved (i.e., coronary heart disease and cancer). The possible role of physique in explaining these differences is not fully explored in the above studies. Section IV deals with specific disease categories, and some attempts are made to control for the possible influence of differences in physique between athletes and nonathletes.

The inquiry by Moorstein (see Chp. 8) indicates that misconceptions (or at least misinformation) about the long-term health effects of athletics exist in the medical profession. Westura notes the need for data on large samples of athletes; such data have been provided by Prout (Chp. 9), with specific reference to crewmen.

The results of Prout's study on Harvard and Yale varsity oarsmen are apparently unique, in showing a greater longevity of athletes compared with their classmates. As we have noted, several cohort studies have shown a consistent (if small) advantage in longevity among nonathletes (vs. athletes). What seems remarkable about Prout's results (Table 9-I), however, is the rather low average length of life of the controls. This suggests the possible role of selection for college athletics on the basis of present and past health, as noted by Rook (Chp. 4) and others (including Prout). Examination of causes of death under age 60 (Table 9-II) supports this idea; the higher frequency of mortality from infectious diseases, including tuberculosis, in the controls is noteworthy. Also, it is unclear whether or not the controls had graduated from college, whereas the oarsmen were described as graduates; thus, some very early deaths (possibly accidents or other nonnatural causes) may have been included in the controls, which could have expected the mean age at death.

As we have noted (see Introduction) Olympic and professional athletes may be even more select in terms of health than college athletes. In Section V, the advantage of athletes in terms of survival to early ages will be discussed. Also, some data on the previous health of college athletes and nonathletes will be presented, which support the idea that athletes are selected in terms of health.

REFERENCES

Carter, J.E.L. 1970 The somatotypes of athletes: A review. Human Biol. *42*:535-569.

Dubos, R. 1965 Man Adapting. Yale University Press, New Haven.

Greville, T.N.E. 1975 Some Trends and Comparisons of United States Life-Table Data: 1900-1971. U.S. Dept. of Health, Education and Welfare Publication No. (HRA)75-1150, Rockville, Maryland.

Jacobson, P.H. 1964 Cohort survival for generations since 1840. Milbank Mem. Fund Quart. *42*:36-53.

Montoye, H.J. 1967 Participation in athletics. Canad. Med. Assoc. J. *96*:813-820.

Montoye, H.J., W.D. Van Huss, H. Olson, A. Hudec, and E. Mahoney 1956 Study of the longevity and morbidity of college athletes. J. Amer. Med. Assoc. *162*:1132-1134.

Montoye, H.J., W.D. Van Huss, and J.W. Neval 1962 Longevity and morbidity of college athletes: A seven-year follow-up study. J. Sports Med. Phys. Fitness *2*:133-140.

Olson, H.W., H. Teitelbaum, W.D. Van Huss, and H.J. Montoye 1977 Years of sports participation and mortality in college athletes. J. Sports Med. *17*:321-326.

College Athletes:
Specific Causes of Death

Follow-up studies on Harvard College men (see Chaps. 6 and 7) suggest that the slightly reduced longevity of athletes (vs. nonathletes) may be related to earlier death from cardiovascular diseases and cancers. The following papers examine these causes of death more closely in this same population. First, mortality from renal diseases among Harvard College athletes and nonathletes is considered; short-term changes in renal function related to athletics (and other types of exercise) have suggested the possibility of long-term effects on the kidney.

Chapter 10

MORTALITY FROM RENAL DISEASES AMONG FORMER COLLEGE ATHLETES*

ANTHONY P. POLEDNAK, Ph.D.

Abstract

In a cohort study of 8393 men attending Harvard College between 1880 and about 1912, data on mortality from renal diseases were obtained from death certificates. Mortality from all renal diseases and from nephritis alone was compared by birth decade (1860-1869, 1870-1879, and 1880-1889) and athletic status in college (major athlete, minor athlete, or nonathlete). Differences in percentages of deaths attributed to renal diseases (underlying or contributory cause) among the three athletic groups were small and statistically insignificant. Among men with renal disease listed as the underlying cause of death, the mean age at death was significantly higher for athletes than for nonathletes. These findings do not support the belief that strenuous exercise (as in college athletics) has long-term adverse effects on the kidney.

GARDNER (1) has summarized evidence that strenuous exercise or athletic competition has deleterious effects on the kidney. Urinary abnormalities reported among college athletes in various sports (2, 3) were believed to be transient, but recent evidence on military recruits (4, 5) suggests that the effects of strenuous exercise on the kidney may be more severe (1). Alyea and Parish (2) raised the question of whether recovery from kidney damage among college athletes was complete or

*From *Annals of Internal Medicine*, 77:919-922, 1972.
   Supported in part by a predoctoral fellowship (5-F01MH-43833-02) from the National Institute of Mental Health, Bethesda, Md., and by the Fund for Research and Teaching, Department of Nutrition, Harvard University School of Public Health, Boston, Mass.

135

whether this damage "leaves the tubular element in a weakened or more vulnerable condition."

As Gardner observes (1), there is "no documented evidence of an increased incidence of renal disease in athletes." In fact, there are no published data on mortality from renal diseases among athletes and suitable control subjects. Such data, now presented for Harvard College athletes and their classmates, may help determine whether there are long-term adverse effects from athletic competition on the kidney.

Subjects and Methods

The subjects have been described in detail elsewhere (6-8). Initially, they included 11,169 men measured anthropometrically while at Harvard University between 1880 and about 1912. These men were born between 1860 and 1889; they were divided into 3 birth decades (1860-1869, 1870-1879, and 1880-1889). To ensure greater homogeneity of the sample and that all subjects had an opportunity to participate in college sports, only those men were included who had spent 2 or more years in Harvard College. Exclusion of dropouts and graduate students reduced the number of subjects to 8743. Further exclusion of men who were lost (n = 81) or who were known to be dead but on whom there were no death certificates (n = 289) yielded a study group of 8393 men.

The subjects were classified into three groups, according to athletic participation: (1) major athletes (n = 845) — men who received one or more awards ("letters") in varsity sports (baseball, football, track, crew, ice hockey, tennis, and golf); (2) minor athletes (n = 1776) — men who participated in varsity sports without winning a letter or in sports for which letters were not awarded (for example, interclass sports); and (3) nonathletes (n = 5772) — men with no record of participation in formal college sports or men who participated only as freshmen. All subjects were interested in exercise to some extent, since all had applied for gymnasium locker rental. Data on exercise habits after college were unavailable.

Causes of death were obtained from death certificates and

coded according to the International Statistical Classification of Diseases (ICD) (9). The first-listed or "underlying" cause of death was used in some analyses, but "contributory causes" were also recorded and analyzed. Renal disease was defined as including "acute" and "chronic" nephritis (ICD 590-594), "infections of the kidney" (ICD 600), and "other diseases of the kidney" (ICD 601-603), and "uremia" (ICD 792).

As of 30 June 1967, 1831 of the 1834 men (99.8%) born in 1860-1869 had died, as had 2812 of the 2967 (94.7%) born in 1870-1879 and 2581 of the 3582 (72.1%) born in 1880-1889. Thus, a total of 7224 out of 8393 men, or 86.1%, had died. Table 10-I shows their distribution by birth decade and athletic category.

Table 10-I

DEATHS OF HARVARD MEN*
BY ATHLETIC STATUS AND BIRTH DECADE

	Birth Decade			Total
	1860-1869	1870-1879	1880-1889	
	←	no.		→
Major athlete	204	290	249	743
Minor athlete	295	436	698	1429
Nonathlete	1332	2086	1634	5052
Total	1831	2812	2581	7224

*Dead of known cause, as of 30 June 1967.

Results

Table 10-II shows mortality from renal diseases (underlying cause) by athletic status and birth decade. In each birth decade the percentage of such deaths is slightly (but insignificantly) higher among major athletes than among minor or nonathletes. The mean age at death from renal diseases, however, is consistently higher among athletes than among nonathletes. For all three birth decades combined (Table 10-II), mean age at death is significantly higher among major athletes than among nonathletes (70.4 years versus 62.4 years; $P < 0.01$, t test). The differences between major and minor athletes and between minor and nonathletes are not statistically significant. For all

Table 10-II

MORTALITY FROM RENAL DISEASES* (UNDERLYING CAUSE)
AMONG HARVARD MEN, BY ATHLETIC STATUS AND BIRTH DECADE

	1860 1869		1870 1879		1880 1889		All Decades Combined			
	Percent*	Mean Age at Death	Percent	Mean Age at Death	Percent	Mean Age at Death	Total Deaths	Percent	Mean Age at Death	SD
		yr		yr		yr	no.		yr	yr
Major athlete	5.4	72.7	4.5	69.8	2.4	67.6	30	4.0	70.4	13.4
Minor athlete	5.1	67.5	2.5	69.4	2.3	64.0	42	2.9	66.7	14.7
Non athlete	4.3	63.6	3.6	61.5	2.2	62.5	169	3.3	62.4	16.9
Total	4.5	65.5	3.6	63.5	2.2	63.4	241	3.3	64.2	16.4

* ICD code 580-594, 600-603, and 792 (9). Percentages are calculated as a percentage of deaths from known cause (proportional mortality rate).

Table 10-III

MORTALITY FROM NEPHRITIS* (UNDERLYING CAUSE)
AMONG HARVARD MEN, BY ATHLETIC STATUS AND BIRTH DECADE

	Deaths						All Decades Combined			
	1860-1869		1870-1879		1880-1889		Total Deaths	Percent	Mean Age at Death	SD
									yr	
	no.	*%*	*no.*	*%*	*no.*	*%*	*no.*			
Major athlete	7	3.4	7	2.4	2	0.9	16	2.2	65.2	14.4
Minor athlete	12	4.1	6	1.4	7	1.0	25	1.7	63.2	14.1
Nonathlete	36	2.5	46	2.2	16	1.0	98	1.9	56.1	14.8
Total	55	3.0	59	2.1	25	1.0	139	1.9	56.6	15.8

* ICD code 590-594 (9). Percentages are calculated as a percentage of deaths from known cause.

three birth decades combined, the percentage of deaths from renal diseases (Table 10-II) is slightly higher in major athletes and lowest in minor athletes, but none of the differences is statistically significant. When both groups of athletes (major and minor) are combined, this percentage is identical with that of nonathletes — 72 of 2172 (3.3%) for athletes and 169 of 5052 (3.3%) for nonathletes. The nonathletes, however, died significantly earlier than the athletes from renal diseases — 68.2± 14.3 years for athletes versus 62.4 ± 16.9 years for nonathletes (*P* < 0.01, *t* test).

Mortality from nephritis (ICD 590-594) is analyzed separately (Table 10-III), in view of the suspected deleterious effects of strenuous exercise (1, 3). The findings are similar to those in Table 10-II; namely, athletes died from nephritis about as frequently but significantly later than nonathletes. For the mean age at death from nephritis (Table 10-III), the differences between major athletes and nonathletes and between minor athletes and nonathletes were both statistically significant (*P* < 0.05).

The World Health Organization Expert Committee on Health Statistics (10) and others (11) have recommended removing the distinction between "underlying, contributory and incidental" conditions reported on death certificates. Presumably, this would provide more complete information on the pathological conditions identified at death. This procedure has been followed in this report; all renal diseases, whether listed as underlying or contributory causes, have been analyzed (Table 10-IV). The differences among the three athletic groups in percentages of death certificates mentioning nephritis or any renal disease were small and statistically insignificant (Table 10-IV).

Discussion

Tables 10-II to 10-IV show an apparent decline in the frequency of renal diseases across the three birth decades; this holds whether renal disease is listed as an underlying or contributory cause of death. But, since all men in this study have not died, age-specific death rates for renal diseases should be compared to the three birth cohorts. These data will be pre-

Table 10-IV

FREQUENCY OF RENAL DISEASES
LISTED AS UNDERLYING OR
CONTRIBUTORY CAUSES OF DEATH*

	Birth Decade						
	1860 1869		1870 1879		1880-1889		Total
	no.	*%*	*no.*	*%*	*no.*	*%*	*no.*	*%*
Any renal disease								
Major athlete	17	8.3	21	7.2	14	5.6	52	7.0
Minor athlete	26	8.8	21	4.8	26	3.7	73	5.1
Nonathlete	111	8.3	143	6.9	65	4.0	319	6.3
Total	154	8.4	185	6.6	105	4.1	444	6.1
Nephritis								
Major athlete	9	4.4	10	3.4	5	2.0	24	3.2
Minor athlete	22	7.5	16	3.7	13	1.9	51	3.6
Nonathlete	72	5.4	84	4.0	33	2.0	189	3.7
Total	103	5.6	110	3.9	51	2.0	264	3.7

* Individuals whose death certificate mentioned nephritis (ICD 590-594) or any renal disease (ICD 590-594, 600-603, 792). Frequency percentages of deaths from renal disease or nephritis calculated as a percentage of deaths from known cause.

sented in another report.

The problems and limitations of using death certificates to determine disease frequency have been discussed elsewhere, both in general terms (11, 12) and with specific reference to renal diseases (13, 14). It may be more meaningful and improve accuracy somewhat to take into account all causes of death mentioned on death certificates (12). In addition, Abramson, Sacks, and Cahana (12, p. 427) have observed that: "For epidemiological purposes, the fact that the certificate data are not a very valid indicator of the prevalence of diseases at death need not in itself be a major handicap, provided that the discrepancies are due to chance alone." The three athletic categories were compared by birth decade, a procedure that presumably minimized time trends in age at death, cause of death, and diagnosis.

In view of the inherent inaccuracies of death-certificate diagnoses, the results of this study allow only some cautious conclusions about the long-term effects of exercise or athletic competition on the kidney. First, renal diseases apparently account for about an equal percentage of deaths among former college athletes and nonathletes. This holds whether renal disease is listed as an underlying or contributory cause on death certificates. Second, the mean age at death is significantly higher among athletes than among nonathletes certified as dying from renal disease (underlying cause). Does exercise (or athletics) therefore have a protective effect on the kidney, increasing resistance to infection, trauma, or other noxious agents? Without comparable data from other studies, we can only speculate. Several other possible explanations might be considered.

First, the difference in mean age at death from renal disease might be part of a general trend toward increased longevity among athletes compared with nonathletes. In fact, however, Harvard major athletes (lettermen) lived slightly shorter lives compared with nonathletes (7, 8), in agreement with other cohort studies. Also, Harvard lettermen died slightly earlier than nonathletes from coronary heart disease and neoplasms (7). These findings contrast with those reported above on mean age at death from renal diseases. Second, the intercollegiate sports involved here may not have been strenuous enough to produce long-term renal damage. Short-term urinary abnormalities have been reported (2, 3), however, among athletes in both contact and noncontact sports. Thus, the present findings do not support Alyea and Parish's (2, p. 813) belief that the temporary renal damage among athletes "leaves the tubular element in a weakened or more vulnerable condition."

Third, college athletes may have been selected — both by self-selection and by medical examination — for the absence of conditions (such as previous infectious diseases) that might predispose to early death from renal disease. Of the 139 deaths attributed to nephritis, 109 (or 78.4%) were listed as "chronic" nephritis. The role of previous streptococcal infection in chronic (versus acute) glomerulonephritis is obscure. Hansen and Susser (15), however, noted a decline in U.S. and British death rates from both chronic nephritis and known manifestations of streptococcal infection (rheumatic fever, rheumatic heart disease, and scarlet fever): These authors suggested that "this is the expected relationship if both scarlet fever deaths in childhood and chronic nephritis deaths in later life had a common source in streptococcal infections in childhood" (p. 41). The clinical data do not support the idea of a definite relationship between chronic nephritis and a history of acute nephritis or antecedent infection, but this is still a subject of debate (16).

Table 10-V

PREVIOUS INFECTIOUS DISEASES
REPORTED BY HARVARD MEN*
(BORN 1860-1869), BY ATHLETIC STATUS

	Major Athlete ($n = 204$)		Minor Athlete ($n = 295$)		Non-athlete† ($n = 270$)	
	no.	%	no.	%	no.	%
Rheumatic fever	1	0.5	1	0.3	1	0.4
Rheumatic heart disease	0	0.0	0	0.0	1	0.4
Scarlet fever	5	2.5	8	2.7	8	3.0
Pneumonia	8	3.9	14	4.7	14	5.2

* During medical and anthropometric examination at Harvard University, at a mean age of 19.3 years.
† A sample of every fifth consecutive nonathlete measured.

Table 10-V shows selected previous infectious diseases reported by Harvard men (born 1860-1869) at the time of their medical examination (at a mean age of 19.3 years). Differences between athletes and nonathletes, in percentages of men reporting a history of scarlet fever, rheumatic fever, rheumatic heart disease, and pneumonia, are small and statistically insignificant. It is difficult to interpret these small differences as influencing age at death from chronic nephritis, expecially in view of the uncertain etiologic role of previous streptococcal infection. This role will be examined further in a case-control study of previous infectious disease and chronic nephritis among Harvard men.

REFERENCES

1. GARDNER KD JR: Athletic nephritis: pseudo and real. *Ann Intern Med*

75:966-967, 1971.
2. ALYEA EP, PARISH HH JR: Renal response to exercise — urinary findings. *JAMA* 167:807-813, 1958.
3. GARDNER KD JR: "Athletic pseudonephritis" — alteration of urine sediment by athletic competition. *JAMA* 161:1613-1617, 1956.
4. SCHRIER RW, HENDERSON HS, TISHER CC, et al: Nephropathy associated with heat stress and exercise. *Ann Intern Med* 67:356-376, 1967.
5. SCHRIER RW, HANO J, KELLER HI, et al: Renal, metabolic and circulatory reponses to heat and exercise: studies in military recruits during summer training, with implications for acute renal failure. *Ann Intern Med* 73:213-233, 1970.
6. POLEDNAK AP, DAMON A: College athletics, longevity and cause of death. *Hum Biol* 42:28-46, 1970.
7. POLEDNAK AP: Longevity and cause of death among Harvard College athletes and their classmates. *Geriatrics.* In press, 1972.
8. POLEDNAK AP: Longevity and cardiovascular mortality among former college athletes. *Circulation.* In press, 1972.
9. WORLD HEALTH ORGANIZATION: *Manual of the International Statistical Classification of Diseases, Injuries, and Causes of Death,* 7th ed. Geneva, Switzerland, World Health Organization, 1957.
10. WHO EXPERT COMMITTEE ON HEALTH STATISTICS: *Epidemiological Methods in the Study of Chronic Diseases. WHO Tech Rep Ser* No. 365, 1967.
11. FEINSTEIN AR: Clinical epidemiology. II. The identification rates of disease. *Ann Intern Med* 69:1037-1061, 1968.
12. ABRAMSON JH, SACKS MI, CAHANA E: Death certificate data as an indication of the presence of certain common diseases at death. *J Chronic Dis* 24:417-431, 1971.
13. KESSNER DM, FLOREY CDuV: Mortality trends for acute and chronic nephritis and infections of the kidney. *Lancet* 2:979-982, 1967.
14. MODAN B, MOORE BP, PAZ B: Mortality from renal disease in Israel: some epidemiological aspects. *J Chronic Dis* 22:727-732, 1970.
15. HANSEN H, SUSSER M: Historic trends in deaths from chronic kidney disease in the United States and Britain. *Am J Epidemiol* 93:413-424, 1971.
16. RELMAN AS: Clinical aspects of chronic glomerulonephritis, in *Diseases of the Kidney,* 2nd ed., edited by STRAUSS MB, WELT LG. Boston, Little, Brown and Co., 1971, p. 488.

Chapter 11

CORONARY HEART DISEASE IN FORMER FOOTBALL PLAYERS*

WILLIAM C. POMEROY, M.D. AND PAUL D. WHITE, M.D.

Abstract

The health records of a group of 355 men who had distinguished themselves at football in the years 1901 to 1930 inclusive were studied for factors that might predispose a man to coronary heart disease. The cause of death was ascertained in 87 cases and was found to be coronary heart disease in 25. Comparisons were made between former athletes still living without coronary heart disease and former athletes, living or dead, with coronary heart disease, with respect to data that had been recorded during health examinations while they were in college and noted in the years since their graduation. The coronary and noncoronary groups did not differ significantly with respect to body build as recorded in college, but the family histories of the coronary group showed a higher incidence of unfavorable family health and the coronary group gained more weight after leaving college. Little difference was found in this study between heavy smokers and abstainers and between heavy drinkers and abstainers, but it is noted that the groups were small and did not manifest any wide diversity in ways of life. The most interesting finding concerned the amount of exercise taken habitually during the lifetime of these men. Those in the coronary group engaged in less vigorous exercise than did the others, and no individual in this study who maintained a heavy exercise program happened to develop coronary heart disease.

THE health and longevity of athletes has been of considerable interest for 100 years or more and is still a

---

*From *JAMA, 167*:711-714, 1958. Copyright 1958, American Medical Association.

problem of great importance. Not many satisfactory studies have been carried out and published concerning this question, especially as it relates to so-called heart strain and the development of heart disease. Now and then, in the past, some interesting observations have been made, which include a book entitled "University Oars," by Morgan, dated 1873, which discusses the longevity of members of the Oxford and Cambridge crews in the years 1829-1869. Dr. Morgan concludes as follows:

> On the whole the results obtained by the Life Tables, in so far as they bear upon the duration of life of the Cambridge University Oarsmen, must be deemed decidely favourable; the lives of each one of the 32 crews to which they refer extended over 334 instead of 320 years (expected for the male population at large). Hence each individual who rowed is likely to survive the race, on an average, some 42 instead of 40 years.
>
> The lives of the Oxford men are on the whole decidedly better than those of the Cambridge Oars, the former averaging 43.7 years instead of 40 after the race. This is due to the fact that out of the 16 Oxford crews which rowed between 1829 and 1869 only 15 men died within those years, while the deaths among the Cambridge men, who took part in the same races, amount to 24.

Dr. Morgan stated that 11 men died from fever, 7 from consumption, 2 from other forms of chest disease, 6 from accidental causes, 3 from heart affections, 2 from diseases of the brain, 2 from inflammatory attacks, 1 from general paralysis, 1 from calculus, 1 from erysipelas, 1 from Bright's disease, 1 from cancer, and 1 from lupus erythematosus.

Another report of interest was that of Gaines and Hunter, who wrote a paper entitled "Mortality Among Athletes and Other Graduates of Yale University" in the *Transactions of the Actuarial Society of America,* in 1905. The author summarized some of the results as follows:

> Combining crew, football, track and baseball and tracing members to the end of 1904, the death rate was nearly 25 per cent lower than among graduates of the Academic Department. Among the 55 deaths there were 12 from tuberculosis of the lungs and 5 from typhoid fever, conditions which would not appear nowadays. A synopsis of the experience of the

Yale graudates from 1701 through 1777 indicates a high death rate at ages under 35, nearly three times that in this present generation. It was not until the age group 70 and over that the mortality rates compare with the current ones.

It is well known that coronary heart disease tends to be more common in men of the mesomorphic body type than in those of other (endomorphic and ectomorphic) types. In view of this propensity, it was believed to be desirable to study a group of individuals with this body build, with reference to the possible influence of various environmental factors upon the coronary circulation.

Present Study

It was hoped that Harvard football lettermen of a generation ago would furnish a suitable group for a study of this sort. Questionnaires were sent to all "H" winners in football for Harvard from 1900 to 1930 (except the years 1918 and 1919 when no intercollegiate games of football were played by Harvard because of World War I). Further information was obtained where possible by individual letters to families and to personal physicians. Also, the death certificates for the Commonwealth of Massachusetts were examined for causes of death in cases where no other information was available.

According to the Harvard College alumni records, 424 men won football "H's" in the years 1902 to 1930 inclusive. Of these, 292 were known to be alive, 6 were lost to follow-up, and 126 were known to have been dead as of the date of 1955 on completion of these data. The cause of death was known for 87 of the 126 men. Of the grand total of 424, some information was available concerning 355 persons. It is of interest that, of these, 34 were known to have or to have had definite coronary heart disease.

Findings

The causes of death in 87 former football players are enumerated in Table 11-I. For purposes of comparison, the causes of death in adult white males in Massachusetts for the year 1940 are listed in Table 11-II. These data were chosen because the median year of death for the group being studied was 1936, and the vital statistics for 1940 were the nearest available for Massachusetts.

A comparison of the percentages of coronary disease in the two groups is difficult because of the vague nature of "chronic myocarditis and myocardial degeneration." Certainly many of these are cases of hypertensive or coronary heart disease. If the cases attributed to cardiovascular disease in each group are compared, it is noted that the former football players have but a slightly lower percentage of death from that cause. It is presumed, of course, that the football players were free of rheumatic and congenital heart lesions at the time of their participation in the sport. They were all carefully examined at that time.

Table 11-I

CAUSES OF DEATH OF EIGHTY-SEVEN
HARVARD FOOTBALL PLAYERS
OF A GENERATION AGO

Causes of Death	Cases	
	No.	%
Coronary heart disease		
(thrombosis or angina pectoris)*	25	28.8
Malignancies and tumors	11	12.6
Pneumonia	9	10.3
War injuries	9	10.3
Accidents	8	9.2
Suicide	4	4.6
Cerebral hemorrhage*	3	3.4
Typhoid	2	2.3
Generalized artheriosclerosis*	3	3.4
Nephritis	2	2.3
Uremia	2	2.3
Congestive heart failure*	2	2.3
Miscellaneous (1 case each)	7	8.0

* Cardiovascular disease in 33 (37.9%) apparently was due to arteriosclerosis or/and hypertension without congenital, rheumatic, or syphilitic heart disease.

Table 11-II

CAUSES OF DEATH OF ADULT WHITE MALES
IN MASSACHUSETTS IN 1940

Causes of Death	Deaths	
	No.	%
Diseases of circulatory system	10,084	42.0
Chronic myocarditis and myocardial degeneration*	3,988	16.6
Other diseases of myocardium	697	2.9
Diseases of coronary artery	3,477	14.5
Angina pectoris	127	0.5
Chronic affections of valves and endocardium	688	2.9
Other diseases of circulatory system (including 351 cases of arteriosclerosis)	1,107	4.6
Suicide	424	1.8
Cancer and other tumors	3,273	13.6
Accidents	1,359	5.7
Cerebral hemorrhage	1,690	7.0
Pneumonia	1,165	4.8
Typhoid	6	0.0
Chronic nephritis (not arteriosclerotic kidney)	863	3.6
Acute nephritis	24	0.1
All other causes†	5,138	21.3
Total	24,026	100.0

* Includes hypertensive heart disease.

† Includes tuberculosis, 1,015 cases; diabetes, 535; cirrhosis of liver, 265; diseases of digestive system, 866; arteriosclerotic kidney, 526; and hypertrophy of the prostate, 266.

An attempt was made to compare the longevity and mortality of these Harvard football players with that of healthy males of comparable age in the general population or indeed among Harvard graduates who had not played football, but adequate data for any such statistical comparison were lacking. The principal objective of the study, the evaluation of the influence of various factors upon the incidence of coronary heart disease in this group, was approached in two ways.

First, the lettermen with known coronary heart disease were compared with a control group in reference to the factors under

Table 11–III

COMPARISON OF DATA OF EXFOOTBALL PLAYERS
WITH AND WITHOUT CORONARY HEART DISEASE

General Data	Group Living Without Coronary Disease, per Class Grouping						Coronary Group, Both Dead and Living
	1901-1905	1906-1910	1911-1915	1916-1920	1921-1925	1926-1930	
Body build							
Av. height in college, ft.-in.	6-0	5-11½	5-11	6-0	5-11½	5-11½	5-11
Av. weight in college, lb.	˙173	184	171	187	182	179	182
Av. weight in later life, lb.	175	190	182	199	193	190	200
Marital status, %							
Married	95	86	88	100	98	91	90
Unmarried	5	9	12	0	2	7	3
Divorced	0	5	0	0	0	2	7
Children, av. no.	2.6	2.0	2.4	2.2	2.6	2.3	2.5
Family history of coronary heart disease, %							
None	67	71	62	82	67	57	67
Mild	0	5	0	0	2	6	0
Moderate	33	14	38	18	26	31	13
Severe	0	10	0	0	5	6	20
Habits of exercise, %							
None	0	5	4	8	0	1	18
Minimal	5	32	15	15	17	31	12
Light	19	32	22	31	38	23	52
Moderate	71	22	55	38	37	39	18
Heavy	9	9	4	8	8	6	0
Use of tobacco, %							
None	14	9	26	8	23	25	18
Unspecified amount	10	18	11	8	6	8	10
Minimal	14	14	0	3	3	3	0
Moderate	48	41	33	46	38	34	28
Heavy	14	18	30	38	29	30	44
Use of alcohol, %							
None	0	18	22	8	14	9	11
Unspecified amount	5	18	7	8	5	7	5
Minimal	29	23	4	8	8	11	21
Moderate	57	41	56	76	67	65	52
Heavy	9	0	11	0	6	8	11
Caloric intake, %							
Moderate	100	86	100	67	90	96	77
Heavy	0	14	0	33	10	4	23
Fat intake, %							
Light	20	14	17	0	24	8	0
Moderate	80	72	83	100	59	84	75
Heavy	0	14	0	0	17	8	25
Cholesterol intake, %							
Light	20	0	17	33	10	4	0
Moderate	80	57	50	67	59	64	83
Heavy	0	43	33	0	31	32	17

study. As a control group, the former football players who are living and have no evidence of coronary heart disease were chosen. The comparison between the coronary group and the control group is made in Table 11-III. It will be noted that the control group is broken down into groups of five graduating classes (1901 to 1905, 1906 to 1910, and so on). This breakdown was made so that it would be possible to note any changing trends during the 30 years covered by this study.

If Table 11-III is examined, it will be seen that the body build in college of the coronary group did not differ significantly from that of the control group. The coronary group did, on the whole, gain more weight than the control group. There was a definite difference here, though not of great magnitude. The family status of the coronary group does not differ markedly from that of the control group except that there were more divorces in the group with coronary heart disease. This may or may not represent a factor of stress. With reference to a family history of coronary heart disease, the exathletes who eventually developed coronary heart disease had a definitely higher occurrence of "unfavourable family health." This meant, in most cases, that both parents had had coronary heart disease.

The most interesting finding of the entire study concerning the amount of exercise. As can be seen from Table 11-IV, the men in the coronary heart disease group engaged in less vigorous exercise than did those without heart disease. The objection might be raised that these figures are from the period after the onset of heart disease and thus represent a curtailing of normal activity. This is not the case, since the lifelong habits of exercise were investigated. This is an important finding.

With reference to the use of tobacco, there were a few more heavy smokers than nonsmokers in the coronary heart disease group. This is not of statistical significance. The use of alcohol was about the same in both groups.

With reference to diet, it is difficult to draw definite conclusions because of the probable inaccuracies of estimation by those filling out the questionnaires. There seems to be little difference with reference to caloric intake. The coronary group

Table 11-IV
COMPARISON OF EXTREMES IN DATA ON WEIGHT GAIN,
EXERCISE, AND USE OF TOBACCO AND ALCOHOL
IN EXFOOTBALL PLAYERS

Current Data	1901-1905	1906-1910	1911-1915	1916-1920	1921-1925	1926-1930	Total
Marked weight gain (40 lb. or more)							
Living and well	0	2	1	2	6	8	19
Coronary heart disease	2	2	2	0	0	1	7
Other significant disease	4	0	3	0	0	5	12
Little or no weight gain (5 lb. or less)							
Living and well	3	1	1	2	5	8	20
Coronary heart disease	1	3	0	0	0	0	4
Other significant disease	6	2	5	1	2	5	21
Heavy exercise							
Living and well	0	0	1	1	3	4	9
Coronary heart disease	0	0	0	0	0	0	0
Other significant disease	1	2	2	0	2	1	8
Little or no exercise							
Living and well	1	5	2	3	10	21	42
Coronary heart disease	2	1	1	0	0	2	6
Other significant disease	1	4	3	0	1	7	16
Heavy smoker							
Living and well	2	4	4	5	15	20	50
Coronary heart disease	0	1	3	0	2	0	6
Other significant disease	1	2	4	2	4	7	20
Nonsmoker							
Living and well	3	3	3	1	10	9	29
Coronary heart disease	0	1	2	0	0	1	4
Other significant disease	2	0	4	0	5	12	23
Heavy drinker							
Living and well	1	0	0	0	2	4	7
Coronary heart	0	1	0	0	1	0	2
Other significant disease	1	0	3	0	2	3	9
Nondrinker							
Living and well	0	3	2	1	5	5	16
Coronary heart disease	1	0	1	0	0	0	2
Other significant disease	0	2	4	0	2	3	11

Classes, No. of Persons

generally ate more fat than did the control group, though, as noted above, all of the figures relating to diet are open to question.

The second method of investigating the effect of the various factors being studied was the comparison of the extremes in each instance. These data are listed in Table 11-IV by number of cases. If the "H" men who gained 40 lb. or more are compared with those who had little or no weight gain, it can be seen that there was an increased risk of developing coronary heart disease in those with the marked weight gain. With reference to exercise, although there were relatively few exathletes who continued a strenuous program of physical activity, it appeared that a heavy exercise program tended to protect against coronary disease. On the other hand there seemed to be little difference between heavy smokers and abstainers and between heavy drinkers and abstainers with reference to the development of coronary heart disease, although there were but limited numbers in both of these groups; the average Harvard graduate used tobacco and alcohol in a moderate degree.

Summary and Conclusions

A questionnaire study has been made of the prevalence of coronary heart disease in mesomorphic exathletes and of the influence of various environmental factors upon its development. An attempt was made to follow up 424 Harvard College students who won their football Hs in the years 1901-1930 inclusive. Of these, in 1955, 126 were known to have died and 292 to be alive; 6 could not be traced. The cause of death was known in 87 of the 126. Among these, coronary heart disease was responsible for 25 deaths, or 29%. Cerebral hemorrhage, generalized arteriosclerosis, and congestive heart failure accounted for 8 more cases, making the total 33 cardiovascular deaths, or 38%. Cancer apparently caused 11 deaths, or 13%; pneumonia and war injuries 9 deaths each, or 10%; accidents 8 deaths, or 9%; suicide 4 deaths, or 5%; typhoid 2 deaths; and the balance miscellaneous.

An attempt was made to compare these figures with those of the white male population of the same age group in Massachusetts in whom cardiovascular deaths amounted to 44%, cancer 13%, accidents 7%; and pneumonia 5%. The cardiovascular deaths included an uncertain number of cases of coronary heart disease labeled as such in 13% and probably included under the designation of chronic myocarditis or degeneration, which was recorded as 16%. The mortality of these football players as compared with healthy males of the same age in the general population could not be determined because of the inadequacy of data.

The following relationships in the group of football players were compared for persons whose history showed the presence of coronary heart disease and for those without coronary heart disease: body build, weight gain, personal family status, family history, habits of exercise, use of alcohol and tobacco, and diet.

Body build did not differ significantly, but there was more weight gain in the coronary group than in the other. The family status was not significantly different except that there were more divorces in the coronary group. There was a higher percentage of family history of coronary heart disease in the coronary group than in the control group. One of the most significant findings in the study was the apparent protection afforded by the continuation of a program of heavy exercise. Those who maintained even moderate habits of exercise were less prone to coronary heart disease, and no individual in this study who maintained a heavy exercise program happened to develop coronary heart disease. There was a higher percentage of heavy smokers in the coronary group, but the difference was not marked. Alcohol appeared to have little influence on the development of coronary heart disease. The lack of detailed and accurate information about the dietary habits prevented any satisfactory conclusions in that area.

The chief defect revealed in a study of this sort lies in the uniformity of the ways of life of most Harvard and other college graduates and, therefore, in the difficulty of comparing extremes because of the inadequate numbers represented therein. A study of racial groups, of which certain members, either in the country of their origin or when transplanted elsewhere, live very differently from others of the same race, should prove more instructive.

Chapter 12

LONGEVITY AND CARDIOVASCULAR MORTALITY AMONG FORMER COLLEGE ATHLETES*

ANTHONY P. POLEDNAK, Ph.D.

Abstract

Among 681 former Harvard College athletes (lettermen), longevity and cardiovascular mortality differed not by type of sport but by extent of participation. Relative to one-letter and two-letter athletes, men with three or more letters died slightly earlier from natural causes, and significantly more often and slightly earlier from cardiovascular diseases and (specifically) coronary heart disease. The three-or-more-letter athletes differed in physique, being significantly more mesomorphic (muscular, bony) than the other two groups. Further analysis suggested that physique did not account for these differences; other possible explanations were discussed.

DO certain kinds of sport in college conduce to shorter lives, while others lengthen the life span? Perhaps the extent of participation — number of years and number of sports — is more crucial? Or is the type of participant, particularly in terms of physique, more important? The data relevant to these questions are limited. Apparently, there is only Rook's[1] study of Cambridge University sportsmen which considered longevity and cardiovascular mortality by type of sport.

In addition to type of sport the present study considers extent of participation, as measured by the number of athletic awards

*From Circulation, XLVI:649-654, 1972, by permission of the American Heart Association, Inc.

Supported in part by predoctoral fellowship 5-F01MH-43-833-02 from the National Institute of Mental Health.

won. Such data may help to explain the slightly reduced longevity of lettermen, relative to their less athletic classmates, reported in several cohort studies.[1-5] More broadly, this study relates to the question of whether extensive physical training (such as athletics) has long-term effects on cardiovascular and general health. As Pyörälä et al.[6] have observed: "It is not known whether the cardiovascular changes caused by endurance athletics are wholly reversible [or] . . . whether taking part in endurance athletics modifies the course of cardiovascular disease in later life."

Methods

The present subjects are part of a larger series of 8753 men, 6601 measured anthropometrically,[5] and 2152 measured and photographed for somatotype rating,[4] while at Harvard College between 1880 and about 1912 by D. A. Sargent and two assistants. Only men born between 1860 and 1889 were included; they were divided into 3 birth decades (1860-69, 1870-79, and 1880-89). All 8753 men had attended Harvard College for at least 2 years. Exclusion of men who were lost (N = 81), or known to be dead but lacking death certificates (N = 269), yielded a study group of 8403 men. Of these 8403 men, 855 were lettermen according to Harvard records[7] which listed the number of years an individual won an award in each sport.

Age at death and cause of death were obtained from death certificates. Only the first-listed cause* was used here, coded according to the 1957 International Classification of Diseases.[8] Height and weight measured in college were available for all athletes, and somatotype was available for 177. Somatotype photographs were rated by F. L. Stagg and the late E. A. Hooton, using a modification of Sheldon's[9] technic. Of the 855 lettermen, 753 or 88.1% had died as of June 30, 1967. Exclusion of deaths from causes other than natural ones yielded a study group of 783 lettermen, of which 681 were dead of natural causes and 102 were still alive. As previously noted[4,5] Harvard athletes and nonathletes did not differ in percentage of deaths from nonnatural causes, i.e. accidents (excluding war) or suicides. We are concerned here only with deaths due to natural

---

*i.e., underlying cause of death. (Ed.)

causes, and particularly with cardiovascular deaths.

Results

Type of Sport

In mean age at death from natural causes, differences among the various sports were inconsistent in direction across the 3 birth decades. Combining all 3 birth decades was justified by the similar percentages of lettermen in each sport in each birth decade. Mean ages at death from natural causes were as follows: 65.2 ± 16.2 years for baseball (N = 107); 66.6 ± 15.7 years for football (N = 135); 66.8 ± 16.3 years for crew (N = 133); 66.9 ± 16.7 years for tràck (N = 186); and 67.2 ± 14.0 years for lettermen in two or more sports (N = 85). Differences among these five groups were small and statistically insignificant. Numbers of lettermen in ice hockey (N = 25), tennis (N = 9), and golf (N = 1) were too small for analysis.

Cardiovascular deaths, as a percentage of total deaths from natural causes, were compared among lettermen in different

Table 12-I

CARDIOVASCULAR MORTALITY
BY TYPE OF SPORT;
ALL BIRTH DECADES COMBINED*

Sport	N†	%‡	Age (yr) Mean	sD
Crew	51	38.3	72.9	11.0
Track	73	39.2	73.7	11.6
Football	57	42.2	69.0	12.5
Baseball	47	43.9	69.1	11.9
Two or more sports	42	49.4	71.7	10.2

*This table is based on 646 of the 681 athletes dead of natural causes. Numbers for other sports − ice hockey (N = 25), tennis (N = 9), and golf (N = 1) − were too small for analysis.

†Number of deaths attributed to cardiovascular diseases; first listed cause of death, code 400-468.[8]

‡Cardiovascular deaths as a percentage of total deaths from natural causes.

Table 12-II

HEIGHT, WEIGHT, AND SOMATOTYPE BY TYPE OF SPORT;
ALL BIRTH DECADES COMBINED

| Sport* | N | Height (in) | | Weight (lb) | | N | Somatotype† | | | | | |
| | | Mean | SD | Mean | SD | | Endomorphy | | Mesomorphy | | Ectomorphy | |
							Mean	SD	Mean	SD	Mean	SD
Crew	133	68.9	2.5	152.7	18.7	30	3.77	0.56	3.83	0.82	4.23	0.72
Track	185	69.6	2.4	143.7	15.0	63	3.33	1.16	3.44	0.77	4.84	0.69
Football	136	69.5	2.6	162.7	23.3	23	4.13	0.80	4.39	0.64	3.57	1.17
Baseball	107	68.4	2.5	144.1	15.1	9	4.00	0.47	3.78	0.46	4.00	0.94
Two or more sports	85	69.6	2.3	158.4	18.0	17	3.88	0.53	4.47	0.78	3.76	0.49

* Numbers of lettermen in ice hockey (N = 25), tennis (N = 9), and golf (N = 1) were too small for analysis

† Somatotype was available for 142 of the 646 lettermen included in this table.

sports (Table 12-I). Crewmen had the lowest percentage, but numbers were small and differences were statistically insignificant. Analysis of physique (Table 12-II) showed that the more endomesomorphic groups (football, two or more sports, and baseball) tended to die more often and earlier from cardiovascular diseases than the mesoectomorphic groups (crew and track). This is not unexpected since physique, specifically high endomorphy (fatness, stockiness) and high mesomorphy (robust muscularity), is a significant risk factor in cardiovascular disease.[10,11]

Extent of Participation

It is difficult to rate specific sports objectively in terms of strenuousness or level of physical training required for successful performance. One objective method of measuring extent of participation, however, utilizes the total number of athletic awards (letters) won. This measures both the number of years of competition and the number of sports participated in; it must also reflect, to some extent, the level of physical training achieved.

Mean ages at death from natural causes, by total number of letters won, appear in Table 12-III. In the first birth decade, for which all men had died, longevity decreased as the number of letters increased; this trend was less evident in the next birth decade (1870-79) and absent in the last (1880-89). Since the percentages of men in the three groups (one, two, and three or more letters) were nearly identical in each of the 3 birth decades (Table 12-III), the 3 birth-decade samples were combined. Differences were statistically insignificant. Although percentages still alive (not shown) were nearly identical for the three groups of lettermen, the significance of the general trend, i.e. longevity decreasing as the number of letters increases, may be assessed better when all men have died.

Differences in longevity by number of letters held within each sport. Because of small numbers, one-letter athletes were compared with two-or-more-letter athletes; in the case of lettermen in two or more sports, two-letter athletes were compared

Table 12-III

MEAN AGE AT DEATH (NATURAL CAUSES) BY NUMBER OF LETTERS*

Letters (no.)	Birth decade									Total			
	1860–69			1870–79			1880–89						
	N	%	Mean (yr)	N	%	Mean (yr)	N	%	Mean (yr)	N	%	Mean (yr)	SD (yr)
1	92	47.7	68.3	125	48.3	69.6	109	47.6	63.3	327	47.9	67.1	15.8
2	44	22.8	68.0	66	25.5	65.4	50	21.8	66.3	160	23.5	66.4	16.5
3 or more	57	29.5	62.1	68	26.3	69.2	70	30.6	64.6	195	28.6	65.5	15.8
Total	193	100.0	66.4	259	100.0	68.4	229	100.0	64.3	681	100.0	66.5	16.0

*Percentages still alive, as of June 30, 1967, were: 0.0% for 1860–69; 12 of 271 or 4.4% for 1870–79; and 90 of 319 or 28.2% for 1880–89. This table includes lettermen in ice hockey, tennis, and golf (total N = 35); these men were excluded from the previous tables.

with three-or-more-letter athletes. The roughly similar frequency of each of these two groups in each of the 3 birth decades justified combining the 3 birth-decade samples. Although differences, i.e., 3.2 years (crew), 2.2 years (baseball), 0.2 years (football), 2.5 years (track), and 1.4 years (two or more sports), were statistically insignificant, the consistency in trend was impressive.

As the number of letters increased, mean height and weight also increased (Table 12-IV). Two differences were significant; athletes with three or more letters were heavier ($P < 0.01$) and taller ($P < 0.05$) than those with one letter. The weight difference was due largely to muscle or bone rather than fat (Table 12-IV). This is, three-or-more-letter athletes were significantly more mesomorphic ($P < 0.05$) than either of the other two groups, but did not differ in endomorphy or ectomorphy (linearity, here based on height divided by cube root of weight). One-letter and two-letter athletes did not differ in somatotype.

Could physique (mesomorphy) account for the differences in longevity among the three groups of lettermen (Table 12-III)? Among 2450 Harvard men from the same era as the present subjects,[12] longevity was only slightly, but negatively, associated with mesomorphy. In the present study numbers are too small for the proper analysis, i.e. longevity within each athletic group by specific somatotype categories. A cruder approach limits the analysis to lettermen with a low or moderate mesomorphy rating of 4 or lower on the 7-point scale. A total of 118 of 145 athletes dead of natural causes (for whom somatotype ratings were available) had a mesomorphy rating of 4 or less. Combining all 3 birth decades the difference in mean age at death from natural causes, between 68 men with one letter and 50 men with two or more letters (70.1±15.4 years vs. 67.2±17.5 years), was statistically insignificant, but the same trend was evident as in Table 12-III. Mean somatotype ratings were nearly identical for the one-letter and two-or-more-letter athletes: 3.60 endomorphy), 3.49 (mesomorphy), 4.51 (ectomorphy) for the former (N = 68), and 3.58, 3.56, and 4.46, respectively, for the latter (N = 50).

In all but 1 birth decade (1860-69) athletes with three or more

The Longevity of Athletes

Table 12-IV

HEIGHT, WEIGHT, AND SOMATOTYPE BY NUMBER OF LETTERS;
ALL BIRTH DECADES COMBINED*

Letters (no.)	Height (in)		Weight (lbs)			Somatotype†						
							Endomorphy		Mesomorphy		Ectomorphy	
	N	Mean	SD	Mean	SD	N	Mean	SD	Mean	SD	Mean	SD
1	326	69.2	2.5	149.5	19.1	79	3.64	0.64	3.71	0.80	4.39	1.54
2	160	69.7	2.6	150.8	20.4	31	3.61	0.83	3.65	0.90	4.16	1.06
3 or more	195	69.8	2.4	154.6	19.1	35	3.71	0.66	4.20	0.82	4.20	0.92

*For significance of differences, see text.
†Somatotype ratings were available for 145 (21.3%) of the 681 lettermen dead of natural causes.

Table 12-V

CARDIOVASCULAR DEATHS BY NUMBERS OF LETTERS*

Letters (no.)	1860-69			1870-79			1880-89			Total			
	N†	%‡	Mean (yr)	N	%	Mean (yr)	N	%	Mean (yr)	N	%	Mean (yr)	SD (yr)
1	40	43.5	74.6	47	37.6	73.6	44	40.0	66.1	131	40.2	71.4	12.1
2	14	31.8	75.6	24	36.4	73.2	23	46.0	68.3	61	38.1	71.9	11.7
3 or more	18	31.6	70.7	42	61.8	71.1	37	52.9	68.0	97	49.7	69.9	11.8
Total	72	37.5	73.8	113	43.6	72.6	104	45.2	67.3	289	42.4	71.0	12.0

* For significance of differences, see text.

† Number of deaths attributed to cardiovascular diseases; first listed cause of death code 400-468.[b]

‡ Cardiovascular deaths as a percentage of total deaths from natural causes.

letters had the highest percentage of cardiovascular deaths
(Table 12-V). Combining all 3 birth decades (Table 12-V), this
percentage was significantly higher ($P < 0.05$) for athletes with
three or more letters than for either of the other two groups. In
mean age at death from cardiovascular diseases (Table 12-V),
the three-or-more-letter athletes died earliest in all but the last
birth decade (1880-89). Although differences were statistically
insignificant, 102 lettermen are still alive; conceivably, differences may become greater when all men have died.

Mortality from coronary heart disease (CHD) was analyzed
separately (Table 12-VI). Again, the three-or-more-letter athletes died most often and earliest. In percentage of deaths attributed to CHD, one difference was statistically significant (two
letters vs. three or more; $P < 0.05$) and another approached
significance (one letter vs. three or more; $0.10 > P > 0.05$).
Differences in mean age at death from CHD were statistically
insignificant for these small samples.

Table 12-VI

CORONARY HEART DISEASE (CHD)
BY NUMBER OF LETTERS;
ALL BIRTH DECADES COMBINED*

Letters (no.)	N†	%‡	Mean (yr)	SD (yr)
1	72	22.0	72.6	10.2
2	32	20.0	70.4	13.1
3 or more	57	29.2	70.1	10.1
Total	161	23.6	71.3	11.4

*For significance of differences, see text.
†Number of deaths attributed to CHD; first listed
cause of death, code 420.1.[8]
‡Percentage of total deaths (natural causes) attributed to CHD.

Since mesomorphy is the predominant somatotype component among young men with myocardial infarction,[11] physique
might account for the relatively greater cardiovascular mortality among athletes with three or more letters. Again, we limit

our analysis to the 118 men with a low or moderate meso-morphy rating. For cardiovascular mortality the figures were: 36 of 94 or 38.3% for men with one or two letters (mean age at death, 76.1 years); and 13 of 24 or 54.2% for men with three or more letters (mean age at death, 71.5 years). Differences were statistically insignificant, but the same trend is evident.

Discussion

Although numbers are small there are no significant differences in longevity among prominent college athletes subdivided by type of sport. This finding agrees with Rook's[1] on Cambridge University sportsmen from roughly the same era as the present subjects. Rook's oarsmen had significantly fewer cardiovascular deaths relative to several other groups, while in the present series crewmen also had the lowest percentage of such deaths but differences were not statistically significant. Our somatotype data suggest that this finding may be explained by physique.

The present data show differences in longevity and cardiovascular mortality by extent of participation in college athletics, a novel finding. Relative to one- or two-letter athletes, men with three or more letters died slightly earlier from natural causes, and significantly more often and slightly earlier from cardiovascular diseases (and coronary heart disease). We should note, however, that death-certificate data are reportedly inaccurate in measuring mortality from specific conditions, such as myocardial infarction.[13] In addition, Table 12-V shows that percentages of deaths attributed to cardiovascular diseases in this cohort increased from 37.5 to 43.6 to 45.2 across the 3 birth decades. This secular trend must be due, at least in part, to changes in diagnostic practices and in preparation of death certificates. Since the diagnostic criteria for cardiovascular disease have changed markedly over time — especially since the delineation of coronary heart disease in 1912 — dates of birth, diagnosis, and death should be taken into account. Although it is doubtful that these changes in diagnosis affected one athletic group more than another, this problem has been only partly overcome by analyzing cardiovascular deaths by number of awards within each birth decade. This procedure presumably minimized time trends in diagnosis, as well as in longevity. The number of subjects was too small for a similar analysis of CHD mortality among the three groups of lettermen.

Our data also suggested that physique did not account for the differences in longevity and cardiovascular mortality by extent of participation. Without comparable data from other studies we can only speculate. Other explanations might involve: (1) long-term effects of college athletics, related either to extensive physical training itself, or to the stress of athletic competition; and (2) factors of selection other than physique. We have no data on the life style of athletes after college, for example, exercise habits, relative weight gain, personality, or smoking habits. Speculating further, athletes with three or more letters might be more likely to continue exercise in later life relative to athletes with only one or two letters. If this were true, the effects would most likely oppose the trends observed in this study; two small studies found that former prominent athletes who continued exercise in later life had fewer myocardial infarcts[14] and less symptomatic CHD[6] than less active former athletes.

Another possible explanation involves personality factors. Such attributes as aggressiveness, competitiveness, hard-driving effort, striving for achievement, and commitment to one's occupation, are part of the behavior pattern (type A) significantly associated with smoking[15] and increased risk of CHD.[16] Not unexpectedly, high school[17] and college[18,19] athletes score higher than their less athletic classmates on scales of dominance, aggressiveness, competitiveness, and leadership. The most successful college athletes, such as those with three or more athletic awards, may be more highly selected for such personality traits. Is the kind of participant or the participation itself more important in determining these personality differences? The former seems more likely[20] but there are few longitudinal data on the psychological effects of athletic competition.

REFERENCES

1. ROOK A: An investigation into the longevity of Cambridge sportsmen. Brit Med J 1: 773, 1954
2. DUBLIN LI: College honor men longer lived. Statist Bull Metróp Life Insur Co 13: 5, 1932
3. Montoye HJ, Van Huss WD, Neval JW: Longevity and morbidity of college athletes: A seven-year follow-up study. J Sports Med 2: 133, 1962
4. POLEDNAK AP, DAMON A: College athletics, longevity, and cause of death. Hum Biol 42: 28, 1970
5. POLEDNAK AP: Longevity and cause of death among Harvard College athletes and their classmates. Geriatrics. In Press
6. PYÖRÄLÄ K, KARVONEN MJ, TASKINEN P, TAKKUNEN J, KYRÖN-SEPPÄ H: Cardiovascular studies on former endurance runners. Helsinki, Finland, Reports from the Institute of Occupational Health, No. 19, 1965
7. BLANCHARD JA: The H Book of Harvard Athletics. Cambridge, Harvard University Press, 1923
8. WORLD HEALTH ORGANIZATION: International Classification of Diseases. Geneva, World Health Organization, 1957
9. SHELDON WH, STEVENS SS, TUCKER WB: The Varieties of Human Physique. New York, Harper and Row, 1940
10. DAMON A: Delineation of the body build variables associated with cardiovascular diseases. Ann N Y Acad Sci 126: 711, 1965
11. DAMON A, DAMON ST, HARPENDING H, KANNEL WB: Predicting coronary heart disease from body measurements of Framingham males. J Chronic Dis 21: 781, 1969
12. DAMON A: Physique, longevity, and number of offspring: Possible stabilizing selection in man. (Abstr) Amer J Phys Anthrop 35: 276, 1971
13. ABRAMSON JH, SACKS MI, CAHANA E: Death certificate data as an indication of the presence of certain common diseases at death. J Chronic Dis 24: 417, 1971
14. POMEROY W, WHITE PD: Coronary heart disease in former football players. JAMA 167: 711, 1958
15. JENKINS CD, ROSENMAN RH, ZYZANSKI SJ: Cigarette smoking: Its relationship to coronary heart disease and related risk factors in the Western Collaborative Group Study. Circulation 38: 1140, 1968
16. JENKINS CD, ZYZANSKI SJ, ROSENMAN RH: Progress toward validation of a computer-scored test for type A coronary-prone behavior pattern.

Psychosom Med 33: 193, 1971

17. FLETCHER R, DOWELL L: Selected personality characteristics of high school athletes and nonathletes. J Psychol 77: 39, 1971

18. COOPER L: Athletics, activity, and personality: A review of the literature. Res Quart 40: 17, 1969

19. HUNT D: A cross racial comparison of personality traits between athletes and nonathletes. Res Quart 40: 704, 1969

20. WERNER AC, GOTTHEIL E: Personality development and participation in college athletics. Res Quart 37: 126, 1966

Chapter 13

COLLEGE ATHLETICS, BODY SIZE, AND CANCER MORTALITY*

ANTHONY P. POLEDNAK, Ph.D.

Abstract

Data are presented on mortality from neoplasms as determined from death certificates in a cohort of 8393 college men, according to athletic status in college. Major athletes (lettermen) died significantly more often from neoplasms than nonathletes. Mean age at death from neoplasms (underlying cause) was significantly lower in major athletes than in both minor athletes and nonathletes. After matching major athletes with nonathletes of comparable body size (height and weight), differences in proportional mortality and mean age at death from neoplasms persisted, although not statistically significant for the smaller samples. Correlation coefficients (Pearson r) and partial rs between weight in college and age at death from neoplasms were negative but of low magnitude. Some possible explanations for the differences between major athletes and nonathletes are discussed.

EVIDENCE from animal experiments, reviewed by La Barba,[14] suggests that exercise may alter the response to cancer, but further work is necessary. In humans, the possible effect of exercise on susceptibility to (or mortality from) malignant tumors is largely unexplored. One approach to this question would utilize data on athletes. A few cohort studies of athletes have included analysis of death from neoplasms. No significant differences were reported between athletes and nonathletes, but sample sizes were small and analyses limited.[19] The present cohort study compares the cancer mor-

---

*From *Cancer, 38(7)*:382-387, 1976. Copyright 1976 by the American Cancer Society, Inc.

169

tality experience of men exposed and not exposed to physical exercise and training as young adults. A host factor, body size, is taken into account in this comparison.

Materials and Methods

The subjects have been described in detail elsewhere.[17–19] Between 1880 and about 1920, some 17,000 men were measured anthropometrically by D. A. Sargent and two assistants. About 85% were "Old American" (all four grandparents born in the United States), largely of British ancestry, and another 10% were of immediate British or other Northern European ancestry. To insure greater homogeneity and a chance for all subjects to have participated in college athletics, only those men were included who had spent two or more years at Harvard College. Exclusion of dropouts, graduate students, instructors, and men born after 1889 (many of whom were still alive at the time of last search), reduced the number of subjects to 8743. Further exclusion of men who were lost ($N = 81$), or who were known dead but for whom there were no death certificates ($N = 289$), yielded a study group of 8393 men.

The subjects were divided into three birth-decade cohorts (1860-69, 1870-79, and 1880-89). They were classified into three groups, according to athletic participation (Table 13-I). "Major athletes" were men who received one or more awards ("letters") in varsity sports (baseball, football, track, crew, ice hockey, and tennis). "Minor athletes" were men who participated in varsity sports without winning a letter or in sports for which letters were not awarded (for example, interclass sports). "Nonathletes" were men with no record of participation in formal college sports or men who participated only as freshmen. All subjects were interested in exercise to some extent, since all had applied for gymnasium locker rental. Data were not available on exercise habits after college.

As of June 30, 1967, 1831 of the 1834 men (99.8%) born in 1860-69 had died, as had 2812 of the 2977 (94.5%) born in 1870-79, and 2581 of the 3582 (72.1%) born in 1880-89. Thus, a total of 7224 out of 8393 men, or 86.1% had died.

Table 13-I

SUBJECTS BY ATHLETIC STATUS
AND BIRTH DECADE*

| | Birth Decade | | | |
	1860-69 No.	1870-79 No.	1880-89 No.	Total No.
Major athletes	204	302	339	845
Minor athletes	294	475	1,005	1,776
Nonathletes	1,336	2,200	2,238	5,772
TOTAL	1,834	2,977	3,582	8,393

* Only men dead of known cause or still alive (as of 30 June 1967)
are included.

Causes of death were obtained from death certificates and coded according to the Seventh Revision of the International Statistical Classification of Diseases (ICD).[25] "Malignant neoplasms" (ICD 140-205), "benign neoplasms" (ICD 210-229), and "neoplasms of unspecified nature" (ICD 230-239) were included. Comparisons were made separately for "underlying" cause of death, and for "underlying" and "contributory" causes combined; no major differences were apparent, so that only the latter comparisons are reported. For comparisons of mean age at death from neoplasms, however, only the "underlying" cause was considered, since incidental (clinically silent) neoplasms are frequently found in elderly decedents, especially at autopsy.[22]

The statistical significance of differences in rates of death and in age at death from neoplasms was evaluated by means of a t-test.

Results

Table 13-II shows mortality rates from neoplasms by athletic status in college and decade of birth. In each birth decade, rates are lowest for nonathletes. In general, rates are highest for major athletes and intermediate for minor athletes. For all birth decades combined, mortality rates for neoplasms are significantly higher in major athletes than in nonathletes ($p < 0.05$).

The Longevity of Athletes

Table 13-II
MORTALITY RATES FOR NEOPLASMS,*
BY ATHLETIC CATEGORY AND BIRTH DECADE

			Birth decade				Total	
	1860-69		1870-79		1880-89			
		Rate		Rate		Rate		Rate
	No.	(per 100)	No.	(per 100)	No.	(per 100)	No.	(per 100)
Major athletes	28	13.7	51	16.9	49	14.5	128	15.2
Minor athletes	30	10.1	81	17.1	128	12.7	239	13.3
Nonathletes	131	9.8	301	13.7	277	12.4	709	12.3
TOTAL	189	10.2	433	14.5	454	12.7	1,076	12.9

Note: For significance of differences, see text.
*ICD code 140-239.[25]

Death rates for neoplasms at specific sites are compared by athletic status in Table 13-III. Rates are consistently higher for major athletes than for nonathletes, with the exception of "benign neoplasms" (ICD 210-229) and "neoplasms of unspecified nature" (ICD 230-239). Rates for minor athletes are intermediate for some sites, and lowest for others (Table 13-III). Only one difference is statistically significant ($p < 0.05$), that between major athletes and nonathletes for prostate cancer.

Mean age at death from neoplasms (underlying cause of death) is compared by athletic status and birth decade in Table 13-IV. Mean age at death is consistently lowest for major athletes in all three birth decades. Minor athletes are intermediate, except for the last birth decade (1880-89), in which mean age at death is highest. Combining all birth decade samples, mean age at death was significantly lower in major athletes than in minor athletes ($p < 0.02$) or nonathletes ($p < 0.02$).

Mean age at death is compared by athletic status for neoplasms at specific sites (underlying cause) in Table 13-V. Mean age at death is lowest for major athletes for all categories except "maligant neoplasms of other and unspecified sites" (ICD code 190-199). One difference is statistically significant, i.e., mean age at death from malignant neoplasms of "breast and genitourinary organs" (ICD 170-181), major athletes vs. nonathletes ($p < 0.05$). No cases of breast cancer were reported in this population.

Table 13-III

MORTALITY FROM NEOPLASMS
AT SPECIFIC SITES,
BY ATHLETIC CATEGORY

Site (ICD Code)	Major athlete (845)	Minor athlete (1,776)	Non-athlete (5,772)
		Rates (per 100)	
I. Malignant neoplasm			
140–149 Buccal cavity, pharynx	0.7	0.5	0.5
150–159 Digestive	5.4	4.7	4.9
(153 Colon)	(1.7)	(1.4)	(1.6)
(150–152, 154–159 Other)	(3.8)	(3.3)	(3.3)
160–165 Respiratory	1.5	1.8	1.4
170–181 Breast and genitourinary	4.4	3.3	3.1
(177 Prostate)	(3.6)	(2.3)	(2.2)
190–199 Other and unspecified	1.5	1.5	0.9
200–205 Lymphatic and hematopoietic	1.1	1.3	1.1
II. Benign neoplasm (210–229)	0.2	0.3	0.3
III. Neoplasm of unspecified nature (230–239)	0.2	0.1	0.2
TOTAL	15.2	13.3	12.3

Note: For significance of differences, see text.

From these data it would appear that major athletes are at higher risk for death from neoplasms than minor or nonathletes. Previous studies[18,19] have shown that Harvard major athletes of this era were significantly taller and heavier than minor or nonathletes, while minor athletes were intermediate. If body size were related to cancer risk, the highest neoplastic death rates in major athletes could be explained by their larger body size.

An attempt was made to match each major athlete with the next nonathlete measured who was in the same birth-decade cohort and of similar body size, i.e., within 3 cm in height and 3 kg in weight. Only men dead of natural causes were used in the matching; 650 major athletes were matched with 650 non-

Table 13-IV

MEAN AGE AT DEATH FROM NEOPLASMS

(UNDERLYING CAUSE OF DEATH), BY ATHLETIC CATEGORY

	Birth decade														
	1860–69			1870–79			1880–89			Total		
	No.	Mean (yr)	S.D. (yr)	No.	Mean (yr)	S.D. (yr)	No.	Mean (yr)	S.D. (yr)	No.	Mean (yr)	S.D. (yr)
Major athletes	25	66.4	14.1	38	67.7	13.2	40	65.6	10.5	103	66.5	12.4
Minor athletes	25	69.8	12.3	58	70.9	12.9	103	68.5	12.6	186	69.4	12.6
Nonathletes	106	70.9	13.1	232	71.2	11.9	222	67.6	11.8	560	69.8	12.2

Note: For significance of differences, see text.

Table 13-V

MEAN AGE AT DEATH FROM MALIGNANT NEOPLASMS AT SPECIFIC SITES (UNDERLYING CAUSE OF DEATH), BY ATHLETIC CATEGORY

ICD Code	Major athletes			Minor athletes			Nonathletes		
	No.	Mean (yr)	S.D. (yr)	No.	Mean (yr)	S.D. (yr)	No.	Mean (yr)	S.D. (yr)
140-148	6	66.1	12.0	6	66.2	10.9	23	66.6	11.3
150-159	41	67.2	11.3	71	68.9	11.8	240	70.1	12.0
(153)	(12)	(68.2)	(16.2)	(21)	(74.0)	(9.3)	(74)	(73.0)	(11.4)
(150-152, 154-159)	(29)	(66.8)	(8.9)	(50)	(66.5)	(12.1)	(166)	(68.7)	(12.0)
160-165	12	67.0	10.6	23	70.0	12.9	63	71.2	10.6
170-181	21	68.5	11.4	35	70.7	14.8	123	74.4	8.3
(177)	(15)	(70.9)	(10.3)	(22)	(74.2)	(10.0)	(87)	(74.8)	(8.6)
190-199	11	72.5	14.9	21	70.4	12.2	44	68.1	10.3
200-207	8	56.7	13.6	23	68.6	14.1	44	68.8	13.1

Note: For significance of differences, see text.

Table 13-VI

MORTALITY FROM NEOPLASMS IN MAJOR ATHLETES
AND NONATHLETES MATCHED FOR BODY SIZE*

| Birth decade | Major Athletes | | | | | | Nonathletes | | | | | |
| | Total No. | Neoplasms (all causes) | | Age at death (underlying cause) | | | Total No. | Neoplasms (all causes) | | Age at death (underlying cause) | | |
		No.	%	No.	Mean (yr)	S.D. (yr)		No.	%	No.	Mean (yr)	S.D. (yr)
1860-69	178	27	15.2	25	66.4	14.1	178	19	10.7	15	75.9	11.9
1870-79	251	49	19.5	37	68.6	11.9	251	40	15.9	34	71.9	13.6
1880-89	221	48	21.7	39	65.5	10.6	221	49	22.2	37	64.9	12.2
TOTAL	650	125	19.2	101	66.9	12.0	650	108	16.6	86	69.6	13.3

* Includes men dead of natural causes, matched within 3 kg in weight and 3 cm in height as measured while in college.

athletes, while another 31 major athletes were too large in body size and could not be matched. Proportional mortality rates for neoplasms were obtained (Table 13-VI). The results indicate that the proportion of deaths from (or with) neoplasms was greater among the major athletes, although the overall difference in proportional mortality was not statistically significant (19.2% vs. 16.6%) for these smaller samples. Mean age at death from neoplasms (underlying cause) was also compared in the matched athlete-nonathlete groups, and the overall difference (66.9 vs. 69.6 years, Table 13-VI) was similar to that found in the original comparison (66.5 vs. 69.8 years, Table 13-IV). For the smaller samples in Table 13-VI, however, differences were not statistically significant.

The relationship between body size and age at death from neoplasms (underlying cause) was explored further. Table 13-VII shows correlation coefficients (Pearson r) between age at death from neoplasms and height and weight, including partial correlation coefficients. Weight has the strongest linear relationship with age at death from neoplasms, but correlations are low in magnitude. The negative partial r between weight and age at death, holding height constant, is the consistent finding; this correlation is significant for major athletes ($r = -0.24$, p < 0.01), but not for minor athletes ($r = -0.02$) or nonathletes ($r = -0.08$, p = 0.06).

Table 13-VII

CORRELATION (PEARSON r)
OF HEIGHT AND WEIGHT
WITH AGE AT DEATH FROM NEOPLASMS
(UNDERLYING CAUSE)

	Major athletes ($N = 103$)	Minor athletes ($N = 186$)	Non- athletes ($N = 560$)
Height	−0.15	+0.05	−0.09*
Weight	−0.28*	+0.02	−0.12*
Height (partial)	+0.03	+0.06	−0.02
Weight (partial)	−0.24†	−0.02	−0.08‡

* p < 0.01.
† p < 0.05.
‡ p = 0.06.

Discussion

In view of the inherent inaccuracies of death certificate diagnoses, the results of this study allow only some cautious conclusions about the possible effects of exercise or athletic competition on neoplastic death rates. Death certificates give a fairly accurate indication of the presence of malignant neoplasms as judged by comparison with autopsy data,[1,4] but not of neoplasms at specific sites.[1] When all certificate entries (including contributory causes) are taken into account as in the present study, the sensitivity is increased.[1]

Abramson, Sacks, and Cahana[1] have observed that: "For epidemiological purposes, the fact that the certificate data are not a very valid indicator of the prevalence of diseases at death need not in itself be a major handicap, provided that the discrepancies are due to chance alone." In the present study, death certificate errors in diagnosis may have been randomly distributed among the three categories (major, minor, and nonathletes). In addition, the three athletic categories were often compared by birth decade, a procedure that presumably minimized time trends in cause of death and diagnosis.

The present study indicates an increased death rate from neoplasms in major athletes relative to minor athletes and nonathletes. This difference held for malignant neoplasms at all sites, but not for benign neoplasms. Mean age at death from neoplasms were earliest in major athletes in each birth decade. When analyzed by specific site, numbers were small, but the same pattern held for all sites except "other and unspecified." Conceivably, differences in these various comparisons may become even greater when the entire cohort has died. The consistency in pattern for cancer death rates and age at death suggests a common underlying factor or factors.

It is difficult to separate factors related to selection of persons for athletics from the effects of exercise or athletic competition in attempting to explain the relatively greater mortality from neoplasms in major athletes. Body size, as reflected in height and weight measured in the college years, did not appear to explain the differences found. Information on weight gain in later life was not available. Although it often stated that athletes tend to gain more weight after college than their classmates, the single study[14] of weight gain after college showed no difference between varsity athletes and nonathletes.

The relationship between body size and cancer risk is not well understood. Studies in mice[11] suggest a relationship between obesity due to major genes and certain neoplasms, but other work with animals[5] indicates that the causes of body size differences may be important in influencing findings of studies of tumor susceptibility. In humans, life insurance data[23] suggest a relationship between "overweight" and mortality from some types of tumors. In an occupational cohort, limited data reported suggested a curvilinear or U-shaped relationship between cancer death and "relative weight," defined by life insurance "ideal" weights,[8] but the usefulness of such weights is questionable. Body size or weight has been positively associated with risk of endometrial cancer[7] and breast cancer[24] in females, but not with prostatic cancer.[10] Further studies are needed of specific sites of cancer, with more detailed anthropometric data.

In the present study, body weight was negatively correlated with age at death from neoplasms, but the magnitude of the correlations was low (Table 13-VII). In comparing major athletes with nonathletes, controlling for weight (Table 13-VI) failed to remove the differences in mean age at death from neoplasms. Thus, a linear relationship between weight (in early adult life) and age at death from neoplasms may exist, but it is not very strong.

Other possible explanations for the differences between major athletes and nonathletes may be suggested by the data presented here. Analysis of mortality from neoplasms at specific sites (Table 13-III) suggests that the excess risk among major athletes is greatest in cancer of the prostate and of the digestive tract excluding the colon. Interestingly, the colon is the only digestive tract site not showing an excess male risk in whites; that is, the sexes are about equally affected.[2] A causal role of androgens in prostatic carcinoma has been suggested by the results of orchiectomy and hormone therapy. These considerations could lead to speculation, and hormonal factors may be involved in the athlete-nonathlete differences in cancer mortality. Again, this factor could be related to selection for athletics (e.g., greater masculinity due to androgens), or effects of chronic exercise (e.g., adrenocortical secretion of androgenic hormones). The growth-promotion effects of androgens are well-known,[13] but the role of these hormones in cancer initiation or promotion requires further study. Greenwald et al.[10] found no relationship between morphologic masculinity, which is conditioned by androgens, and prostatic cancer, but this does not preclude a role for androgens in these tumors.

It is likely that mechanical injury from trauma in athletics was not a factor here, since animal evidence for such tumor induction is apparently lacking.[20] Animal experiments provide some evidence for a protective effect of exercise on tumor production or promotion,[12,16,21] and have led to the hypothesis of a "tumoristatic" factor produced by contracting muscle.[12] Experiments on rats suggest that physical exercise early in life may increase survival rates, independently of body weight; specific causes of death, however, have apparently not been studied.[9] On the other hand, chronic exercise may be viewed as a type of "stress;" its profound effects on adrenocortical function[6] are of particular interest in view of the effects of adrenocortical steroids on antibody levels.[3]

Athletes and nonathletes could differ in life-style, occupation, personality, and personal habits that are relevant to cancer risk. Data on smoking habits and alcohol consumption were not available, but major athletes had no appreciably increased risk from respiratory cancer relative to nonathletes; risk of cancer of the buccal cavity and pharynx may have been increased in major athletes, but the numbers of these tumors are small. Thus, these analyses provide no definitive explanations for the apparent differences observed, but do suggest some hypotheses for further testing. The role of male hormones in human tumor production and promotion requires further study. The relationship between physique and specific types of cancer also needs more detailed analysis; such analyses are planned for the present subjects.

REFERENCES

1. Abramson, J. H., Sacks, M. I., Cahana, E.: Death certificate data as an indication of certain common diseases at death. *J. Chron. Dis.* 24:417-431, 1971.
2. Ashley, D. J. B.: Sex differences in the incidence of tumors at various sites. *Br. J. Cancer* 23:26-30, 1969.
3. Batchelor, J. R.: Hormonal control of antibody formation. *In* Regulation of Antibody Response, B. Cinader, Ed. Springfield, Thomas, 1971; pp. 276-293.
4. Beadenkopf, W. G., et al.: An assessment of certain aspects of death certificate data for epidemiologic study of arteriosclerotic heart disease. *J. Chron. Dis.* 16:249-262, 1963.
5. Bloom, J. L.: Body size and lung-tumor susceptibility in outbred mice. *J. Natl. Cancer Inst.* 33:599-606, 1964.
6. Buuck, R. J., and Tharp, G. D.: Effect of chronic exercise on adrenocortical function and structure in the rat. *J. Appl. Physiol.* 31:880-883, 1971.
7. Damon, A.: Host factors in cancer of the breast and uterine cervix and corpus. *J. Natl. Cancer Inst.* 24:483-516, 1960.
8. Dyer, A. R., et al.: High blood pressure — A risk factor for cancer mortality? *Lancet* 1:1051-1056, 1975.
9. Edington, D. W., Cosmas, A. C., and McCafferty, W. B.: Exercise and longevity — Evidence for a threshold age. *J. Gerontol.* 27:341-343, 1972.
10. Greenwald, P., et al.: Physical and demographic features of men before developing cancer of the prostate. *J. Natl. Cancer Inst.* 53:341-346, 1974.
11. Heston, W. E., and Vlahakis, G.: Genetic obesity and neoplasia. *J. Natl. Cancer Inst.* 29:197-209, 1962.
12. Hoffman, S. A., et al.: The influence of exercise on the growth of transplanted rat tumors. *Cancer Res.* 2:597-599, 1962.
13. Kaplan, J. G., et al.: Constitutional delay of growth and development — Effects of treatment with androgens. *J. Pediatr.* 82:38-44, 1973.
14. La Barba, R. C.: Experimental and environmental factors in cancer. A review of research with animals. *Psychosom. Med.* 32:259-276, 1970.
15. Montoye, H. J., et al.: Study of the longevity and morbidity of college athletes. *J. Am. Med. Assoc.* 162:1132-1134, 1956.
16. Newton, G.: Tumor susceptibility in rats — Role of infantile manipulation and later exercise. *Psychol. Rep.* 16:127-132, 1965.
17. Polednak, A. P.: Longevity and cardiovascular mortality among former college athletes. *Circulation* 46:649-654, 1972.
18. Polednak, A. P.: Longevity and cause of death among Harvard college

athletes and their classmates. *Geriatrics* 27:53-64, 1972.

19. Polednak, A. P., and Damon, A.: College athletics, longevity and cause of death. *Hum. Biol.* 42:28-46, 1970.
20. Robbins, S. L., and Angell, M.: Basic Pathology. Philadelphia, Saunders, 1971; p. 87.
21. Rusch, H. P., and Kline, B. E.: The effect of exercise on the growth of a mouse tumor. *Cancer Res.* 4:116-118, 1944.
22. Suen, K. C., Lau, L. L., and Yermakov, V.: Cancer and old age, an autopsy study of 3,535 patients over 65 years old. *Cancer* 33:1164-1168, 1974.
23. Tannenbaum, A.: Relationship of body weight to cancer incidence. *Arch. Pathol.* 30:509-517, 1940.
24. Valaoras, V., et al.: Lactation and reproductive histories of breast cancer patients in greater Athens, 1965-67. *Int. J. Cancer* 4:350-363, 1969.
25. World Health Organization: International Classification of Diseases. Seventh Revision. Geneva, WHO, 1957.

DISCUSSION

Kidney Diseases

IN view of the short-term effects of strenuous physical exercise on urinary abnormalities, the question of the long-term effects of exercise on the kidney was raised by Gardner (1971). Urinary abnormalities among athletes appear to be transient in most cases, as shown in a study of ice-hockey players (Fletcher, 1977). In agreement with Fletcher's findings, Castenfors' (1977) data on participants in an 85-km ski race, and on heavily exercised persons in the laboratory, suggest that changes in renal parameters are transient; there is no indication of renal parenchymal damage during prolonged heavy exercise.

The question of possible long-term effects of athletic competition on the kidney was examined among Harvard men (Polednak, 1972, see Chp. 10). No evidence for adverse effects was found in this study, which involved proportional mortality analysis (i.e., deaths from renal diseases as a proportion of the total number of deaths from known cause). Proportional mortality rates must be interpreted with caution, since a deficiency of deaths from certain causes will increase the proportion of deaths from other causes. Such proportional "rates" do not indicate the actual risk of members of the population dying from the disease in question; differences may exist in the denominations of the compared ratios (i.e., the total number of deaths) and hence in the total death rate, between the population subgroups compared. In the studies of Harvard men, however, previous reports had analyzed overall mortality (by life-table methods) and proportional mortality ratios for many causes of death (see Section III). Nevertheless, a cohort study

183

design using the person-years method* of follow-up would have been useful; the problem in using such a design concerns the difficulty in obtaining stable mortality rates on a large group of controls (e.g., all U.S. males) which would be comparable with the study group (in this case, Harvard men) in terms of characteristics relevant to longevity (e.g., socioeconomic class, education, medical care).

As noted in Chapter 10 (Polednak, 1972a), the sports involved may not have been strenuous enough to produce long-term renal damage, even though short-term urinary abnormalities may have occurred. Gardner (1971) has observed that urinary abnormalities in athletes (and others) seem to depend on the severity and duration of physical stress, as well as on the prior conditioning of the athlete. Further long-term studies on marathon runners, in terms of morbidity and mortality from renal diseases, may be in order.

Cardiovascular Diseases

More work has been done on cardiovascular disease mortality among former college athletes than on any other group of diseases. Adverse effects of athletic competition on the heart have been suspected for many years, as noted by Rook (1954, see Chp. 4). Among Harvard men followed for many years after college (Polednak, 1972b), major athletes died slightly earlier than minor athletes or nonathletes from coronary heart disease (see Section III). In this section, cardiovascular disease mortality was analyzed within the major-athlete group by type of sport and extent of participation. Again, proportional mortality analysis was used, so that the limitations mentioned with respect to the study of kidney disease mortality also apply here.

The most striking differences (Polednak, 1972c, see Chp. 12) were in the comparisons of athletes by extent of participation (i.e., athletes with 3 or more letters vs. those with 1 or 2). The 3-

---

*With this study design, the total number of person-years in a given time interval for a given age group and sex is multiplied by the appropriate mortality rate (specific for time, age, sex, and cause of death) to obtain an "expected" number of deaths. These expected numbers may then be compared with the observed numbers, and the differences evaluated in terms of statistical significance (see Colton, 1974, for a brief description of this method, and Monson, 1974, for a more detailed explanation).

or-more-letter athletes differed from other athletes in somatotype (i.e., mesomorphy); as noted above (Section II), mesomorphy ratings tend to be higher in men with certain types of
coronary heart disease (CHD). A crude analysis suggested that
physique may not have accounted for the differences observed
in proportional mortality (and mean age at death) from CHD.
A more-detailed analysis of CHD mortality by number of letters, within groups defined by mesomorphy rating, would have
been informative, but sample sizes were too small.

Even if the observed differences in cardiovascular mortality
by extent of participation are real, they may not be due to long-
term effects of athletic competition or physical training.
Among the factors of selection mentioned with respect to success in college athletics, personality is of particular interest
because of the evidence for an association between certain personality characteristics prevalent among athletes (see Chapter 3)
and risk of CHD. Jenkins (1976) has reviewed the extensive
evidence that supports the idea of an association between the
"type A" behavior pattern and prevalence of CHD, degree of
atherosclerosis evident in coronary angiography, and possibly
risk of reinfarction in persons with CHD. It would require
investigations of large samples of athletes, with data on physique and personality (behavior types A and B), to examine this
question.

Some readers may have expected mortality from cardiovascular diseases to be lower among former athletes than nonathletes, in view of the short-term effects of exercise (see Section I)
and the possible effect of exercise on the coronary collateral
circulation. The question of the effects of exercise on coronary
collaterals is still an open one. Evidence from studies of
animals (i.e., dogs) is conflicting and is of questionable relevance to the human situation; for example, dogs have larger
and more numerous coronary collateral vessels relative to man.
The factors which stimulate the functioning of coronary collaterals, as well as the degree of protection such collaterals afford
to patients with CHD, are controversial (Helfant and Gorlin,
1972; Lewin, 1974; Bodenheimer et al., 1977). Helfant et al.
(1971), for example, found that death was less frequent in 61
patients with coronary collateral vessels than in 58 without

them, but the difference did not reach statistical significance.

Perhaps of greatest relevance to the assessment of the effects of exercise on risk of cardiovascular disease are studies on former athletes who follow differing patterns of exercise in later life.

Pomeroy and White (1958; see Chp. 11) were able to examine exercise habits after college in a small group of Harvard football players (i.e., lettermen between 1901 and 1930). We shall not discuss Pomeroy and White's findings on cause of death, because the sample size was small and the control group (i.e., adult white males in Massachusetts) was of questionable value. This study was based in part on responses to questionnaires. As noted in the Introduction, studies on humans differ from those on animals in that follow-up in the former studies may be incomplete, raising the possibility of bias in the results.

Of chief interest here are the findings on exercise habits in former football players with and without CHD (Pomeroy and White, 1958; Table 11-III). None of the coronary group reported "heavy" exercise habits, while a small percentage of the group still living (without coronary disease) did report such habits. The number of men in the coronary group is small (i.e., 34), however, and statistical tests were not applied to the data; a larger case-control type study, of similar design, would be of value. Although Pomeroy and White state that "lifelong habits of exercise" were investigated, it is not made clear how variations in a given individual's habits over time were taken into account. This question of the effect of life-long exercise habits on CHD risk, whether in athletes or others, is an important one, to which we shall return in the *Concluding Remarks*. It is important to note that a relatively large proportion of the total group of former athletes reported "moderate" or "heavy" exercise habits (Pomeroy and White, 1958). Thus, studies of larger samples of former college athletes could provide data relevant to the effects of different levels of activity (throughout life) on the risk of CHD and other diseases.

A more recent study (Paffenbarger, Wing and Hyde, 1978) has provided evidence corroborating Pomeroy and White's (1958) conclusion on the importance of lifelong exercise habits on risk of heart disease. These authors investigated a population of 36,500 Harvard male alumni who entered college in 1916-50, and obtained information on physical activity patterns in selected years of later life. Age-adjusted rates of first heart attack were compared in men who were and were not varsity athletes in college, according to their physical activity index (equivalent energy expenditure in kcal/week) in later life. Student varsity athletic participation was not closely related to heart attack rate in later life, but in both athletes and nonathletes the heart attack rate decreased as the physical activity index increased. Thus, continued vigorous physical activity in later life may affect risk of heart attack independently of early activity (such as athletics in college) (Paffenbarger et al., 1978).

It is noteworthy that in the lowest physical activity index group (i.e., less than 500 kcal/week) the heart attack rate was somewhat higher in former varsity athletes than in nonathletes (i.e., 92.7 vs. 70.7 heart attacks per 10,000 person-years of observation). In the higher physical activity index levels (i.e., 500-1999 and 2000+ kcal/week) heart attack rates were nearly equal in former college varsity athletes and nonathletes. It could prove informative to investigate various characteristics (physique, weight gain, health status, and life style) of former college athletes who maintain different levels of activity in later life.

Also in agreement with Pomeroy and White's (1958) findings, Paffenbarger et al. found that a large proportion of former varsity athletes (i.e., 56%) were strenuously active in sports or other physical activities in later life. In comparison, about 38% of former college nonathletes had achieved an adult exercise level sufficient to be in a low risk group for heart attack. As Paffenbarger et al. (1978) observed, this apparent relationship between later exercise level and heart attack risk, if causal, suggests that a program of primary intervention (through physical exercise) "could appreciably lower the overall heart attack risk among Harvard alumni." One goal of such an intervention program would be to increase the physical activity level of the majority of former college nonathletes; studies of the characteristics of the 38% of this group who chose to become active would be useful in this regard. It should be noted, however, that the relationship between exercise level and heart attack risk may not be causal, a point to which we shall return in the final section of this book.

Regarding weight gain after college, Pomeroy and White stated that the coronary group tended to gain more weight than the control group, but this was not made very clear by the manner of presentation of the results. Unfortunately, weight gain in the athletes could not be compared with that in a comparable group of nonathletes. As we have noted, Montoye et al. (see Chp. 5) found no significant difference in weight gain after college between athletes and nonathletes.

Cancer (Malignant Neoplasms)

Few studies have reported in any detail on cancer mortality among athletes and comparable controls. The results of the study on Harvard men (see Chp. 13) are difficult to interpret without similar data from other studies, and due to the many confounding variables which could account for the differences found. The differences in cancer mortality rate between athletes and nonathletes are small in magnitude, albeit statistically significant for these sample sizes. Although these differences may be real, an attempt at their explanation involves considerable speculation (as evident in Chp. 13). In addition to possible effects of exercise, such potential confounding variables as lifestyle and host factors are mentioned.

Exercise may be considered as a form of "stress" (i.e., physical stress, as distinct from the psychological stress of athletic competition). In animal experiments, environmental stresses have been associated with increased risks of certain tumors (Riley, 1975; Seifter et al., 1973), possibly related to immunosuppression due to adrenal-cortical hypersecretion. More work needs to be done on the effects of various stresses on cancer susceptibility in animals; in humans, such effects are more difficult to study.

REFERENCES

Bodenheimer, M.M., V.S. Banka, G.A. Hermann, R.G. Trout, H. Pasdar, and

R.H. Helfant 1977 The effect of severity of coronary artery obstructive disease and the coronary collateral circulation on local histopathologic and electrographic observations in man. Amer. J. Med. *63*:193-199.

Castenfors, J. 1977 Renal function during prolonged exercise. Ann. N.Y. Acad. Sci. *301*:151-159.

Colton, T.R. 1974 Statistics in Medicine. Little, Brown, Boston.

Helfant, R.H. and R. Gorlin 1972 The coronary collateral circulation. Ann. Intern. Med. *77*:995-997.

Helfant, R.H., P.S. Vokonas, and R. Gorlin 1971 Functional importance of the human coronary collateral circulation. New Engl. J. Med. *284*:1277-1281.

Jenkins, C.D. 1976 Recent evidence supporting psychologic and social risk factors for coronary disease (Part 2). New Engl. J. Med. *294*:1033-1038.

Levin, D.C. 1974 Pathways and functional significance of the coronary collateral circulation. Circulation *50*:831-837.

Monson, R.R. 1974 Analysis of relative survival and proportional mortality. Computers Biomed. Res. *7*:325-332.

Paffenbarger, R.S., Jr., A.L. Wing and R.T. Hyde 1978 Physical activity as an index of heart attack risk in college alumni. Amer. J. Epidemiol. *108*:161-175.

Polednak, A.P. 1972a Mortality from renal diseases among former college athletes. Ann. Intern. Med. *77*:919-922.

Polednak, A.P. 1972b Longevity and cause of death among Harvard College athletes and their classmates. Geriatrics *27*:53-64.

Polednak, A.P. 1972c Longevity and cardiovascular mortality among former college athletes. Circulation *46*:649-654.

Riley, V. 1975 Mouse mammary tumors: Alteration of incidence as apparent function of stress. Science 189:465-467.

Seifter, E., M. Zisblatt, N. Levine, and G. Rettura 1973 Inhibitory action of vitamin A on a murine sarcoma. Life Sci. *13*:945-952.

Other Athletes:
Longevity and Mortality

Chapter 14

LONGEVITY AND CAUSES OF DEATH IN MALE ATHLETIC CHAMPIONS*

PETER SCHNOHR, M.D.

Abstract

Information was obtained about 297 (96.7%) of 307 male athletic champions born in Denmark between 1880 and 1910. Mortality among the athletes was compared with the mortality in the general Danish male population. The ratio of observed to expected deaths was 0.61 in the life period from 25 to 49 years, 1.08 from 50 to 64 years, and 1.02 from 65 to 80 years. The male athletic champions had a significantly lower mortality than the general population under the age of 50 years; after 50 years of age the mortality was the same. Death certificates were obtained concerning the 144 who had died before June 1, 1970; the causes of death were the same as in the general population.

Introduction

THE aim of the study was to determine the longevity and causes of death in top athletes compared with the general population.

Previous studies were not concerned with athletes at national or international level. Men rowing in the Oxford/Cambridge boat races between 1829 and 1869 lived about two years longer than the average Englishman judging by insurance tables,[1] and athletes in college lived longer than the average insurance risk.[2-8] College graduates lived longer, however, regardless of participation in athletics.[9]

---

*From *The Lancet*, 1364-1366, December 18, 1971.

This study was supported by grants from the Danish Heart Foundation.

Comparing letter-winners from eight colleges in the eastern United States with their classmates, and taking age 22 as the base for a life table, the expectation of life was 45.71 years for all 38,269 graduates; 45.56 years for athletes, and 47.73 years for honours men. Insured men in the U.S.A. and Canada in the same period could expect 44.29 years.[9] At Harvard University between 1880 and 1902 the life expectancy of major athletes and nonathletes did not differ significantly; but, the trend favoured nonathletes. The group of minor athletes was the longest-living.[10] The findings were similar concerning men enrolled at Cambridge University between 1860 and 1900; the average age of death, from all causes except accidents and war, was 67.97 years for sportsmen, 69.41 years for men on the academic honours list, and 67.43 years for randomly selected classmates. Only the 2-year advantage of men on the honours list was significant ($p < 0.05$).[11] The finding that life expectancy is unaffected by college athletics was confirmed in another study, based on 1212 returned questionaires out of 2260 sent; the difference in life expectancy between athletes and classmates was less than 0.4 years in favour of the nonathletes.[12]

Earlier studies of the distribution of causes of death in athletes[2,3,6 9,13-15] lacked adequate control groups. Recent studies have indicated that athletes do not differ from the general population in death-rate from infections, neoplasms, cardiovascular diseases, or suicide.[10-12,16,17] There was a trend towards a lower death-rate from nervous diseases, and a higher death-rate from accidents.[11,13] Paffenbarger et al.[17] found a significantly smaller percentage of university athletes among future coronary decedents than among controls.

Materials and Methods

The group of athletes consisted of 307 men born between 1880 and 1910 with biographies in the Danish Sportslexicon.[18] Information about 297 (96.7%) was obtained from the population register of the Copenhagen Community, the department of medical statistics of the Danish National Board of Health, and the Danish National Archives.

All the athletes had been Danish champions, recordholders,

Table 14-I

BEST ATHLETIC RESULTS OF THE

297 MALES BORN 1880-1910

Best result	No.	%
World records	4	1·4
Medals at Olympic Games	22	7·4
World championships..	11	3·7
European championships	15	5·0
Nordic championships	21	7·1
Members of Olympic teams	50	16·8
Danish champions, record-holders, or members of national teams	174	58·6
Total	297	100·0

or members of national teams (Table 14-I). 19 different sports categories were represented: soccer (21%), track and field (18%), bicycle racing (8%), rowing (6%), wrestling (6%), boxing (6%), tennis (5%), horse-back riding (5%), gymnastics (5%), fencing (4%), swimming (4%), weightlifting (2%), hockey (2%), cricket (2%), handball (2%), badminton (1%), skating (1%), golf (1%), and walking (1%). 68 were born between 1880 and 1889, 114 between 1890 and 1899, and 115 between 1900 and 1910. Anthropometric data and information about socioeconomic status, smoking habits, and daily physical activity were absent.

The number of deaths at 25-49 years, 50-64 years, and 65-80 years was compared with the expected number of deaths had the mortality been the same as in the general population. The life tables used for computing the expected number of deaths were those prepared by the Danish State Statistical Department for 5-year periods from 1905 to 1969.

The causes of death among the athletic champions were compared with causes of death in Danish males of the same 5-year age-group. The distribution of the causes of death in the year 1961 was chosen for comparison, because half of the athletes died before this year.

Results

Longevity

Of 297 25-year-old Danish males born in the same years as

the top athletes, 27.9 were expected to die before the age of 50; of the athletic champions only 17 died. The ratio of expected to observed mortality in this 25-year period is 0.61. Thus the mortality in the 25-year period is 39% less for the athletic champions than for the general male population ($p < 0.04$).[19] For the life periods 50-64 years and 65-80 years, the ratios of observed to expected deaths are 1.08 and 1.02 (see Fig. 14-1). Thus, athletic champions under the age of 50 years have a lower mortality than the general male population. After this age the mortality was the same as in the general population.

Causes of Death

Of the 297 athletes, 144 were dead as of June 1, 1970. Table 14-II shows the leading causes of death in this group compared

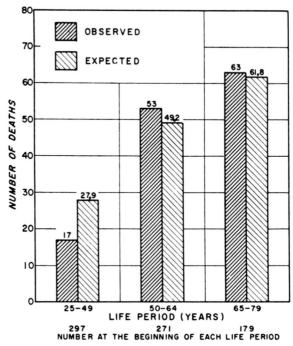

Figure 14-1. Comparison of observed and expected deaths in 297 Danish male athletic champions during three different life periods.

with the causes of death for males dying within the same 5-year age-group as the athletic champions. The difference between observed and expected causes of death was tested by x^2 test. For this purpose infectious diseases and homicide were grouped together with "all other causes." As x^2 is 2.6 (f = 9) the differences were not significant (p > 0.05).

Table 14-II

OBSERVED AND EXPECTED CAUSES OF DEATHS
OF THE 144 ATHLETIC CHAMPIONS

Causes of death	No.	Deaths (%)	
		Observed	Expected
Infectious diseases (including tuberculosis)	5	3·5	1·2
Cancer	34	23·6	25·1
Apoplexia and senility	18	12·5	11·5
Diseases of the heart	50	34·7	36·7
Diseases of the respiratory system	5	3·5	3·7
Diseases of the digestive system	5	3·5	3·7
Diseases of the genitourinary system	8	5·6	4·1
Accidents	6	4·2	4·6
Suicide	7	4·9	3·1
Homicide	1	0·7	0·2
Other causes	5	3·5	6·3
Total	144	100·2	100·2

Discussion

Mortality after the age of 50 is not affected by the degree of past athletic performance. Both the athletic champions investigated in this study and university athletes investigated previously[1-12] have almost the same mortality as comparable male populations.

The finding that athletic champions have a lower mortality than the general male population at ages less than 50 does not agree with previous findings. In college athletes there is a trend to more deaths from accidents than in control groups.[11,13] Although the age at death from accidents was not reported, presumably it was less than 50.

Why former athletic champions survived better at ages less than 50 is uncertain. The leading cause of death in this age-group was not cardiovascular disease.[20] Therefore, better survival probably is not produced by cardiovascular training. In fact, only 36% of the athletes in this study participated in sports involving unusual cardiovascular stress. An alternative interpretation is that the group of athletic champions contained only individuals in excellent health. In previous studies a trend towards fewer deaths from disease at less than 50 years may have been obscured by the higher risk of death from accidents.

Why Danish athletic champions may be less accident prone than their Anglo-Saxon counterparts is uncertain. Probably they were placed lower socially because few of them were enrolled at universities, and they may have had less opportunity for adventurous undertakings.

Neither the former athletic champions nor the less successful athletes studied previously continued vigorous exercise after the years of competition. Therefore, the effect of habitual, vigorous exercise on life is still uncertain. Finnish skiers lived 6-7 years longer than the general male population between 1931 and 1940. This points to a positive effect of training.[21] A firmer conclusion awaits studies with adequate control groups.

In any case, athletics seems to be healthier in our times than in antiquity. Hippocrates wrote about athletes that: "... the truth is, however, that no one is in a more risky state of health than they ..."

REFERENCES

1. Morgan, J. E. University Oars. London, 1873.
2. Meylan, G. L. *Harvard Grad. Mag.* 1904, 9, 362, 543.
3. Anderson, W. G. *Med. Times*, 1916, 44, 75.
4. Hill, A. B. *Lancet*, 1927, ii, 949.
5. Cooper, L., O'Sullivan, J., Hughes, E. *Med. J. Aust.* 1937, i, 569.
6. Knoll, W. *Med. Klin.* 1938, 34, 464.
7. Hartley, P., Llewellyn, G. F. *Br. med. J.* 1939, i, 657.
8. Wakefield, M. C. *Res. Q. Am. Ass. Hlth phys. Educ.* 1944, 15, 2.
9. Dublin, L. I. *Statist. Bull Metropolitan Life Insurance Co.* 1932, 13, 5.
10. Polednak, A. P., Damon, A. *Hum. Biol.* 1970, 42, 28.
11. Rook, A. *Br. med. J.* 1954, ii, 773.
12. Montoye, H. J., Van Huss, W. D., Olson, H., Hudec, A., Mahoney, E. *J. Am. med. Ass.* 1956, 162, 1132.
13. Greenway, J. C., Hiscock, I. V. *Yale Alumni Wkly*, 1926, 35, 1086.

14. Bickert, F. W. *Dt. med. Wschr.* 1929, 55, 23.
15. Van Mervenne, *Ned. T. Geneesk.* 1941, 85, 535.
16. Pomeroy, W., White, P. D. *J. Am. med. Ass.* 1958, 167, 711.
17. Paffenbarger, R. S., Asnes, D. P. *Am. J. publ. Hlth,* 1966, 56, 1026.
18. Lundqvist Andersen, A., Budtz-Jorgensen, J. Dansk Sportsleksikon; vol. I, p. 607; vol. II, p. 695. Copenhagen, 1944.
19. Hald, A. Statistical Theory with Engineering Applications; p. 783. New York, 1967.
20. Causes of Death in the Kingdom of Denmark; p. 158. National Health Service of Denmark, Copenhagen, 1961.
21. Karvonen, M. J., Kihlberg, I., Määttä, J., Virkajarvi, J. *Duodecim,* 1956, 72, 893.
22. Medicorum Graecorum, Galeni Opera (edited by C. G. Kuhn) p. 694, Leipzig, 1821.

Chapter 15

PREVIOUS HEALTH AND LONGEVITY OF MALE ATHLETES*

ANTHONY P. POLEDNAK, Ph.D.

SCHNOHR[1] reported that, under age 50, Danish male athletic champions had a low mortality rate relative to the general male population, and stated that this finding "does not agree with previous findings" on college athletes. At Cambridge University[2] between 1860 and 1900, however, 723 sportsmen had slightly lower mortality rates relative to 362 "intellectual" and 325 randomly chosen classmates up to age 45, and slightly lower than the random group up to age 50.

Table 15-I shows the survival of 7877 Harvard men born between 1860 and 1889, by athletic status. Deaths from causes other than natural were excluded, following Rook's[2] procedure. Major athletes were lettermen in varsity sports, while minor athletes participated in varsity sports without winning a letter, or in nonvarsity (i.e., interclass) sports.[3,4] Up to age 40 or 45 there is little difference between lettermen and nonathletes. In the last birth decade (1880-89) major athletes had the highest survival-rates up to age 45, but differences again were small. Major athletes graduating in later years, after about 1890, had mortality rates much lower than those of earlier classes, but only slightly higher than their less-athletic classmates after age 50.

Somewhat similar trends were reported by Dublin[5] among 38,269 men graduating from 8 colleges in the eastern United States between 1870 and 1905. Athletes graduating in later years (1900-05) reportedly had the lowest mortality rates of all groups. Dublin attributed this improvement to better selection

---

*From Letter to the Editor: *The Lancet,* 711, September 30, 1972.

Table 15-I

HARVARD MEN*:
PERCENTAGES REACHING A GIVEN AGE,
BY ATHLETIC STATUS AND BIRTH DECADE

Age (yr.)	Birth decade								
	1860–69			1870–79			1880–89		
	Major athlete	Minor athlete	Non-athlete	Major athlete	Minor athlete	Non-athlete	Major athlete	Minor athlete	Non-athlete
20	100·0	100·0	99·8	100·0	99·8	100·0	100·0	99·8	99·9
25	98·4	98·6	98·8	98·5	98·9	98·7	99·4	98·9	99·2
30	96·4	96·8	95·8	96·3	97·5	97·6	98·4	97·8	97·9
35	94·3	94·6	93·3	94·4	96·9	96·1	97·8	96·8	96·0
40	90·2	91·4	90·7	93·0	95·1	94·3	96·9	94·3	95·0
45	87·0	88·1	88·4	90·7	93·0	92·3	93·1	92·4	92·9
50	80·8	86·0	85·4	86·3	89·2	88·9	87·8	89·1	90·1
55	76·7	81·3	80·2	82·2	85·2	84·7	84·1	85·1	87·1
60	69·9	75·9	75·2	74·8	76·0	77·7	75·6	79·9	80·6
65	59·1	67·6	68·1	68·1	69·2	69·0	68·4	72·9	73·7
70	45·1	56·1	53·7	55·2	57·3	58·4	57·5	63·2	62·0
75	34·4	41·4	40·0	45·6	47·6	44·4	49·1	51·4	50·0
No. in group	190	279	1260	270	445	2072	320	942	2099

* Men dead of natural causes or still alive as of June 30, 1967.

of college athletes by medical examination, which became "standard practice" in later years.[5]

It has been suggested[1,2] that selection for general health — both by self-selection and by medical examination — may explain the lower mortality among athletes up to age 50, reported by Schnohr[1] and in the above-mentioned studies of college athletes. We have no data on the health status of Harvard athletes while they were in college. At the time of anthropometric examination in college (at a mean age of about 19 years), however, each man was asked about previous illnesses. The checklist included four pulmonary diseases — pneumonia, bronchitis, pleurisy, and asthma. Among men in the 1860-69 birth decade (Table 15-II), a significantly higher percentage of nonathletes than major athletes reported a previous pulmonary disease (12.0% vs. 6.3%; p < 0.05, *t* test). On this criterion, therefore, major athletes were indeed healthier than their classmates. All men in the present series were interested in exercise to some extent, since all had voluntarily rented a gymnasium locker. Thus, the nonathletes may have been healthier than the general student population, which makes the differences found more meaningful. Parenthetically, we note that in another study of Harvard men,[6] significantly more men without previous pulmonary disease were still alive than those with such disease.

Table 15-II

PREVIOUS PULMONARY DISEASES
REPORTED* BY HARVARD MEN
(BORN 1860-69),
BY ATHLETIC STATUS

Type of disease	Major athlete ($N = 190$)	Minor athlete ($N = 279$)	Non-athlete ($N = 250$)†
Pneumonia ..	6	13	11
Bronchitis ..	3	12	10
Pleurisy	1	5	5
Asthma	2	2	5
Total no. of cases	12	32	31
Total no. of men‡	12 (6·3%)	30 (10·8%)	30 (12·0%)

    * During anthropometric examination at Harvard University.
    † A sample of every fifth consecutive non-athlete measured, who was dead of natural causes.
    ‡ None of the major athletes reported two pulmonary diseases, versus 2 minor athletes and 1 non-athlete; none of the subjects reported more than two pulmonary diseases.

Relative to the general male population, Danish national champions must be an even more select group (in terms of general health) than college athletes relative to their classmates. This may account for the rather large difference in survival to age 50 between Danish champions and controls,[1] relative to the small differences reported between college athletes and their classmates. After age 50 other factors must have offset the early advantage shown by the Danish champions. One such factor could be physique, as has been suggested for college athletes.[3,4]

REFERENCES

1. Schnohr, P. *Lancet*, 1971, ii, 1364.
2. Rook, A. *Br. med. J.* 1954, ii, 773.
3. Polednak, A. P., Damon, A. *Hum. Biol.* 1970, 42, 28.
4. Polednak, A. P. *Geriatrics* (in the press).
5. Dublin, L. I. *Statist. Bull. Metropolitan Life Insurance Co.* 1932, 13, 5.
6. Damon, A., McClung, J. P. *J chron. Dis.* 1967, 20, 59.

Chapter 16

LONGEVITY OF MAJOR LEAGUE BASEBALL PLAYERS*

METROPOLITAN LIFE INSURANCE COMPANY

FROM the first pitch on opening day till the last out of the World Series, season in, season out, baseball fans watch their favorite players perform, grow older, and retire. But only on occasion, such as a Hall of Fame election, or the report of the death of a baseball "great" like Roberto Clemente, Gil Hodges, Jackie Robinson, or Ducky Medwick does the question of the longevity of the "boys of summer" arise.

A study made by the Statistical Bureau of the Metropolitan Life Insurance Company of the survivorship of major league players indicates that professional team members experience very favorable mortality, significantly below that for white men born in the same years in the general population of the United States. This conclusion was drawn from a study of 10,079 major league players who were professionally active at any time prior to the end of the 1973 season.† Because the necessary birth and death records were unavailable, an additional 1,077 players were excluded; 877 of these entered the major leagues before 1901.

The number of major league players by team years played and by period of commencement of professional activity is shown in Table 16-I. It is of particular interest to note that most players had careers of less than five years' duration. For all ages combined, these major league players registered mortality just 72 percent of that among cohorts of white males in the general population. Wide differences in mortality obtained, however, with respect to period of entry into the major leagues.

---

*From *Statistical Bulletin*, 2-4, April 1975. Courtesy of Metropolitan Life Insurance Company.
†Including those who played on any of the professional major league teams that have existed since 1876.

For example, the 1,399 players who had careers beginning before 1901 experienced a mortality rate just under that of white males in the United States population; the 8,680 whose careers began after 1900 registered mortality less than two thirds of that expected.

Table 16-I

Team Years Played†	Number of Players	
	1876-1900	1901-1973
1	352	2,693
2-4	416	2,754
5-9	314	1,796
10-14	203	974
15-19	84	379
20 or more	30	84

†Each time a man played for a different major league team in a single season he was credited with a team year. Many of those who played for only one year either had less than 25 "at bats," or pitched less than 25 innings.

The considerable improvement in mortality experienced by major league players over the years is illustrated in Table 16-II. From the earliest period, the ratio of the mortality of professional baseball players to that of contemporaneous white males in the United States population has declined for every age group under consideration. For example, among players at all ages combined whose professional careers began before 1901, the mortality ratio was 97 percent of that expected; the ratio was 64 percent for those who began playing professionally in 1902-30, and 55 percent in the 1931-73 period.

Further details of the mortality experienced by major league players are shown by attained age and length of career in Table 16-III. For players professionally active before 1901, the ratio of actual to expected deaths was 117 percent at ages under 40 (generally the playing years) and 94 percent at ages 40 and over. In contrast, for men who played for a major league team after

Table 16-II

TREND OF MORTALITY

MAJOR LEAGUE BASEBALL PLAYERS

1876-1973

Mortality Ratio*

Players Who Had
Careers Beginning

Attained Age	1876-1900	1901-1930	1931-1973
All Ages	97%	64%	55%
Under 40	117	58	43
40 and over	94	65	59
40-49	123	71	62
50-59	105	80	62
60-69	101	75	51
70 and over	83	53	42

* Based on mortality rates among cohorts of white males in the general population of the United States.

1900, mortality was lower both under age 40 and at ages 40 and over. The 3,233 who played five or more years experienced mortality 34 percent of that for comparable white males at ages under 40, and 79 percent at ages 40 and older. The mortality of the 5,447 men who played for less than five years was 64 percent of that in the general white male population at ages under 40, and 58 percent at ages 40 and above.

Of the 471 men who have been managers of major league baseball teams during the periods under review, birth and death information was lacking for 40, limiting the investigation to 431; of these, 309 were managers less than five years. A summary by team years as manager is shown in Table 16-IV.

The mortality among men who were managers at any tme before the end of the 1973 season was 92 percent of that for white males born in the same years. Analysis by period indicates that those who were managers before 1901 had overall mortality somewhat above that of their contemporaries in the white male population (see lower tier of Table 16-III).

Expected mortality for the managers was calculated from the

Table 16-III

MORTALITY OF MAJOR LEAGUE BASEBALL PLAYERS
AND MANAGERS COMPARED WITH WHITE MALES
IN UNITED STATES POPULATION

Attained Age	Deaths	Mortality Ratio*	Deaths	Mortality Ratio*	Deaths	Mortality Ratio*

Players Who Had Careers Beginning

	1876-1900		1901-1973			
			played less than 5 years		played 5 or more years	
All Ages	1,391	97%	1,763	59%	935	72%
Under 40.......	211	117	194	64	59	34
40 and over	1,180	94	1,569	58	876	79
40-49	163	123	178	62	117	79
50-59	189	105	342	72	192	81
60-69	280	101	489	72	241	68
70 and over ...	548	83	560	45	326	78

	Managers Who Had Careers Beginning				Members of the Hall of Fame	
	1876-1900		1901-1973		1876-1973	
All Ages	152	106%	139	80%	73‡	82%‡
Under 40.......	6	†	2	†	‡	‡
40-49	17	105	13	91	7	77
50-59	25	111	16	55	16	113
60-69	42	140	41	91	13	58
70 and over ...	62	99	67	84	37	86

* Based on mortality rates among cohorts of white males in the general population of the United States.
† Fewer than 10 deaths.
‡ Experience under age 40 was excluded to allow for the Hall of Fame election requirement of at least 10 years as a player in the major leagues.
Source of basic data: *The Baseball Encyclopedia,* 2d ed. New York, Macmillian Publishing Co., Inc. 1974.

Table 16-IV

Team Years as Manager	Number of Managers
1	161
2-4	148
5-9	69
10-19	41
20 or more	12

earliest age at which their managerial careers started. For those 279 men who became managers at any time during the period 1901-73, mortality was 80 percent of that in the white male population. The managers' mortality record, while favorable overall, was generally poorer than that of the players and may reflect the severe pressure-to-win to which managers are subjected. One manager, however, Cornelius McGillicuddy — "Connie Mack" — remained active to age 88 and died at the age of 93, winning nine pennants and five World Series during his 65-year career as player and manager.

Among the highly select group of 118 baseball players elected to the Hall of Fame at Cooperstown, New York, the mortality experience at ages 40 and over was 82 percent of that expected for contemporaneous white males, or slightly less favorable than that registered by all men whose careers began during 1901-73. As was the case with all major league baseball players and team managers, there were wide variations in mortality by attained age among the Hall of Fame members.

The greater longevity of major league baseball players may be accounted for in part by the superior physical condition required for successful performance and the close supervision of players' health by team physicians in the playing years. During retirement — generally after age 40 — the relative mortality of major league players increased considerably, but continued to remain appreciably below that of their contemporaries in the white male population.

Chapter 17

STATISTICAL ANALYSIS OF DEATHS FROM CORONARY HEART DISEASE ANTICIPATED IN A COHORT OF MARATHON RUNNERS*

Paul Milvy, Ph.D.

Introduction

MANY reports have appeared in the last decade that describe epidemiological studies of the relationship between physical activity and mortality, especially mortality from coronary heart disease (CHD). (For recent general reviews, see References 1-6). The methodological and epidemiological problems encountered by these studies are extreme, and valid conclusions are notoriously difficult to achieve.[7-10] In particular, controversy has developed over the point of view, expressed by Bassler in the most extreme form in 1972, that "a search of the literature failed to document a single death due to coronary arteriosclerosis among marathon finishers"[11] and in 1973, "when the level of vigorous exercise is raised high enough, the protection appears to be absolute. The American Medical Joggers Association (AMJA) has been unable to document a single death resulting from coronary heart disease among marathon finishers of any age."[12] The implication seems to be that after completing a 26.2 mile marathon at some point in one's life, the individual is then protected from death from CHD for the remainder of his life. The controversy engendered by this assertion has continued in the last several years, as may be seen by consulting several recent letters to the editors of several medical and scientific journals.[13-17] We do not know

*From *Annals of the New York Academy of Sciences*, 301:62-626, 1977.

what significance we are to place upon Bassler's communications: we do not know how many deaths of marathoners — from all causes — was revealed by the search of the literature conducted by Bassler, nor do we know the number of autopsies performed or reviewed by the AMJA: both crucial facts for establishing statistical significance to their findings.

In general, epidemiology utilized two general approaches to establish an association between variables that may be involved in human disease: the prospective study and the retrospective (or retrospective-prospective) study (causation, as opposed to association, can only be rigorously proven by the clinical trial, where randomization of variables can be achieved). The following analysis demonstrates the futility of informally applying these epidemiological approaches to a cohort of U.S. marathoners with the expectation of arriving at an evaluation of the influence of marathoning on the incidence of mortality from ischemic and related heart disease.

Materials and Methods

In 1975, 10,482 men and women completed a marathon road race.*[18] Approximately 5% of these runners were women and have not been included in the data base, leaving 9,958 male marathoners. In the remainder of this article an estimate is made of the number of men expected to die from ischemic and related heart disease for a cohort of 9,958 white American males whose age distribution is the same as these marathoners, but whose relative weight and smoking habits are the same as the general American male population. The two factors of weight and cigarette consumption place the general male population at substantial risk from CHD. However, marathoners, as a group, are almost invariably thin and not addicted to smoking. It is well known that marathoners have certain characteristics in common. Almost to a man (or to a woman) they do not smoke, they drink little alcohol, and they are very thin. The average sub-3-hour marathoner who is under 35 years old weighs in pounds about twice the numerical measure of his

---

*This includes AAU certified and uncertified marathon courses. In 1976, 20% more completed one.

height in inches. This is on the order of 15% to 20% less than the weight of the average American man of similar age. Older marathoners although slightly heavier are proportionally even lighter than men of similar age in the general population. Thus, two important risk factors in CHD are absent in virtually all marathoners. But it must be stressed that it has never been established that running *causes* men to be thin and not to smoke. Many men who have never run are still thin and do not smoke, and it is acknowledged that this is likely to be the result of multiple causation, which may but does not necessarily include running. The motivation to run is complex. Several motives that suggest themselves are certainly sheer pleasure; probably competitiveness and aggression; and possibly hostility, masochism, vanity, conceit, or public recognition. In addition, concern for one's health and well-being is probably a motivation for many. This would require the ancillary belief by the runner in the widely accepted but basically unproven proposition that running helps achieve good health to a greater degree than is achieved from participation in any other hobby that one enjoys and which may be said to add to the quality of one's life. The same concern for health and well-being is a motivation not to smoke and not to become overweight. The nonsmoking thin runner may achieve this status by virtue of a complex of causal factors. The scheme that suggests that running is the independent variable, and nonsmoking and thin body the dependent variable cannot be easily demonstrated. There may also be other risk factors affecting most Americans that are substantially absent among marathoners. For example, the poorer social classes (classes 4 and 5) are very underrepresented among marathoners, and marathoners to a greater degree carry life insurance than the typical American, both of which are factors that place the runner in a lower mortality risk category.[19,20]

Appropriate corrections will be applied to the estimated mortality for a cohort of men that is reasonably equivalent to the 9,958 male marathoners, save that they do not run or engage in physical exercise more than does the general insured American male population. Thus, an estimate will be made of the number of marathoners that would be expected to die per year in this cohort, independent of any postulated "protection" that marathoning per se might afford.

Procedure

Table 17-I presents the distribution of the mean relative body weight of male smokers and nonsmokers in a population of over 900,000 men and women studied by Hammond and Garfinkel.[21] The distribution of weights for the two primary smoking categories is seen not to differ substantially. Table 17-

Table 17-I

DISTRIBUTION OF MEAN RELATIVE WEIGHTS
AND CIGARETTE CONSUMPTION FOR MALES

Smoking Habits (Cigarettes per Day)	Relative Weight Distribution				Mean Relative Weight
	<90%	90%–109%	110%–119%	≥120%	
Never smoked regularly	13.2	62.8	16.7	7.3	102.0%
1–9	20.2	61.7	12.8	5.3	99.3%
10–19	26.4	60.3	9.8	3.5	97.0%
20–39	24.5	60.7	11.1	3.7	97.6%
40+	17.8	60.3	15.1	6.8	100.6%
Average all smokers	23.6	60.7	11.5	4.2	98.0%

* Relative weight $= (w/<w>) \times 100\%$, where w is a subject's weight and $<w>$ is the average weight of all subjects normalized for height.

Table 17-II

PERCENT OF MEN WHO SMOKE ONLY CIGARETTES, BY AGE*

Cigarette Consumption (Cigarettes per Day)	Age			
	35–44	45–54	55–64	65–74
Never smoked regularly	25.1	25.3	31.4	48.4
1–9	5.2	5.3	7.1	9.6
10–19	11.7	12.0	14.5	15.3
20–39	48.5	48.1	40.2	24.4
40+ †	10.4	11.2	7.3	3.1
Average	21.3	21.4	18.2	11.6

* Data from Appendix Table 2a and Appendix Table 3a from Hammond[22] were used to construct this table.

† For calculation of the average number of cigarettes, the category "40+" was arbitrarily (but reasonably) set equal to 50.

II presents a profile of the smoking habit of the American male population. This table was extracted from the data contained in the NCI Monograph No. 19.[22]

Table 17-III presents data from Hammond and Garfinkel[21] that has been recalculated to show mortality normalized to 1.00 for the "non or slight cigarette smoker" of weight at least 10% under the average weight for this large cohort. The first three columns of Table 17-IV show the distribution by age of the 9,958 male marathoners and the percent in each age category. The annual mortality is given in column 4 and is taken from the *Statistical Bulletin* data on mortality for ischemic and related heart disease in 1973 for Metropolitan Standard ordinary policy holders.[19] Column 5 shows the number of deaths expected per annum for each age category in this cohort, without

Table 17-III

NORMALIZED MORTALITY RATIOS

Cigarette Consumption per Day	Age	Relative Weight *			
		< 90%		90%–109%	
		A †	B †	A †	B †
None or slight	40–49	1.00 ‡	—·	1.70	—
	50–59	1.00	1.00	1.54	1.54
	60–69	1.00	1.00	1.06	1.06
	70–79	1.00	1.00	1.06	1.06
Intermediate	40–49	4.00	2.51	3.84	—
	50–59	4.00	2.51	4.12	2.59
	60–69	4.00	2.51	4.36	1.74
	70–79	4.00	2.51	3.16	1.99
20.0 (Average of "Intermediate" and "20+")	40–49	4.28	—	6.27	—
	50–59	4.28	2.76	4.96	3.21
	60–69	4.28	2.76	4.55	2.94
	70–79	4.28	2.76	3.72	2.40
20+	40–49	4.56	—	8.71	—
	50–59	4.56	3.01	5.79	3.82
	60–69	4.56	3.01	4.74	3.13
	70–79	4.56	3.01	4.28	2.83

* See Table 17-I.

† Column A is normalized to the death rate for the 40–49-year-old nonhypertensive male who smokes slightly or not at all and weighs <90% of the mean relative weight. Because the death rate for 40–49, none or slight smoker, is not known accurately, column B· is presented, normalized to the 50–59-year-old male with other variables remaining the same. This data is taken from Table 7 of Reference 21.

‡ Too little data to determine accurately.

adjustment for smoking or weight factors. Columns 6 and 7 show the smoking-weight combined risk factors, which were presented in Table 17-III columns A and B, respectively, with the conservative assumption that all men are in the 90%-109% relative weight category. For these columns the assumption that cigarette consumption is 20 per day to age 59 and "intermediate" at older ages is also made. The two extreme right columns "Adjusted Mortality" (np/f where f represents the smoking-weight risk factors) present the annual mortality expected from 9,958 men who do not smoke and are less than 90% of average adjusted weights. That is, this is the mortality per annum that might reasonably be expected in 1976 from the real 9,958 man cohort that completed a marathon in 1975, without consideration of physical inactivity as a risk factor.

Discussion

The last two columns of Table 17-IV present the deaths per year expected from a cohort equivalent in age distribution, smoking habit, and in weight to the 9,958 males who ran a marathon in 1975 in the United States, but these columns reflect the mortality for a cohort that *did not* run a marathon and were no more physically active than the metropolitan ordinary insured policy holders. From this group we may anticipate one or two deaths per annum from ischemic and related heart disease. (From a 9,958 cohort whose weight and smoking profiles were similar to the weight and smoking distributions of the *insured* population, but who were similar in age distribution to the marathoners, we would anticipate 5.37 deaths from ischemic and related heart disease, as shown in Table 17-IV column 5.) To detect the relatively rare event of one or two such deaths per year against a background of over 330,000 U.S. men who die annually from ischemic and related heart disease is a formidable task for the epidemiologist, even were he to have access to the best national registry.

In summary, if marathoning conferred absolute protection from death from ischemic and related heart disease, we would expect no CHD deaths per year from the 10,000 cohort of male

Table 17-IV

EXPECTED MORTALITY FOR COHORT

Age	n	%	Mortality p *	np	Risk Factors † f_1	f_2	Adjusted Mortality np/f_1	np/f_2
⩽ 29	5540	56.0	1.8 ‡	0.10	8.4 §	5.00 §	0.012	0.020
30–39	2393	24.0	20.5	0.49	7.3 §	4.50 §	0.067	0.109
40–49	1439	14.0	122.0	1.71	6.27	4.00 §	0.273	0.428
50–59	463	4.6	403.0	1.85	4.96	3.21	0.373	0.576
60–64	79	0.8	841.0	0.66	4.36 ¶	1.74 ¶	0.151	0.379
64–69	32	0.3	1234.0	0.39	3.76 ¶	1.87 ¶	0.104	0.208
⩾ 70	12	0.1	1704.0	0.17	3.16 ¶	1.99 ¶	0.054	0.158
Total	9958	99.8		5.37			1.02	1.89
All ages **	9958		237.0	23.6				

* Mortality is per 10^5

† f_1 based upon Table 17-III column A; f_2 based upon Table 17-III column B. For explanation, see text.

‡ Estimated mortality; too few deaths to compute accurately.

§ Risk factors estimated based upon observed trend with age. Note that total adjusted mortality in columns 8 and 9 is insensitive to variations in these risk factors: they contribute less than 8% to the total mortality.

¶ Based upon "intermediate" category of cigarette consumption from Table 17-III.

** Distribution of ages reflecting general insured public.

marathoners. If it provided 50% protection, we would expect about one runner per year would die from this disease, while if it provided no protection, we would expect an average of one or two runners per year to die. In addition to the formidable problems of discovering these deaths, were death to occur at all, it is clear that the statistics, which under alternative initial conditions achieve only a difference of at most 2 deaths per year, are not able to assess meaningful differences (in risk factors) in the two cohorts, let alone provide evidence that marathoning prevents CHD. It is no wonder that Tom Bassler has not observed a single infarct among American marathoners. If he had, the proposition that marathoning might be deleterious to general health must be entertained, and I might seriously consider ending my marathon çareer forthwith, in spite of the tremendous pleasure and gratification that it has given me.

Conclusion

What we seek to assess, the validity of the proposition that marathoning may confer absolute, limited, or no protection from CHD to the American male, cannot be easily proven without a formal marathon cohort and recourse to formal epidemiological methods. By formal, we intend to convey the concept of a study in which several thousand marathoners are maintained under observation for a number of years as in conventional prospective epidemiological studies. Clearly under such conditions in which the study is maintained for many years with a carefully selected matched control group in which no known confounding factors complicate the analysis, it would be anticipated that valid data can be collected and valid conclusions achieved. But this is a formidable task.

REFERENCES

1. BLACKBURN, H. 1974. Disadvantages of intensive exercises therapy after myocardial infarction. *In* Controversy in Internal Medicine. F. Ingelfinger, Ed. Vol. 2: 162-172. W. B. Saunders Co. Philadelphia, Pa.
2. BRUCE, R. A. 1974. The benefits of physical training for patients with coronary heart disease. *In* Controversy in Internal Medicine. F. Ingelfinger, Ed. Vol. 2: 145-161. W. B. Saunders Co. Philadelphia, Pa.
3. FEJFAR, Z. 1975. Prevention Against Ischaemic Heart Disease. A Critical Review, Modern Trends in Cardiology, 3, pp. 465-499. Ed. by M. F. Oliver, Butterworths, Boston.
4. FOX, S. M., III, J. P. NAUGHTON & W. L. HASKELL. 1971. Physical activity and prevention of coronary heart disease. Ann. Clin. Res. 3: 404-432.
5. FROELICHER, V. F. & A. OBERMAN. 1972. Analysis of epidemiologic studies in physical inactivity as risk factor for coronary artery disease. Prog. Cardiovasc. Dis. 15 (1, July/August): 41-65.
6. MILVY, J., W. F. FORBES & K. S. BROWN. 1977. A review of epidemiological studies of physical exercise and its relationship to health and mortality. Ann. N.Y. Acad. Sci. This volume.
7. TAYLOR, H. L., R. W. PARLIN, H. BLACKBURN & A. KEYS. 1966. Problems in the analysis of the relationship of coronary heart disease to physical activity or its lack, with special reference to sample size and occupational withdrawal. *In* Physical Activity in Health and Disease. E. Evang & K. L. Anderson, Eds.: 242-261. William & Wilkins, Baltimore, Md.
8. KEYS, A. 1970. Physical activity and the epidemiology of coronary disease.

In Physical Activity and Aging. Medicine and Sport. D. Brunner, Ed. Vol. 4: 250. University Park Press. Baltimore, Md.

9. KEYS, A. 1975. Coronary heart disease — The global picture. Atherosclerosis 22: 149-192.

10. FOX, S. M., III. 1972. Physical activity and coronary heart disease. *In* Controversy in Cardiology. E. K. Chang, Ed.: 201-219. Springer Verlag. New York, N.Y.

11. BASSLER, T. J. 1972. Letter to the editor. Lancet ii: 711.

12. BASSLER, T. J. 1973. Long distance runners. Science 128: 1083.

13. BASSLER, T. J. 1970. Marathon vs. distance running (letter). New Eng. J. Med. 294(2): 114.

14. CORDELLO, F. 1976. Letter to the editor. New Eng. J. Med. 294(2): 115.

15. STEINER, R. 1976. Letter to the editor. New Eng. J. Med. 294(2): 115.

16. BASSLER, T. J. 1975. Marathon running and immunity to heart disease. Phys. Sports Med. 3: 77-80.

17. OPIE, L. H. 1976. Heart disease in marathon runners. New Eng. J. Med. 294(19): 1067.

18. YOUNG, K. 1975. U.S. Distance Rankings for 1975. National Running Data Center, University of Arizona, Tucson, Ariz.

19. STATISTICAL BULLETIN. 1975. Socioeconomic Mortality Differentials. Metropolitan Life Insurance Co., January.

20. BLACKBURN, H. & R. W. PARLIN. 1966. Antecedents of disease: Insurance mortality experience. Ann. N.Y. Acad. Sci. 134: 965-1017.

21. HAMMOND, E. C. & L. GARFINKEL. 1969. Coronary heart disease, stroke, and aortic aneurysm. Arch. Env. Health 19: 167-182.

22. HAMMOND, E. C. 1966. Smoking in relation to the death rates of one-million men and women. National Cancer Institute Monograph #19. : 127-204. January.

DISCUSSION

THESE chapters serve to illustrate the probable importance of the effect of selection of athletes (on the basis of health) on subsequent mortality. Schnohr's (1971) Danish champion athletes (see Chp. 14) showed lower mortality relative to the general population up to the age of 50 years. Schnohr states that this finding is not in agreement with the findings of other studies. As noted in Chapter 15, other studies (on college athletes) have shown slight differences in survival to age 40 or 50 in favor of athletes (vs. nonathletes) (see Rook, 1954, Chp. 4). This is further supported by the data on survival of Harvard athletes and nonathletes (Polednak, 1972, Chp. 15) to various ages.

The greater advantage in survival to early ages shown by Danish athletes vs. controls, than shown by college athletes vs. nonathletes, may be due to the more stringent selection involved for Olympic and other prominent athletes. The meagre data on previous pulmonary diseases reported by college athletes and nonathletes (Polednak, 1972, Chp. 15) illustrates the selection for athletics on the basis on health; differences in previous health may have been even greater between Danish champion athletes and the general population. The effect of differences in history of disease (e.g., pulmonary diseases) on subsequent mortality is difficult to assess quantitatively. As noted in Chapter 15, there is some evidence for a reduced longevity of men reporting (during college) previous pulmonary disease compared with those not reporting such disease. Other evidence suggests that respiratory illness during childhood may be an important risk factor for the development of obstructive lung disease in adult life (Burrows et al., 1977). After long-term follow-up, college men who reported a history of asthma had higher death rates from diseases of the respiratory system than

217

men who did not report this disease, although the overall mortality rate did not differ between the two groups (Polednak, 1975). Evidence from recent studies (reviewed by Anon, 1977) involving follow-up of asthmatic children suggests that the prognosis is not always good; the disease may be chronic and a small proportion of asthmatic children eventually die of asthma.

Schnohr's control group, the general Danish male population, may have been less comparable (in terms of past medical history) to the Danish athletes than college athletes are comparable to nonathletes, which may account for the considerable differences in early death rates reported by Schnohr. A similar explanation may hold for Karvonen et al.'s (1974) findings on Finnish champion skiers who were compared with the general male population; the median length of life favored the skiers by several years.

Schnohr cites some evidence for a higher mortality from accidents among athletes than among control groups, and speculates on why Danish athletes may be less "accident prone" than other athletes. Such speculation may be unnecessary, however, since the evidence on accidental deaths in athletes vs. nonathletes is inconclusive. Studies of Harvard College athletes (see Section III) show no consistent differences in proportional mortality among the groups compared. Rook's (1954, see Chp. 4) study, cited by Schnohr, involved incomplete data (in that not all death certificates were obtained).

The lower mortality of major league baseball players in comparison with the general United States male population is not unexpected. As noted in Chapter 16, the mortality ratio (baseball players vs. U.S. males) was less than 100%, and only 43% for ages under 40 years for players whose careers began in 1931-73. The players' "superior physical condition" and supervision by team physicians are cited as possible explanations; the former explanation seems much more likely than the latter.

A probable analogy to the finding of lower mortality in various groups of athletes relative to the general population, due to selection for health and physical condition, is the "healthy worker effect," well known to epidemiologists. Most industrially employed groups have lower mortality rates than the general population, due to the fact that employable persons are relatively healthy (see Goldsmith et al., 1975).

The interesting theoretical estimates provided by Milvy (1977, Chp. 17) indicate the possible magnitude of the influence of some selection factors on studies of mortality among athletes and controls. These analyses emphasize the point that long-term studies are needed to provide adequate data for statistical analyses of hypotheses regarding the effects of physical training, even if large sample sizes are involved. The small numbers of expected deaths from coronary heart disease, after adjustment for hypothetical differences in smoking habits and relative body weight, are due largely to the young age of the marathon runners (see Table 17-IV). Mortality rates increase dramatically with age; as this cohort ages, therefore, the expected number of deaths will also increase. Hopefully, actual cohort studies of groups such as these 9,958 marathon runners will be conducted. Careful consideration of factors of selection, as indicated by theoretical analyses of Milvy, would require collection of data on these variables (e.g., smoking, weight) in the athletes and comparable controls.

REFERENCES

Anon. 1977. Long-term prognosis of asthma. Lancet 2:1015.

Burrows, B., R.J. Knudson, and M.D. Lebowitz 1977 Relationship of childhood respiratory illness to adult obstructive airway disease. Amer. Rev. Respir. Dis. 115:751-760.

Goldsmith, J.R., P.E. Enterline, W.R. Gaffrey, A.J. McMichael, and S.G. Hayes 1975 What do we expect from an occupational cohort? J. Occup. Med. 17:126-131.

Karvonen, M.J., H. Klemola, J. Virkajarvi, and A. Kekkonen 1974 Longevity of endurance skiers. Med. Sci. Sports 6:49-51.

Polednak, A.P. 1975 Asthma and cancer mortality. Lancet 2:1147-1148.

Section VI

Sudden Death of Athletes

Chapter 18

SUDDEN DEATH IN YOUNG ATHLETES*

THOMAS N. JAMES, M.D., F.A.C.P., PETER FROGGATT, M.D.,
AND THOMAS K. MARSHALL, M.D., M.C. Path.

SUDDEN unexpected death of a young athlete is not an unfamiliar event, but as part of the uniquely poignant tragedy it represents there are often few medical facts to report. In such deaths there is a limited number of possible mechanisms, of which a sudden cardiac arrhythmia is one. For this reason we have recently studied the hearts of two young athletes who died suddenly although previously considered to be in good health and in whom the routine necropsy provided no explanation. Special examination of the cardiac conduction system was performed in both cases, and in one it was possible to obtain a clinical and electrocardiographic survey of many surviving members of the family.

Case Histories

Patient J.W.M. (Case 1)

While playing football this 18-year-old young man suddenly died. Before the game he had felt well and cycled 8 miles with his brother to the playing field. After 10 min of the match he told his brother, who was also playing, that he "felt very tired," and in about 30 sec he collapsed. Only a few minutes later, on admission to the local rural hospital located beside the football ground, he was dead.

*From *Annals of Internal Medicine,* 67(5):1013-1021, 1967. (Abridged.)

This study was supported in part by a grant from the Michigan Heart Association, Detroit, Mich., and by grants H-5197 and H-7108, National Heart Institute, National Institutes of Health, Bethesda, Md.

Further history was obtained from his parents and family. The only possible teratogenic factor unearthed was a febrile illness that kept his mother in bed for about 2 weeks during the fourth or fifth month of pregnancy. His childhood was spent in good health until the age of 13, when he began to complain of tiredness, headache, loss of appetite, and difficulty in sleeping. His doctor then noticed a slow irregular pulse for which the boy was referred for outpatient consultation in a small rural hospital. There the pulse was described as 58/min and "irregular," and an apical systolic murmur was noted; a chest X ray was negative, but an electrocardiogram (EKG) was not done. At the age of 14 he was again seen in consultation, but again no EKG was made: At rest the pulse was about 42/min with coupled beats; on exercise it sped up to 70/min and was regular without coupling. A systolic murmur in the pulmonic area was now described, but the examiner felt that the symptoms were mainly of emotional origin. A sedative was prescribed, and he was referred to a child guidance clinic.

About 2½ years before death he was working as message boy on a bicycle when he was found one day disoriented with occipital abrasions. It was assumed that his head injury was caused by falling off his bicycle, but this was never established. At the hospital he said that he had caught his foot on the pedal and must have fallen and hit his head, but his father suggested that the boy had "blacked out" first. He was probably unconscious for a short period. At an examination, 1 hr later, the pulse was 80/min and regular, and a skull X ray was negative. He was discharged after 3 days. There is no clear history of any subsequent episodes of loss of consciousness or orientation, although they cannot be entirely ruled out since he would never discuss his health with anyone, even his family. They thought he worried about something all the time, but the object is not known.

FAMILY HISTORY: Both parents are members of very large sibships. There is no history of relevant or suspicious symptoms in the members traced except as noted below. Specifically, there is no history of sudden unexpected death, deafness, epileptoid seizures, breath-holding episodes; respiratory distress syndromes, heart condition, or consanguinity. The propositus had two sisters and a brother. The brother and one sister were asymptomatic and had normal EKGs; the other sister has been extremely apprehensive about her heart since her brother's death and complains of palpitation and indigestion. She is considered a nervous woman. Her physical examination and EKG were normal except for premature beats of supraventricular origin. The two children of this sister are normal. Information is available about 75 uncles, aunts, and cousins of the propositus and is pertinent in only 2. A maternal aunt had blackouts before a hysterectomy for menorrhagia some years ago, presumably due to anemia since they stopped after the operation; examination included an EKG and was normal. A male first cousin, aged 12 years, is the son of the maternal aunt and was well until he fainted while watching television one evening; his EKG is normal (rather prominent U waves in V_2 and V_3), but an electroencephalogram was interpreted to show "well-marked epileptic response to photic stimulation over a wide range of flash rates."

Both parents are 58 years old, have no complaints pertinent to the case, and have essentially normal physical examinations. EKGs were made on each parent on two occasions 6 months apart. On both occasions that of the father was within normal limits, with a PR interval of about 0.21 sec. In the first tracing of the mother there were repeated episodes of transient sinus arrest, but these were not present on the second examination; other features of the EKG were normal.

NECROPSY FINDINGS: Only the heart was abnormal. The coronary arteries, pericardium, cardiac valves and septa, and myocardial thickness and architecture were all normal. The arteries supplying both the atrioventricular (AV) node and the sinus node originated from the right coronary artery at the usual sites (1-3). Gross examination of the conduction system was normal except for some ecchymoses near the posterior margin of the sinus node. The area of sinus node was originally screened with sections from 17 serial blocks each about 2 mm thick and that of the AV node and the His bundle, from 10 similar blocks. In regions requiring additional examination, serial 6-μ sections were subsequently made from the original blocks so that a total of 85 slides were studied. The ventricular

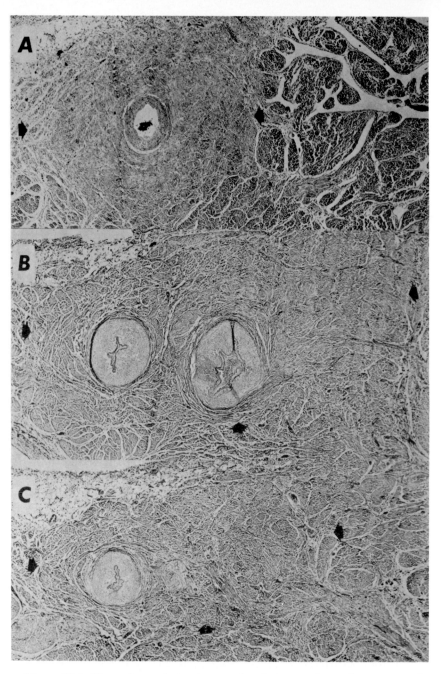

Figure 18-1. These three photomicrographs of sinus node are from a normal heart *(A)* and at points 4 mm apart in the abnormal sinus node of the patient in *Case 1 (B* and *C)*. The region of the sinus node is outlined by arrows in each photograph. The epicardium is above and free wall of right atrium to the right. Note the difference in thickness of the normal and abnormal sinus node arteries. Magnification in *A* is 35 times and in *B* and *C* is 45 times. The normally collagenous sinus node is more distinct in *A* with a trichrome stain than in *B* and *C*, which are stained with Verhoeff-van Gieson, but structure of the artery is better defined in the latter.

myocardium was histologically normal, and the significant histopathology was in and near the conduction system.

The most striking changes were in the sinus node. For a distance of several millimeters the sinus node artery was markedly narrowed by a bizarre medial hyperplasia, and at several points the pinhole lumen was completely occluded by additional intimal proliferation (Figure 18-1). This change in the sinus node artery is identical to that observed in a variety of diseases in which arrhythmias have been documented (4-9). There were foci of both old (scars) and recent (hemorrhage and degeneration) injury within the sinus node and its adjacent nerves and ganglia. Minor changes in the AV node and the His bundle consisted of a small amount of intimal proliferation in one branch of the AV node artery with moderate narrowing of its lumen and unusually heavy deposits of collagen partitioning portions of both the AV node and the His bundle. Slips of AV nodal fibers extended into the central fibrous body in blind pockets, and a few of these fibers were degenerating without inflammatory reaction. A tiny degenerative focus no more than a few microns across was present in part of the left bundle branch.

Patient A.C. (Case 2)

On an autumn afternoon this 15-year-old boy was playing with five companions on some grassy waste ground. They had formed two teams of three each and were wrestling, the object being to hold an opponent down on his back. They had been playing for 10 or 15 min during which time this boy had occasionally somersaulted forward and at least once had stood on his head. There was a bank of clay soil dumped by contractors who were digging foundations near by, and this contained some stones and a few bricks. At one stage he fell on this bank and rolled down the slope to the foot. When he got up he was clasping his left side, but after a few seconds he carried on playing again. Three minutes later he sat down in the field and said that he felt sick. Then he lay down on his back and turned blue. He did not speak after that, and the boys called two men.

One tried artificial respiration, and the other sent for an ambulance. He was unconscious but still alive when the ambulance left for the hospital but was dead on arrival there 17 min after first complaining of feeling sick.

These events were in midafternoon. After his lunch he had bought some apples from a mobile shop, and it is thought that he had eaten more than one of these on his way down to the waste ground. All considered him in good health, and he had recently been working as a lorry helper. At the age of 8 years he had an operation for a depressed fracture of the skull, and when 13 years old he received treatment of a rupture. He last saw a doctor 9 months before death because of a septic throat. He was one of a large family (10 or 11 siblings), and there is apparently no history of untoward attacks, although efforts to obtain more specific information from the family have been unsuccessful.

NECROPSY FINDINGS: The case initially appeared as one of natural death, but an intra-abdominal injury due to the fall needed to be excluded, as did choking and laryngeal shock due to aspiration of food, although the latter seemed unlikely in view of his speaking after feeling ill. At necropsy there was no internal injury. There was 1 oz of straw-colored fluid in each pleural cavity, some regurgitated food just above the vocal cords and a few particles in the trachea, a slight excess of yellow watery fluid in the abdominal cavity, and nothing else. A few necrotic muscle fibers with round-cell infiltration were observed widely scattered in 4 of 13 representative sections of left ventricular myocardium, and there was a small amount of nonspecific perivascular fibrosis with occasional focal medial degeneration in small coronary arteries and arterioles. In the lungs there were some congestion and edema with a few patches of aspiration autolysis. None of these findings was considered an adequate explanation for his sudden unexpected death, and attention was then concentrated on the cardiac conduction system.

Except as noted above, cardiac findings outside the conduction system were not remarkable. The regions of sinus node, AV node, and His bundle were prepared in a manner similar to that for Case 1, with a total of 198 sections being studied. A number of microscopic foci of degeneration were present in the AV node and the His bundle, but all but one of these were old scarring; the exception was an area approximately $100\,\mu$ across at the posterior margin of the AV node where there was recent necrosis with round-cell infiltration. As in the first case, however, the more impressive pathology was in the sinus node. The main sinus node artery was thickened, but one of its major branches supplying nutrient circulation to the node was nearly occluded by medial hyperplasia and intimal proliferation. Downstream from this point of occlusion there was a relatively large focus of degeneration in the sinus node, including a number of adjacent nerves and ganglia.

Discussion

There is a saddening paradox in the sudden death of a young athlete, representing as it does the abrupt end of vigor, strength, and youth, qualities that seem the essence of continuing life. Partly because of the unavoidable personal feelings stirred by such death there has been growing recent interest in the problem out of proportion to its numerical frequency among all deaths. High school football deaths are a notable example, where any may be rightfully considered too many. Those interested in sports medicine have constantly improved protective equipment to prevent dangerous injuries and have continually revised game rules to reduce accidents. Despite these efforts, however, a number of sudden deaths in games remain unexplained, and it is relative to these that the present observations have particular pertinence.

The findings are best interpreted as compatible with a terminal cardiac arrhythmia, but the prevalence of changes in the sinus node raises some questions as to how a lethal arrhythmia may have developed. It must be conceded that the lesser magnitude of histopathologic changes in the atrioventricular (AV) node and the His bundle does not necessarily mean lesser functional significance, and it is not difficult to understand how abrupt heart block, for example, may be fatal. Prudence suggests that the grosser pathology be considered most carefully, however, particularly when it was not only similar in both cases but also resembled that observed in a number of other diseases associated with sudden death (4-9).

Among deaf children with spells who die suddenly a very similar lesion has been observed in the sinus node (8, 9), and the same question arose as to how such a lesion could be fatal. In the deaf children two factors were considered. The first was the presence of a prolonged QT interval (characteristic of the syndrome), causing increased duration of the ventricular vulnerable period, during which a critically timed atrial premature beat or even atrial fibrillation may lead to a ventricular arrhythmia (10, 11). On the basis of this reasoning it was predicted that continued observations in deaf children with long QT intervals and syncopal attacks should lead to documentation of paroxysms of ventricular arrhythmia (8, 12), and these have now been reported by several observers (13-15). Unfortunately, neither of the two young athletes had had an electrocardiogram. Among the family of one an electrocardiographic survey was conducted partly to look for QT prolongation, which is a heritable trait, and a search was made for the congenital deafness that is often (but not always) associated. No significant QT prolongation was found, but this does not eliminate its possible presence in either of the deceased. Furthermore, even those with significant QT prolongation do not always show this change on serial study.

The other factor among the deaf children with injuries in the sinus node that was considered contributory to the development of a lethal cardiac arrhythmia was hemorrhage and degeneration in the region of juxtanodal nerves and ganglia. If these led to neuroflexes, those originating in the ganglia (and some of the nerves) must be vagal since it is generally thought that there are no adrenergic ganglia in the heart. Cholinergic reflexes at the time of intracardiac neural ischemia must suppress sinus pacemaking and AV conduction and may simultaneously suppress the ability of other efficient pacemaking sites (such as the AV node or the His bundle) to provide an efficient escape rhythm. Thus, the occluded sinus node artery might not only alter function of the sinus node directly but by leading to vagal discharge might further depress sinus and other efficient mechanisms as well as impair AV conduction.

Among the kindred of Patient 1 a significant abnormality was present in the electrocardiogram of his mother on one occasion but not later. This was intermittent sinus arrest, which has also been observed in some deaf children and their kindred (9). This, as well as other disorders of normal sinus pacemaking, would actually be the type of functional abnormality one might anticipate with sinus nodal ischemia. Of further significance in this regard is the clear record of marked bradycardia in the first case, which may also be interpreted as a form of abnormal function of the sinus node, whether the actual rhythm during the slow heart rate was sinus bradycardia or sinus arrest with an escape bradycardia of ectopic origin. Recent studies by Han, DeTraglia, Millet, and Moe (16) have demonstrated that a slow heart rate itself produces conditions favorable to the development of ectopic beats and fibrillation because of the greater range of refractory periods at various points in the ventricles.

It has long been known that well-trained athletes characteristically have a slow heart rate. A number of studies have been conducted to determine the physiologic mechanism of this observation, which is at least partly dependent on a high level of vagal tone. Neither of the subjects of the present study could properly be considered a highly trained athlete, but the findings in their hearts may be important relative to those athletes with extensive training. If the training process does produce a vagal effect, one manifestation of which is sinus bradycardia, then the additional presence of disease in the sinus node may be compounded, and it may be the latter that is the lethal factor in those athletes who die suddenly and unexpectedly. This should be relatively simple to determine by examining the cardiac conduction system in such fatal cases, an investigation that has not previously been done to our knowledge.

But easily the most important practical point of the present observations is the probability that under ideal conditions both boys could have been resuscitated. Conditions during athletic games are not always ideal, particularly in rural and other isolated areas, but a number of sudden deaths in young athletes have occurred within a short distance of medical facilities for emergency resuscitation. Undoubtedly some physicians with a special interest in sports medicine have considered the possibility of an arrhythmia as the lethal event in sudden deaths, but it is probably accurate to say that many have not. The findings in these two young athletes indicate that this possibility must be promptly considered, in addition to the more obvious extracardiac injuries, whenever a young athlete collapses suddenly. In both of these cases the general myocardium was well-preserved, and with normal electrical activity it should have supported not only life but continued vigor.

Summary

The sudden unexpected deaths of two young athletes and the findings in their hearts at necropsy are described. Based on the histopathology in and around the sinus node, which was the same in both hearts, a terminal cardiac arrhythmia is postulated as the mechanism of death. Ways in which ischemic pathology in and near the normal cardiac pacemaker may lead to a lethal arrhythmia are discussed. Stress is placed on the importance of considering a cardiac arrhythmia when examining athletes who have suddenly collapsed, since the present observations indicate that appropriate treatment should produce complete recovery.

REFERENCES

1. JAMES, T. N.: *Anatomy of the Coronary Arteries.* Hoeber Medical Division, Harper & Row, Inc., New York, 1961.
2. JAMES, T. N.: Anatomy of the human sinus node. *Anat. Rec.* 141: 109, 1961.
3. JAMES, T. N.: Morphology of the human atrioventricular node, with remarks pertinent to its electrophysiology. *Amer. Heart J.* 62: 756, 1961.
4. JAMES, T. N.: Observations on the cardiovascular involvement, including the cardiac conduction system, in progressive muscular dystrophy. *Amer. Heart J.* 63: 48, 1962.
5. JAMES, T. N., FISCH, C.: Observations on the cardiovascular involvement

in Friedreich's ataxia. *Amer. Heart J.* 66: 164, 1963.

6. JAMES, T. N., FRAME, B., SCHATZ, I. J.: Pathology of the cardiac conduction system in Marfan's syndrome. *Arch. Intern. Med. (Chicago)* 114: 339, 1964.

7. JAMES, T. N.: An etiologic concept concerning the obscure myocardiopathies. *Prog. Cardiov. Dis.* 7: 43, 1964.

8. FRASER, G. R., FROGGATT, P., JAMES, T. N.: Congenital deafness associated with electrocardiographic abnormalities, fainting attacks and sudden death. A recessive syndrome. *Quart. J. Med.* 33: 361, 1964.

9. JAMES, T. N.: Congenital deafness and cardiac arrhythmias. *Amer. J. Cardiol.* 19: 627, 1967.

10. PRESTON, J. B., McFADDEN, S., MOE, G. K.: Atrioventricular transmission in young mammals. *Amer. J. Physiol.* 197: 236, 1959.

11. MOORE, E. N.: Microelectrode studies on concealment of multiple premature atrial responses. *Circ. Res.* 18: 660, 1966.

12. Annotation: Congenital cardiac arrhythmia. *Lancet* 2: 26, 1964.

13. BARLOW, J. B., BOSMAN, C. K., COCHRANE, J. W. C.: Congenital cardiac arrhythmia (letter to the editor). *Ibid.*, p. 531.

14. GAMSTORP, I., NILSEN, R., WESTLING, H.: Congenital cardiac arrhythmia. *Ibid.*, p. 965.

15. WARD, O. C.: A new familial cardiac syndrome in children. *J. Irish Med. Ass.* 54: 103, 1964.

16. HAN, J., DeTRAGLIA, J., MILLET, D., MOE, G. K.: Incidence of ectopic beats as a function of basic rate in the ventricle. *Amer. Heart J.* 72: 632, 1966.

Chapter 19

SUDDEN DEATH AND SPORT*

Lionel H. Opie, M.D.

Abstract

Of 21 sudden deaths in sportsmen, 18 were thought to be caused by heart-attacks either during or after sport. There was firm evidence of ischaemic heart-disease in 9, strongly suggestive evidence in 7, but in 2 there was only suggestive clinical evidence. As a group, these subjects were characterised by (1) a mean age above thirty (above twenty-five for rugby players); (2) a family history of early heart-attacks; and (3) antecedent symptoms of chest pain or pressure in 9, fatigue or blackout in 4, and minor complaints in 2. Most were known to their medical practitioners. Psychological factors were thought to be important in 8. Doctors, players, and referees should be aware that severe sporting exertion as in rugby football involves a risk which for most players is relatively minor, but in the minority predisposed to heart-attacks by family history, smoking, or age (as in referees) the risk is more serious. To reduce the hazard of sudden death in exercise, players and referees should be warned against smoking and informed of the serious implications of the development of chest pain, pressure, or undue tiredness before, during, or after sport.

Introduction

ALTHOUGH exercise may have a place in the prevention and therapy of ischaemic heart-disease,[1-3] exercise is also believed to precipitate arrhythmias and myocardial infarction in certain individuals.[4-12] This article draws attention to a series of sudden deaths (occurring within an hour of

---

*From *The Lancet*, 263-266, February 1, 1975.

the onset of symptoms) associated with rugby football and other sports in South Africa.

Methods

Collection of Information and Case-reports

Information on sudden death in sport was obtained from: (i) a search, sustained for eighteen months, of the daily and weekly South African newspapers (assisted by their librarians); (ii) the director of the regional St. John Ambulance Association; (iii) the police mortuary (who are required to perform a necropsy in cases of unexplained sudden death). South Africa is a sports-loving country and sudden deaths at sport are given great publicity, especially if rugby football is involved. After obtaining the name and address of the patient, the relatives were contacted and a full history obtained. The general practitioner or other attendant doctor was also questioned. Whenever possible, close relatives of the deceased were interviewed, examined, and tested for risk factors of ischaemic heart-disease. Necropsy material, when available, was inspected.

Results

Data on 21 sportsmen who died suddenly are given in Tables 19-I to 19-IV. 2 rugby players, 1 who died with a subarachnoid haemorrhage and one who had congenital absence of one kidney, were thought not to have died from heart-attacks and were excluded from a full study. There were 19 other instances of sudden death due to proven or possible heart-attacks, a term which here is used to include both fatal cardiac arrhythmias and/or acute myocardial infarction.

Features of Coronary-artery Disease (Table 19-I)

Coronary-artery disease and its consequences were evident in most of the 21 subjects. Excluding the 2 who died from non-cardiac causes, 18 of 19 subjects had definite or suggestive fea-

Table 19-I

SUDDEN DEATH AND FEATURES OF
CORONARY-ARTERY DISEASE IN
21 SPORTSMEN

—	Number of subjects
Firm evidence for coronary-artery disease:	
Necropsy evidence of advanced coronary atheroma	7
E.C.G. signs of acute infarction	1
Past myocardial infarction	1
Strongly suggestive clinical picture:	
Chest pain preceding death	4
Other symptoms preceding death	2
Collapse associated with angina and positive E.C.G. exercise test	1
Clinical picture only suggestive	2
No evidence for coronary-artery disease	1
Evidence for non-cardiac disease:	
Unilateral absence of kidney	1
Subarachnoid hæmorrhage	1

Table 19-II

SPORT AND AGE OF MEN WHO DIED SUDDENLY

Type of sport	No.
Rugby football	7 (17, 21, 25, 28, 29, 29, 33)
Referees	4 (48, 52, 55, 58)
Soccer (association football)	2 (34, 53)
Golf	1 (40)
Mountaineering	1 (47)
Tennis	2 (53, 55)
Jogging	1 (46)
Yachting	1 (38)

Ages of subjects are given in parentheses.

tures of coronary-artery disease. A definite pathological diagnosis was only made in 7 subjects, but the data of Friedman et
al.[9] show that coronary-artery disease is almost certainly the
cause of sudden death (including instantaneous death in their
classification) associated with exercise.

Table 19-III

FACTORS PREDISPOSING TO HEART-ATTACKS IN SPORTSMEN WHO DIED SUDDENLY*

Predisposing factors	No.
Smoking:	
No data	3
Non-smokers	3
Heavy (20 + per day)	11
Moderate (10–20 per day)	2
Family history heart-attacks or angina:	
Heart attacks below 45 yr.	4
Angina pectoris	3
Heart-attack at age 70	1
Lipid disorders:	
Definite	3
Probable	3
Hypertension:	
Mild	2
Normotensive	8
No data	9
Previous angina, heart-attack, or intermittent	
claudication	8
Fitness:	
Unfit	4
Obese	3
Decrease in fitness	4
Fit	3
Very fit	4
No data	1

16 subjects had more than one predisposing factor.
* Omitting 2 men who died from non-cardiac disease.

Table 19-IV

RECENT SYMPTOMS PRECEDING SUDDEN DEATH IN SPORTSMEN*

—	No. of subjects
Chest pain or pressure:	
Recent onset of typical or probable angina	3
Suspected myocardial infarction 10 days before	1
Established, recurrent angina	1
Recurrent chest pain after previous infarction	1
Recent heavy feeling on chest with increasing tiredness	1
Severe pain in left arm and shoulder just before match	1
Repetitive chest pains, some on exertion	1
Other major complaints:	
Dizziness and exhaustion during rugby, " passed out " afterwards	1
" Very tired " after rugby practice	1
Extreme fatigue	1
Fatigued, highly strung	1
Minor complaints:	
Painful tendo achilles with injection of local anæsthetic (without adrenaline) on morning of match	1
Peculiar non-exertional pain left side of face	1
No complaints, subject not known to doctors	4

* Omitting 2 men who died from non-cardiac disease.

Blood-lipids (Table 19-III)

There was information on the blood-lipids in only 3 subjects, and evidence for familial hyperlipidaemias in another 3. 1 patient had serum-cholesterol concentrations of 373 and 380 mg per 100 ml with xanthomatosis. A second was reported as having a "very high" cholesterol (value unknown) and xanthomatosis. A third had a cholesterol of value 290 mg per 100 ml when aged thirty-eight. A twenty-seven-year-old brother of another patient had type-II hyperlipidaemia with a blood-cholesterol value of 296 mg per 100 ml. A fifteen-year-old brother of the seventeen-year-old schoolboy had a blood-cholesterol value of 295 mg per 100 ml. The brother of yet another patient had a "lipid disorder" and a heart-attack at the age of thirty-five. No data were available on the other subjects.

Type of Sport (Table 19-II)

Thirteen players or referees took part in rugby or soccer, which are hard, competitive sports. One tennis player was in a club championship, the yachtsman was in an open race, and the jogger "fought" his heart-disease by running 7 miles a day. Thus, competitiveness was a feature in 16 of 19 cases.

"Fitness" (Table 19-III)

Fitness was assessed subjectively, usually by the medical practitioner, wife, or fellow sportsmen. Of the 19 subjects, 11 were unfit, relatively unfit, or obese.

Psychological Factors

Personality factors were thought to have been important in 8 sportsmen. The yachtsman had had a suspected heart-attack ten days before, but he ignored advice not to go yachting and died during a difficult race in bad weather. The jogger had had a heart-attack seven years before, which he "fought by running" up to 7 miles a day, and he died while running. A tennis player was club champion and was defending his title against a much younger player. Because he was determined to win he continued to play despite symptoms and died shortly afterwards. A champion athlete with xanthomatosis, son of a man who died aged thirty-seven from a heart-attack, had been warned about the danger of "early coronary occlusion" but refused medical management and collapsed in the dressing-room after rugby. A champion rugby player had "passed out" in the changing-room three weeks before he died, but he ignored medical advice not to play again. A fifty-five-year-old tennis player felt tired and experienced pressure on the chest; he refused a medical examination and died a few days later. A fifty-five-year-old referee with angina pectoris and a positive exercise electrocardiogram (ECG) test ignored the advice of a consultant physician not to referee again. A referee left the field with chest pain and was advised to go to hospital immediately by the ambulance men, but he insisted on first taking a shower, during which he died.

Recent Symptoms Preceding Sudden Death (Table 19-IV)

9 subjects had had chest pain or pressure before death, 4 had complained of tiredness or exhaustion, and 2 had had other apparently minor complaints (i.e., facial pain and pain in the Achilles tendon). Only 4 subjects were not known to local doctors.

Sudden Death versus Instantaneous Death

Sudden death is variously defined as death occurring within one to twenty-four hours of the onset of symptoms; here all subjects died within an hour. Friedman et al.[9] distinguished between instantaneous death (within thirty seconds of the onset of symptoms) and sudden death (occurring minutes to twenty-four hours after the onset of symptoms. In the present series, it was difficult to differentiate between instantaneous and sudden death according to the criteria of Friedman, perhaps because minor transient symptoms in these sportsmen were more readily apparent to onlookers. However, 2 deaths were obviously instantaneous (i.e., the tennis player who dropped down while jumping for a ball and the yachtsman who fell off the yacht) while another 6 were probably instantaneous. Of these 8 subjects, 3 had advanced coronary-artery disease in the absence of thrombi and 4 had a history of angina or infarction. According to Friedman et al.[9] only instantaneous deaths are associated with moderate or severe physical activity.

Incidence of Rugby Deaths

Special efforts were made to ascertain the incidence of rugby deaths over one football season (March-October, 1973). 2 of the 7 rugby players who died had participated in matches of Western Province Rugby Union, which have an estimated 2100 players out each Saturday or playing public holiday. If each game lasts about ninety minutes (including injury-time) there would be about 100,000 "rugby-hours" per season. Thus the incidence of deaths in this group of rugby players is about 1 per 50,000 "rugby-hours." When it comes to referees, 1 referee died per 3000 "referee-hours" in these same rugby matches. In addition, two referees participating in school rugby matches in same area (with an estimated 6000 "referee-hours") died. The risks for referees with an average age over fifty were considerably higher than for rugby players (with an average age of twenty-six years).

Discussion

Ventricular fibrillation and severe exertion are associated in maximum-effort testing. Bruce[4] found four attacks of ventricular fibrillation during 18,000 maximum-effort tests. Rochmis and Blackburn[5] reported that in 170,000 exercise tests 16 subjects died and 40 were admitted to hospital with chest pain or arrhythmias. Thus in these elderly or middle-aged patients with suspected coronary-artery disease, exercise precipitated features of myocardial ischaemia in about 1 of 4000 to 5000 tests, and sudden death in about 1 of 10,000 tests. The risk of precipitating ventricular fibrillation could be as high as 2 episodes per

1000 hours of physical activity in a population predisposed to coronary attacks.[6] Newspaper reports in Ontario, Canada, suggest an incidence of one attack of ventricular fibrillation per 2500 gymnasium-hours in middle-aged business men.[7] In the present series the death-rate for middle-aged referees was also about 1 death per 3000 referee-hours, but the rate in the young, active rugby players was much lower (1 death per 50,000 rugby-hours or nearly 6 years of continuous playing).

In several studies of sudden death, exercise has been incriminated as the precipitating factor.[9–12] Friedman et al.[9] found that more than half the subjects dying within 30 seconds of the onset of symptoms did so during or immediately after severe or moderate physical activity, and the probable cause was an arrhythmia, since there were only old occlusions of major coronary arteries. Three American studies reported that sudden deaths and/or coronary-artery disease in young soldiers could be positively linked to vigorous exercise.[10–12] In a community study, sudden cardiac death was associated with strenuous activity in only 20% of 300 patients but with mild or moderate activity in another 60%; those sudden deaths which were monitored at the time suggested that ventricular fibrillation was the cause of death.[13]

Heart-attacks During Exercise

A heart-attack during exercise in a person with coronary-artery disease could be the consequence of either increased myocardial oxygen demand outstripping the blood-supply, or disturbances of the cardiac rhythm and conduction induced by exercise; both effects are more likely to develop in the presence of coronary-artery disease.[8] Since exercise could trigger arrhythmias in those with advanced coronary-artery disease, it is not surprising to find an association between exercise and sudden death. Furthermore, Master reported that exercise could precipitate infarction in those with impending infarction.[14]

Heart-attacks after Exercise

In three subjects, heart-attacks developed soon after rugby

matches. The period after cessation of vigorous exercise has been referred to as the post-exercise vulnerable period,[15] and arrhythmias may be more frequent immediately after stopping exercise than during exercise itself.[16,17] Jokl and Cluver[18] reported that an apparently fit rugby international player died while taking a hot bath after a test game. He had narrowed coronary arteries, and peripheral vasodilatation was thought to have precipitated his death, but heat may also precipitate arrhythmias.[19]

In such cases of postexercise heart-attacks a biochemical mechanism may also be considered. After exercise, blood-free-fatty-acids (F.F.A.) increase more in unfit than in fit people,[20] and very high F.F.A. concentrations may be one of several factors contributing to the development of arrhythmias[21] and arterial thrombosis.[22] Furthermore, blood-catecholamines are increased by exercise and may remain raised for some time[19]; catecholamines may precipitate both myocardial ischaemia and arrhythmias in the presence of coronary-artery constriction,[23] and F.F.A.-associated arrhythmias may only be manifest at higher levels of catecholamine activity.[24] Players who are smokers would also tend to smoke after a sports event, with a consequent rise in blood F.F.A.[25] and release of catecholamines[26]; one of the present series died while smoking after golf.

Prevention

Heavy smoking was a risk factor for sudden death in the Framingham study, and arguments for giving up smoking to reduce the risk of ischaemic heart-disease in the general population[26] are even more applicable to sportsmen, who are at greater risk of sudden death. Most of Friedman's subjects who had heart-attacks related to physical activity were heavy smokers,[9] and arrhythmic deaths, cigarette smoking, and catecholamine excretion seem to be linked.[27]

Should "fitness" be encouraged? Even an excellent overall physical condition does not guarantee against sudden death in the presence of coronary-artery disease, as was found in 4 subjects and as reported elsewhere.[18,28] Nor did fitness protect well-trained American middle-aged men from st-depression and arrhythmias after maximum stress.[29] Nevertheless, sudden and unaccustomed physical activity is believed to be more likely to precipitate heart-attacks in the unfit.[6,30] Respiratory infections, held by some to predispose to sudden death,[31] are discounted by others.[6]

Doctors, players, and referees should be aware that severe exertion, as in rugby or in association football (soccer), involves a risk which for most players is relatively minor but for a majority is more serious, especially if they are over thirty (younger for rugby). Players and referees should be warned of possible seriousness of the development of chest pain, pressure, or severe tiredness, especially in relation to sport. Chest pain occurring before, during, or after a match should be viewed with great alarm, the player rested at once, and a doctor called urgently. The player should not be allowed to walk off the field (as happened in 4 of the reported subjects; 1 even walked into the hospital ward). However, sportsmen may be prevented from seeking or accepting medical advice by their psychological constitution and competitive feelings. Psychological factors could have played a role in nearly half the subjects in this series, either because exercise was associated with aggressive activity and emotional conflicts,[32] or because advice not to play, or to stop playing, was ignored.

The links between sporting exercise and sudden death recorded here do not constitute statistical evidence against the possible benefits of exercise training in the prophylaxis and treatment of ischaemic heart-disease. Not everyone dare play every sport,[33] but exercise training may be considered on its own merits[2,3,34,35] and is held to be a safe procedure even in the presence of coronary-artery disease, provided supervision and defibrillators are available.[6,35] Nevertheless, the present report and others linking physical activity with sudden cardiac death[6,7,9-12,35] suggest that the benefits of exercise have to be balanced against a small risk of sudden death. To minimise the risk, Fox[2] has suggested that measurements during exercise could define an intensity of exertion which would give an acceptably low risk of sudden cardiac death but would improve fitness.

REFERENCES

1. Turner, R., Ball, K. *Lancet*, 1973, ii, 1137.
2. Fox, S. M. *in* Exercise Testing and Exercise Training in Coronary Heart Disease (edited by J. P. Naughton and H. K. Hellerstein); p. 3. New York, 1973.
3. Opie, L. H. *Am. Heart J.* 1974, 88, 539.
4. Bruce, R. A. Personal communication.
5. Rocnmis, P., Blackburn, H. *J. Am. med. Ass.* 1969, 217, 1061.
6. Shephard, A. J. *Br. J. Sports Med.* 1974, 8, 101.
7. Shephard, A. J. *Can. Fam. Physn*, 1973, 19, 57.
8. De Maria, A. N., Vera, Z., Amsterdam, E. A., Mason, D. T., Massumi, R. A. *Am. J. Cardiol.* 1974, 33, 732.
9. Friedman, M., Manwaring, J. H., Rosenman, R. H., Donlon, G., Ortega, P., Grube, S. M. *J. Am. med. Ass.* 1973, 225, 1319.
10. Yater, W. M., Traum, A. H., Spring, S., Brown, W. G., Fitzgerald, R. P., Geisler, M. A., Wilcox, B. B. *Am. Heart J.* 1948, 36, 334.
11. French, A. J., Dock, W. *J. Am. med. Ass.* 1944, 124, 1233.
12. Moritz, A. R., Zamcheck, N. *Archs Path.* 1946, 42, 459.
13. Liberthson, R. R., Nagel, E. L., Hirschman, J. C., Nussenfeld, S. R., Blackbourne, B. D., Davis, J. H. *Circulation*, 1974, 49, 790.
14. Master, A. M. *Am. Heart J.* 1968, 75, 809.
15. Adams, C. W. *Am. J. Cardiol.* 1972, 30, 713.
16. Gooch, A. S., McConnel, D. *Prog. cardiovasc. Dis.* 1970, 13, 293.
17. Goldschlager, N., Cake, D., Cohn, K. *Am. J. Cardiol.* 1973, 31, 434.
18. Jokl, E., Cluver, E. H. *in* Exercise and Cardiac Death (edited by E. Jokl and J. T. McClellan); p. 153. Baltimore, Maryland, 1971.
19. Taggart, P., Parkinson, P., Carruthers, M. *Br. med. J.* 1972, iii, 71.
20. Johnson, R. H., Walton, J. L., Krebs, H. A., Williamson, D. H. *Lancet*, 1969, ii, 452.
21. Kurien, V. A., Yates, P. A., Oliver, M. F. *Eur. J. clin. Invest.* 1971, 1, 225.
22. Hoak, J. C., Poole, J. C. F., Robinson, D. S. *Am. J. Path.* 1963, 43, 987.
23. Raab, W., Van Lith, P., Lepeschin, E., Herrlich, H. C. *Am. J. Cardiol.* 1962, 9, 455.
24. Opie, L. H., Norris, R. M., Thomas, M., Holland, A. J., Owen, P., Van Noorden, S. *Lancet*, 1971, i. 818.
25. Kershbaum, A., Bellet, S., Dickstein, E. R., Feinberg, L. J. *Circ. Res.* 1961, 9, 631.
26. Ball, K., Turner, R. *Lancet*, 1974, ii. 822.
27. Warren, J. Y. *Circulation* 1974, 50, 415.

28. Jokl, E., Melzer, L. *S. Afr. J. med. Sci.* 1940, 5, 4.
29. Pollock, M. L., Miller, H. S., Jr., Linnerud, A. C., Royster, C. L., Smith, W. E., Sonner, W. H. *Br. J. Sports Med.* 1973, 7, 222.
30. Wyndham, C. H. *S. Afr. med. J.* 1974, 48, 571. ˙
31. Kocnar, K., Rous, J. *Br. J. Sports Med.* 1973, 7, 166.
32. Engel, G. L. *Ann. intern. Med.* 1971, 74, 771.
33. *Lancet,* 1973, ii, 1066.
34. Bannister, R. *Br. med. J.* 1972, iv, 711.
35. Bruce, R. A., Kluge, W. *J. Am. med. Ass.* 1971, 216, 653.

DISCUSSION

THE studies discussed earlier in this book concerned long-term follow-up of athletes in terms of mortality. The studies reported in this section indicate the importance of sudden death during or immediately after participation in athletics.

James et al. (Chp. 18) present detailed pathologic evidence supporting the role of cardiac arrhythmias in the sudden death of young athletes. An interesting suggestion is that underlying disease in the sinus node,* along with a vagal effect of intensive physical training manifested in sinus bradycardia, may be involved in some cases of sudden death among athletes. That is, an occluded sinus-node artery may alter SA node and by leading to vagal discharge might depress sinus mechanisms and impair AV conduction. There is considerable interest in the role of the autonomic nervous system in the pathogenesis of arrhythmias (Levy, 1977). Assymetries or imbalances within either autonomic division or between the two divisions may cause certain unusual responses in the heart. An animal model of spontaneous syncope and sudden death involves vagal depression of the sinus node (Branch et al., 1977). The possible role of emotional stimuli (mediated through the vagi) in cardiac arrhythmias also comes to mind (e.g., from the work of W. B. Cannon), as discussed below.

Unfortunately, as James et al. observe, neither of the two young athletes studied had had an electrocardiogram. It would have been of interest to correlate electrocardiographic findings with SA node pathology, as has been done in other studies (of nonathletes). In 111 patients with various arrhythmias (and other electrocardiographic abnormalities), for example, They

---

*The sinus or sinoatrial (SA) node is also known as the Keith-Flack node, after two investigators who described it (Keith and Flack, 1907).

et al. (1977) examined pathology of the sinoatrial node. Chronic sinoatrial block was associated with extensive lesions (mainly fibrotic) of the SA node, occasionally combined with lesions in the AV (atrioventricular) node region. James et al. (Chp. 18) also noted some AV node injury in their cases. Thery et al. (1977) were unable to find evidence of an ischemic origin in the majority of their cases, while James et al. reported evidence of thickening or occlusion of the sinus node artery. Hopefully, advances in methods of histochemical diagnosis will help elucidate the etiology of SA node lesions (Thery et al., 1977).

Whatever the pathological processes involved, the probable role of arrhythmias in some types of sudden death is becoming increasingly recognized. In a study of instantaneous and sudden deaths, Friedman et al. (1973) found that instantaneous deaths from coronary heart disease often occurred during or immediately after physical exertion, and death appeared to result from primary arrhythmias. In contrast to the athletes described by James et al., none of the hearts in Friedman et al.'s series showed discernible pathology of the SA or AV nodes; instead, old occluded coronary arteries were frequently present.

Coronary occlusion was not present in the two young athletes described by James et al. (above) but was involved in at least some of the sudden deaths described by Opie (Chp. 19), who also discussed the probable role of arrhythmias. In physically untrained (sedentary) persons, intense and unusual exercise, sometimes associated with emotional excitement, is often an immediate factor precipitating heart attack (Kavanagh and Shephard, 1973). It is likely that previous disease (especially coronary atherosclerosis) is involved in such cases. Well-trained men, however, are not protected against arrhythmias and electrocardiographic abnormalities after maximum physical stress, as pointed out by Opie. It is unclear whether the majority of physically trained men who die suddenly from heart attacks during or after exercise have previous coronary disease, but Opie's data (Chp. 19) indicate that many have a history of such disease, while others have one or more "risk factors" associated with heart disease (i.e., cigarette smoking, positive family history, lipid disorders). McHenry et al. (1976) report some limited data suggesting that in persons without clinical evidence of heart disease, exercise-induced ventricular arrhythmias are not associated with an increased risk of sudden death or future coronary heart disease. Parenthetically, the apparent relation between exercise heart rate and exercise-induced ventricular arrhythmias reported by McHenry et al. (1976) is supported by evidence from experiments on exercised dogs (Thompson and Lown, 1976).

Opie (Chp. 19) mentions the possible role of psychological factors, including the aggression and emotional aspects of athletic competition, in sudden death of athletes. It is difficult to differentiate the psychological from the physical aspects of athletic competition. Athletic coaches, however, are subject primarily to the psychic stress associated with competitive events. A group of football and basketball coaches were monitored continuously, with a radioelectrocardiographic device, throughout athletic games (Gazes et al., 1969). Along with tachycardia, some coaches developed rare premature ventricular beats and others rare premature atrial beats; one coach with known coronary disease had multifocal premature ventricular beats.

Other studies indicate that emotional stress precipitates a variety of disturbances in cardiac rhythms, including atopic beats and atrial fibrillation (Berman et al., 1954; Nakamoto, 1965). There is evidence that psychological stimuli can profoundly affect the susceptibility of the heart to fatal arrhythmias (Verrier et al., 1975), possibly through the arrhythmogenic effect of the sympathetic nervous system (via catecholamines). In an extensive review of the literature, however, Lynch et al. (1977) note the paucity of work on the direct, long-term effects of psychological states and emotional factors on cardiac arrhythmias.

The physiological effects of psychological aspects of exercise or athletic competition are suggested by data on psychoendocrine reactions in men in anticipation of exhausting exercise. Mason et al. (1973) observed consistent individual responses with significant elevations of plasma cortisol and norepinephrine during a 20-minute period prior to exhausting exercise.

In addition to cardiac arrhythmias, heat stroke may be involved in some cases of sudden death among athletes. The potentially serious consequences of heat stroke in athletes were emphasized by Barcenas et al. (1976), who reported on an obese fifteen-year-old boy who died soon after his first football practice. Myofibrillar degeneration, a nonspecific morphologic indicator of cardiac injury, was found at autopsy.

The impact on society of sudden deaths (whatever their mechanisms or pathology) in young athletes is pointed out by James et al., with particular reference to high school football deaths. Evidence on high-school, college, and professional or semiprofessional football players indicates a considerable number of deaths due to "direct" (blocking and tackling) and "indirect" (heart failure, heat stroke) causes in 1955-59 and 1960-64 (Anon., 1965). Direct causes are not of major interest in this discussion, but it is important to note that fatalities in organized tackle football due to direct causes involve mostly head and neck injuries (Torg et al., 1977).

As James et al. (Chp. 18) have observed, physician awareness of the possibility of lethal cardiac arrhythmias could lead to appropriate treatment and recovery. Opie considers several aspects of prevention of sudden death in sport, indicating the need for education of players, referees and coaches, as well as physicians, to the possible role of risk factors (e.g., smoking, family history of heart disease) and the recognition of early signs of heart trouble.

REFERENCES

Anon. 1965 Competitive sports and their hazards. Stat. Bull. *46*:1-3.

Barcenas, C., H. P. Hoeffler, and J. T. Lie 1976 Obesity, football, dog days and siriasis: A deadly combination. Amer. Heart J. *92*:237-244.

Berman, R., E. Simonson, and H. Heron 1954 Electrocardiographic effects associated with hypnotic suggestion in normal and coronary sclerotic individuals. J. Appl. Physiol. 7:89-92.

Branch, C. E., B. T. Robertson, S. D. Beckett, A. L. Waldo, and T. N. James 1977 An animal model and spontaneous syncope and sudden death. J. Lab. Clin. Med. *90*:592-603.

Friedman, M., J. H. Manwaring, R. H. Rosenman, G. Donlon, P. Ortega, and S. M. Grube 1973 Instantaneous and sudden deaths: Clinical and pathological differentiation in coronary artery disease. J. Amer. Med. Assoc. *225*:1319-1328.

Gazes, P. C., B. F. Sovell, and J. W. Dellastatious 1969 Continuous radioelectrocardiographic monitoring of football and basketball coaches during games. Amer. Heart J. *78*:509-512.

Kavanagh, T. and R. J. Shephard 1973 The immediate antecedents of myocardial infarction in active men. Canad. Med. Assoc. J. *109*:19-22.

Keith, A. and M. Flack 1907 The form and nature of the muscular connections between the primary divisions of the vertebrate heart. J. Anat. Physiol. *41*:172-189.

Levy, M. N. 1977 Neural mechanisms in cardiac arrhythmias. J. Lab. Clin. Med. *90*:589-591.

Lynch, J. J., D. A. Paskewitz, K. S. Gimbel, and S. A. Thomas 1977 Psychological aspects of cardiac arrhythmia. Amer. Heart J. *93*:645-657.

Mason, J. W., H. Hartley, T. A. Kotchen, E. H. Mougey, P. T. Ricketts, and L. G. Jones 1973 Plasma cortisol and norepinephrine responses in anticipation of muscular exercise. Psychosom. Med. *35*:406-412.

McHenry, P. L., P. N. Morris, M. Kavalier, and J. W. Jordan 1976 Comparative study of exercise-induced ventricular arrhythmias in normal subjects and patients with documented coronary artery disease. Amer. J. Cardiol. *37*:609-616.

Nakamoto, K. 1965 Psychogenic paroxysmal cardiac arrhythmias. Jap. Circulation J. *29*:701-717.

Thery, C., B. Gosselin, J. Lekieffre, and H. Warembourg 1977 Pathology of sinoatrial node. Correlations with electrocardiographic findings in 111 patients. Amer. Heart J. *93*:735-740.

Thompson, P. L. and B. Lown 1976 Coronary occlusion before, during and after strenuous exercise. Cardiovas. Res. *10*:385-388.

Torg, J. S., T. C. Quedenfeld, R. A. Moyer, R. Truex Jr., A. D. Spealman, and C. E. Nichols III 1977 Severe and catastrophic neck injuries resulting from tackle football. J. Amer. College Health Assoc. *25*:224-226.

Verrier, R. L., A. Calvert, and B. Lown 1975 Effect of posterior hypothalamic stimulation on ventricular fibrillation threshold. Amer. J. Physiol. *228*:923-927.

Concluding Remarks

As the above studies indicate, there is no strong evidence for significantly reduced longevity of former athletes (college or other) relative to controls. The small, consistently reported differences in favor of college nonathlete controls may be real, or due to selection of athletes on factors relevant to longevity. The differences in overall longevity appear to be due mainly to cardiovascular diseases and certain types of cancer, according to limited data on college athletes and nonathletes. These differences in mortality from certain causes are rather small in magnitude, although statistically significant. In the few studies available on Olympic and professional athletes, the problem of adequate control groups make the findings difficult to interpret. The greater longevity of these athletes relative to the general male population is not unexpected, in view of the highly select nature of the former groups.

There is no clear evidence for a long-term protective effect of athletics on health (as reflected in longevity). Such an effect might have been expected in view of the results of some animal experiments on exercise and longevity, and the apparent short-term effects of exercise (including some changes that run counter to those seen with "aging") reported in some studies of athletes and other groups. The reversibility of these changes related to exercise (i.e., their dependence on continuity of training), however, is a consistently reported finding. In any event, it appears from the studies on longevity of athletes that one cannot "store up" any benefits of earlier physical exercise and training (as involved in athletic participation) (Fox and Haskell, 1968). Habitual exercise at a strenuous level, if continued through life, seems more likely to produce beneficial effects which may be reflected in health and longevity.

The slightly greater longevity of minor athletes at Harvard College relative to major athletes and nonathletes is intriguing,

251

but difficult to interpret without comparable data from other studies. Again, selection may be involved in these slight differences, if they are indeed real. Persons who chose to exercise moderately, whether in college or later in life, may be a distinct group in terms of psychological factors and personal habits, which in turn may influence health and mortality. A similar situation may hold in studies of the general population, in which level of exercise at work and during leisure time have been examined in relation to health or risk factors of disease. Hickey et al. (1975), for example, studied habits of physical activity at work and during leisure in 15,171 men aged 25 to 74. The results suggested the possibility that the often reported reduction in coronary heart disease incidence associated with physical exercise may not represent a direct effect of exercise. Men who are physically active during their leisure time may differ from less active men in smoking and dietary habits or medical history; this was suggested by the apparent relation between physical activity during leisure time (but not during work) and certain coronary risk factors (Hickey et al., 1975).

A potential problem with studies of the effects of exercise in the general population is that habitual levels of physical activity may vary so little that any potential effects of strenuous exercise may be difficult to detect. One may cite the results of community surveys by Montoye and his colleagues (Cunningham et al., 1968; Taylor and Montoye, 1975; Montoye, 1975), showing the participation of Tecumseh (Michigan) men of various ages in leisure-time activities in terms of multiples of the basal metabolic rate (BMR). A very small percentage of men (i.e., less than 1%) engaged in leisure activities whose peak loads were 8 times the BMR or greater; carrying objects weighing 20-44 lbs requires a ratio of 5, and hammering or sawing a peak load of 6 (Reiff et al., 1967), and these are not extremely demanding or strenuous activities. In contrast, some former college athletes (see Chp. 11) may continue to exercise strenuously in later life.

Former athletes who continue to exercise at varying levels would be interesting groups to follow-up in terms of longevity, health, and "life satisfaction." Problems of selection would exist, however, in comparing men at different levels of activity, as in other studies, unless random assignment to activity levels were possible. As noted by Webb et al. (1977), cooperation among researchers may facilitate studies of older champion athletes (such as participants in the World Masters Championships). As Milvy's (1977) calculations suggest, large sample sizes and long-term follow-up over many years may be required for such studies to be productive in terms of testing of hypotheses of the effects of exercise on longevity and mortality. As discussed above with reference to Pomeroy and White's (1958) study of former college athletes with and without coronary heart disease, however, case-control studies may also be useful.

Results of such studies of active athletes may serve to indicate the maximum effects that may be expected from physical training in view of the strenuous levels involved, as well as the constitutional characteristics of the athletes. At present, programs of high-intensity physical training may be impractical in the general population (Taylor, Buskirk, and Remington, 1973). Techniques for improving participation in (and adherence to) high-intensity exercise programs, however, may be developed for large groups such as industrial workers or students. As with weight reduction programs, the challenge is to maintain participation in order to maintain beneficial effects. Exercise programs, optimal with respect to improvement in cardiovascular health, need to be designed for specific groups depending on their age, present health, and fitness level. Levels of fitness approaching those of trained active athletes may never be reached in much of the general population, even with intensive training, but nonattainment of such levels does not preclude the possibility of beneficial effects.

REFERENCES

Cunningham, D. A., H. J. Montoye, H. L. Metzner, and J. B. Keller 1968 Active leisure time activities as related to age among males in a total community. J. Gerontol. *23*:551-556.

Fox, S. M. and W. L. Haskell 1968 Physical activity and the prevention of coronary heart disease. Bull. N.Y. Acad. Med. *44*:950-967.

Hickey, N., R. Mulcahy, G. J. Bourke, I. Graham, and K. Wilson-Davis 1975

Study of coronary risk factors related to physical activity in 15,171 men. Brit. Med. J. *1*:507-509.

Milvy, P. 1977 Statistical analysis of deaths from coronary heart disease anticipated in a cohort of marathon runners. Ann. N.Y. Acad. Sci. *301*:620-626.

Montoye, H. J. 1975 Physical Activity and Health: An Epidemiologic Study of an Entire Community. Prentice-Hall, Englewood Cliffs.

Reiff, G., H. J. Montoye, R. D. Remington, J. A. Napier, H. L. Metzner, and E. H. Epstein 1967 Assessment of physical activity by questionnaire and interview. *In:* Karvonen, M. J. and A. J. Berry (Eds.) Physical Activity and the Heart. Charles C Thomas, Springfield, Illinois.

Taylor, H. L., E. R. Buskirk, and R. D. Remington 1973 Exercise in controlled trials of the prevention of coronary heart disease. Feder. Proc. *32*:1623-1627.

Taylor, H. L. and H. J. Montoye 1975 Physical fitness, cardiovascular function and age. *In:* Ostfeld, A. M. and D. C. Gibson (Eds.) Epidemiology of Aging. U.S. Dept. Health Educ. Welfare Public. No. (NIH) 75-711, U.S. Public Health Service, Washington, D.C., pp. 223-241.

INDEX